Between Altars and Alliances
The Diplomatic Formation and Legacy of Pope Francis

Dimitri Tsakas, PhD

Blakrok Insight
Brisbane, Australia
2025

Published by
Blakrok Insight
Brisbane, Australia

© 2025 Dimitri Tsakas

Blakrok Insight™ is a trademark of Dimitri Tsakas.
All rights reserved. No part of this publication may be reproduced, stored in a retrieval system, or transmitted in any form or by any means—electronic, mechanical, photocopying, recording, or otherwise—without the prior written permission of the author, except for brief quotations used in reviews or scholarly works.

ISBN: 978-1-7641486-0-3 (Paperback)

Printed in Australia

www.blakrokinsight.com

For Michelle,
who stood in the silence between chapters.
For Andrew and James,
who reminded me where the heart lives.
And for Pope Francis,
whose diplomacy made space for the Spirit to breathe.

Contents

Foreword v

Preface viii

Acknowledgements x

Introduction xi

PART I: Faith, Formation, and Foreign Affairs: The Jesuit Pope's Diplomatic Inheritance 1

Chapter One: From Fisherman to Statesman The Historical Foundations of Papal Sovereignty 2

Chapter Two: Between Rome and the World An Introduction to Mapping the Diplomatic Legacy of Pope Francis 25

Chapter Three: The Diplomatic Imagination of Pope Francis 33

Chapter Four: Jesuit Spirituality as Diplomatic Formation and the Inner Life of a Global Actor 62

Chapter Five: The Legacy of Vatican II in the Francis Pontificate 87

PART II: Francis in the World: Relations with the United States, Russia, and China 108

Chapter Six: Francis and the American Imperium 109

Chapter Seven: Pope Francis and the Geopolitics of Russia 133

Chapter Eight: The Dragon and the Cross Pope Francis and China 158

Chapter Nine: Legacies in Light and Shadow The Horizons of Pope Francis 189

Epilogue: From Francis' Legacy to Leo's Dawn 197

BIBLIOGRAPHY 204

Foreword

Ian Hall

In retrospect, perhaps, the election of Pope Leo XIV ought not to have come as such a surprise. And yet it did, perhaps because outside observers are only now coming to terms with the impact that his predecessor, Pope Francis, had upon the Catholic Church. It is increasingly clear that more than any recent pope – indeed, likely more than any pope in centuries – Francis transformed the Church's long-standing claim to universality into an institutional reality, with dramatic effect. Appointing cardinals from more than two dozen countries not hitherto represented in the College, Francis pushed European cardinal electors into a minority. Giving voice in this way to the billion or so Catholics who live beyond Europe's borders, in Africa, the Americas, Asia, and the Pacific, he has decisively tipped the balance of power within the Church.

We may soon find that the election of an American and Peruvian pope with both European and African ancestry to succeed Francis is only the most obvious consequence of this transformation. It may be that the work that the late pontiff did to reorient Catholic thinking about the world and the Vatican's role in international relations was just as important. After all, as Dr. Dimitri Tsakas shows in this perceptive book, Francis brought to his papacy a different way of looking at international affairs and at the place of the Church in world politics to earlier popes. Indeed, he constructed a new kind of papal diplomacy.

This novel approach was at times controversial, both within the Church and outside it, and remains so today. Francis' establishment of a new *modus vivendi* with the Chinese Communist Party, which promised more space for the faithful, but which came at the price of more governmental oversight, was not welcomed by all, including by some of his fellow bishops. His diplomatic outreach to Russia and the Russian Orthodox Church, which included the first ever meeting between Pope and Russian Patriarch, was praised in some quarters and strongly criticised in others. His responses to Russia's invasion of Ukraine prompted further ire – especially in Europe – but were consistent with his belief that in a multipolar world, channels of communication must be kept open with all parties. In parallel, Francis' handling of relations with the United States, before and after the rise of Donald J. Trump, as well as with the fractious American Church, were also much debated. And his efforts to heal rifts with Muslim communities, which included a landmark visit to Indonesia, and his public concern for the plight of Palestinians, the Rohingya, and Uyghurs were arguably better received, but did not pass without comment.

Dr. Tsakas explores these interventions, their motivations, and their effects. But he also goes deeper, exploring the ideas that informed Francis' distinctive engagement in international relations. Dr. Tsakas shows how Francis drew upon a variety of ideas over the course of his life and his papacy, teasing out ways of thinking about the world, and weaving them back together into a robust philosophy capable of defining equally robust action. Francis' childhood in Argentina, membership of the Jesuit Order, experience of dictatorship, intellectual engagement with Liberation Theology, and understanding of the urgency and importance of the agenda laid out for the Church by Second Vatican Council all played parts, Dr. Tsakas shows, in shaping his 'unconventional' approach to papal diplomacy.

I am delighted to see this book in print – and not just because of the intrinsic importance of the subject. It was my pleasure to work with the now Dr. Tsakas on an earlier doctoral thesis on the diplomacy of Pope Francis which he completed at Griffith University. For me, the experience was an education, despite my formal role as an academic mentor and supervisor. When the research proposal was first pitched to me, I will admit, I was sceptical about the project. I recognised, of course, that the Catholic Church is a significant diplomatic actor and that past popes, notably John Paul II, have played important – even decisive – global roles. But when some years ago Dr. Tsakas and I began to talk about Francis, I was not as convinced as I now recognise that I should have been about his capacity to change the Church, its thinking, and its diplomacy. At that time, I did not fully appreciate Francis' distinctiveness and his capacity to affect the politics of a disordered world. Nor was I convinced that the moment was right, as it were, for a pope – who is, first and foremost, the Bishop of Rome, an ancient European city – to shape contemporary international affairs, defined, as they increasingly are, by non-Western powers.

Yet as the project developed and Dr. Tsakas made his case, I was increasingly persuaded of the intellectual importance of Francis' ideas and the power of his approach to papal diplomacy. And I am sure that other readers of this book will be similarly convinced, even if they might dissent from Francis' views on this or that issue. This book is not, in any case, a defence of Francis' diplomacy or some kind of apologia. Rather, it explores how and why Francis came to see the world as he did and to act in it as he did. It invites us to look from Francis' perspective and to understand his mind as well as his actions. Beyond the detailed analysis, the book's great strength is here, in the intellectual sympathy and consideration Dr. Tsakas rightly extends to a man who thought deeply and acted thoughtfully in the world.

Preface

This book began with a simple but persistent question: what made Pope Francis' approach to international diplomacy so unconventional, and yet consequential? In an age of resurgent nationalism, institutional mistrust, and global fragmentation, the Vatican's voice has continued to carry weight on the international stage. Under Francis, however, it assumed a more singular, unpredictable, and at times disruptive tone. This study seeks to explore and evaluate that tone within the wider arc of modern papal diplomacy.

Pope Francis may have been the first Jesuit pope, the first from the Global South, and the first to bear the name of *Il poverello of Assisi*, but these firsts were not merely symbolic. They represented a convergence of history, spirituality, and strategy that transformed expectations placed on the papacy itself.

The ensuing reflections are the result of my doctoral research investigating the international diplomacy of Pope Francis. That research involved sustained engagement with primary sources, historical records, and contemporary scholarship on Vatican diplomacy. This material helped to unpack how Francis' pontificate intersected with the practice of global diplomacy. While it derives from academic method, the text is written for a broader audience interested in the interplay between global politics, the Catholic church, and international leadership.

The impetus for this work lies in the belief that Francis' diplomatic strategy remains understudied in its totality. While his theological and pastoral priorities have been widely discussed, his geopolitical vision and the intellectual framework underpinning it have often been overlooked or misrepresented. Yet in an increasingly fragmented world order, the role of a global religious leader who speaks across ideological and national lines, often to both power and the powerless, invites serious attention.

At a time when diplomacy itself is under strain, the legacy of Francis offers an example of international initiative that was relational, fluid, and open to fresh potential. Whether one agrees with his choices or not, the legacy of his pontificate challenges us to rethink what diplomatic power can look like in the modern world, and what it means for the Church to act not simply in defence of itself, but in service of the common good of humanity.

At its core then, this book asks a simple but far-reaching question: *What does it mean for a pope to act as a diplomat in today's world?* And how did Pope Francis define that role in ways that both challenged and revitalised the Church's international presence?

Dimitri Tsakas, PhD
Brisbane, Australia
June 2025

Acknowledgements

This book, like the doctorate that gave rise to it, was not written alone. It was woven through long nights, countless hours, and the quiet patience of those who walked beside me.

I am deeply grateful to my wife, Michelle — companion of many seasons — for her enduring grace amid the long and often inconvenient hours this work demanded. Her patience has been the silent architecture behind every paragraph, and her presence a quiet strength beyond words.

To our children, Andrew and James, whose laughter and love reminded me daily of life beyond the page, I offer heartfelt thanks. They bore the distance my thoughts often travelled and gently anchored me when I needed returning.

I also wish to acknowledge Professor Ian Hall — scholar, mentor, and steadfast guide. His intellectual generosity, steady encouragement, and ever-open door shaped not only this book, but also the way I think. I could not have asked for a better supervisor, nor a more gracious companion on the academic road.

Introduction

Francis' pontificate unsettled the comfortable and roused the contemplative. It provoked reflection, ignited controversy, and inspired admiration. With his 2013 election, the papacy entered uncharted territory, Latin American in origin, Jesuit in spirit, and radically repivoted in its diplomatic posture and global perception. *Between Altars and Alliances* aims to offer insight into the extraordinary diplomatic legacy of Pope Francis. The present work explores his theological, cultural, and strategic formation and how it moulded his foreign policy in a multipolar world. In particular, it traces the footprint of Francis' diplomacy through three case studies: his relations with the United States, Russia, and China.

This study contends that Pope Francis did not merely inherit the instruments of papal statecraft as a fixed legacy, but received them as a living language, inflected with the cadence of his formation and the imprint of his global vision for the Church. Unlike some of his predecessors who operated within frameworks defined by European sensibilities and Atlantic alliances, Francis brought to the world stage a style born of the Latin American global South. His posture, at once pastoral and political, spiritual and strategic, offered an acutely personal model of international engagement: not grounded in geopolitical supremacy or triumphalism, but in dialogue, accompaniment, and a diplomacy of encounter.

Contours of Conviction

To understand Francis' diplomatic imagination, one must first return to his formation. Bergoglio's worldview was forged not in Roman palaces or European seminaries, but in the barrios of Buenos Aires, amidst political volatility, economic upheaval, and ecclesial transformation. He was a priest of the streets before he became a prince of the Church.

His years as a Jesuit provincial during Argentina's Dirty War taught him the limits of idealism and the consequences of silence. His complex relationship with liberation theology revealed both his proximity to the poor and his discomfort with ideological rigidity. These early tensions did not produce a binary thinker, but a leader trained to dwell in ambiguity, to discern rather than dictate, to listen more than to lecture.

The Ignatian tradition in which Bergoglio was steeped privileged discernment over dogma, and reality over abstraction. Jesuit engagement is not simply a set of techniques; it is rather, a posture that accepts paradox, embraces tension, and sits comfortably with relational ambiguity in politics. For Francis, diplomacy was not merely a tool of statecraft but an extension of his priestly calling. As such, it was imbued with pastoral sensitivity, ethical intentionality, and spiritual resonance.

This disposition was enriched by the Second Vatican Council, whose influence on Francis cannot be overstated. The Council's emphasis on dialogue with the contemporary world and its universal call to solidarity provided the architecture for Francis' diplomatic outlook. His pontificate consistently sought the implementation Vatican II in full. The *aggiornamento* called for by Pope John XXIII found in Francis a global executor. Where others saw Vatican II as a closed chapter or a point of contestation, Francis regarded it as an unfolding imperative.

From Universal Shepherd to Global Statesman

Francis' international diplomacy must also be read in light of his vision of the Church not as a fortress besieged by secularism, but as that of a 'field hospital' tending the wounds of humanity. In this, he saw the Vatican, not simply a as guardian of doctrine but as a prophetic voice in international affairs.

Where previous popes relied upon old alliances, Francis often appeared to sidestep them. His diplomacy favoured multilateralism, nonalignment, and what might be called strategic polycentrism. He welcomed a multipolar world not as a threat but as a providential opportunity to de-Westernise the Church's global imprint. In his preference for dialogue over domination and his pursuit of relations with non-Western powers, including those known for authoritarianism, Francis directed his own geopolitical compass.

His approach was not without controversy. Critics accused him of naïveté, of moral relativism, or of downplaying the suffering of those oppressed by some of the very regimes he sought to engage. Others argued that his gestures of openness masked strategic calculation. But such critiques often fail to grasp the deeper logic of Francis' diplomacy, which frequently privileged long-term goals over short-term triumph.

Choreographing Complexity: Francis in the World

A core of this book examines three case studies that illuminate the distinctive features and contradictions of Francis' diplomatic legacy.

His engagement with the United States reveals a pope unafraid to challenge a superpower both within and beyond ecclesial boundaries. His criticisms clashed with American exceptionalism. His 2015 visit to Washington, D.C., and his historic address to Congress reflected both reverence for American ideals and deep unease with their global implications.

In contrast, his approach to Russia displayed a cautious but persistent effort to foster dialogue with the Orthodox world. Despite geopolitical tensions over Ukraine,

Crimea, and NATO expansion, Francis sought to preserve channels of communication with Moscow, both religious and political. His meeting with Patriarch Kirill in 2016, the first in history between a pope and a Russian patriarch, symbolised his desire to reconcile East and West.

The China dossier stands as the most delicate and contested of all. Francis' détente with Beijing, resulting in the 2018 Provisional Agreement on episcopal appointments, represented a radical gamble. For some, it was a diplomatic breakthrough; for others, a betrayal of underground Catholics and a concession to authoritarianism. Yet here again, Francis' logic was long-term: to preserve the unity of the Church in China, to protect its fragile future, and to create openings where previous pontificates saw only impasse. The strategy mirrored the Jesuit missions of the early modern period, adaptation, patience, and the quiet work of mutual concession.

In all three contexts, Francis demonstrated a diplomacy not of dominance but of discernment. His pontificate invites us to rethink what it means for the pope to be a global actor in the 21st century. He neither retreated from the world nor submitted to its logic. Instead, he engaged it with the tools of a different arsenal: encounter, flexibility, and the tensions inherent with diversity.

This reimagined diplomacy did not please all. Within the Church, Francis met formidable resistance from traditionalist factions, conservative policy institutes, and media voices wary of his tenor. On the international stage, his challenge to dominant liberal models of globalisation and his sporadic provocations brought unease among those who preferred clarity over complexity. Francis was thus either cast as an inspirational global leader or dismissed as a political opportunist. His critics saw inconsistency; his defenders discerned adaptation. His diplomacy moved between shadows and light, too fluid to be boxed, too deliberate to be dismissed.

Between Legacy and Horizon

This book does not seek to canonise or condemn Pope Francis' diplomatic project. Rather, it aims to trace its sources, examine its strategies, and assess its consequences. It asks how a Jesuit pope, shaped by the crucible of Latin America, came to define Vatican diplomacy in an age of fragmentation, doing so not by inheritance, but on his own terms. It explores Francis' vision of a Church in dialogue with history: discerning the world it must speak to, and becoming the voice that fractured humanity might yet heed.

The chapters that follow are arranged both thematically and chronologically. Part I traces the historical and theological foundations of papal diplomacy, explores Francis' intellectual and spiritual formation, and examines the institutional legacy he inherited from the Second Vatican Council. Part II explores his relations with three geopolitical giants, Washington, Moscow, and Beijing, with each chapter unpacking the tensions, triumphs, and trade-offs of his diplomatic encounters. The final chapter reflects on the long-term significance of his pontificate before the transition to his successor, Pope Leo XIV.

Ultimately, this book argues that Pope Francis conceived of diplomacy not as a detached extension of statecraft, but as a living expression of the Church's mission in the world. He approached diplomacy not merely as the art of negotiation, but as a ministry of presence. Though his legacy continues to unfold, it already poses a quiet provocation to future pontiffs, diplomats, and theologians: to reimagine the Church's role in a world marked by fracture and flux.

PART I: Faith, Formation, and Foreign Affairs: The Jesuit Pope's Diplomatic Inheritance

Chapter One: From Fisherman to Statesman The Historical Foundations of Papal Sovereignty

The figure of the pope, once cloaked in temporal majesty and feudal power, has undergone a profound metamorphosis, emerging in the modern era as a sovereign global actor, shaped by history and the urgencies of modern diplomacy. This transformation did not occur overnight, nor was it the product of a singular theological insight or political reform. Rather, it unfolded through a centuries-long negotiation between spiritual authority and temporal ambition.

Beginning with the reforms of Pope Gregory VII (1073–1085), the papacy in the eleventh and twelfth centuries increasingly asserted its authority over secular rulers. The Investiture Controversy (1075–1122), for example, directly challenged the right of monarchs to appoint bishops, reflecting a broader struggle over the boundaries of ecclesiastical and temporal power. Combined with the earlier establishment of the Papal States (756) and the later trauma of their dissolution (1870), these developments contributed to the emergence of a distinctive papal conception of sovereignty, one that navigated the complex terrain between spiritual leadership and geopolitical agency.

As the unified authority of Christendom fragmented, it gradually gave way to the Westphalian system, a political order established in the seventeenth century that recognised the sovereignty of individual nation-states and the separation of religious and political authority. The *Peace of Westphalia* (1648) marked a turning point, seeking to end the devastating Catholic-Protestant wars of religion that had engulfed Europe from 1524 to 1648.

Within this emerging framework, and later within the broader international system of modern states, the papacy was progressively compelled to reimagine its global posture and diplomatic role. No longer commanding armies or ruling territories, it cultivated alternative and renewed forms of presence that would prove increasingly consequential in the twentieth and twenty-first centuries.

This chapter traces the historical genesis of that transformation, illuminating how the papal office acquired, lost, and ultimately reconceived its role on the world stage. It explores the foundations of modern papal diplomacy: how the papacy became a sovereign global actor, how its identity evolved, and how it functions within the contemporary international system. From ancient bishopric to modern global diplomatic stature, the papacy has undergone one of the most remarkable institutional evolutions in the history of international relations. This transformation was neither linear nor uncontested. It unfolded through doctrinal assertion, imperial patronage, geopolitical necessity, and at times sheer survival.

Contemporary papal authority is both immense and constrained. A pope governs Vatican City and directs Catholic diplomacy, but he cannot arbitrarily change Church doctrine or deviate from scripture and normative interpretations of Catholic tradition. This balance between power and limitation, and between the spiritual and the temporal, is essential to understanding what Pope Francis' role in the theatre of international affairs was. His papal office served as a unifying symbol for the global Catholic Church, both internally and in its ministry among and within secular states. Throughout most of its history, the Church has seen itself as necessarily engaged in world politics. Each pope must navigate the paradox between the *realpolitik* of global affairs and the idealism found in the Church's ecclesial self-understanding. This is the perennial paradox of the Church itself: how to be in the world, yet not of it.

From Catacombs to Crowns: The Ascent of the Papal Office

The papacy stands as one of the oldest continuous institutions in global politics, its longevity eclipsing that of most contemporary nation-states. Across two millennia, successive popes have traversed the rise and fall of empires, the upheavals of revolution, and the shifting tides of ideology. They have crowned emperors and challenged monarchs, mediated conflicts and shaped moral discourse, leaving an indelible imprint on the trajectory of Western civilisation.

Though stripped of its former territorial dominion, the Holy See endures as a singular entity, both spiritual and sovereign, whose diplomatic influence, paradoxically, has only deepened in the wake of its temporal decline. In an international order defined by power blocs and shifting alliances, the Vatican offers a distinct voice: unarmed, often underestimated, yet remarkably resilient. Philosopher Thomas Hobbes once described the papacy as "the ghost of the deceased Roman Empire sitting crowned upon its grave" (Hobbes, Stanlick, and Collete 2016, 274). He was not entirely wrong. The Roman Church did arise from the ruins of the empire it once served. Yet what Hobbes did not foresee was the remarkable durability, adaptability, and diplomatic reach that the papacy would continue to display.

The Catholic Church has long demonstrated a particular capacity to translate spiritual foundations into political authority. Central to this evolution is the *Petrine Commission*—Christ's words to the Apostle Peter: "You are Peter, and on this rock I will build my church" (Matthew 16:18). For Catholics, this passage serves not merely as a theological cornerstone but as the legitimating source of papal primacy. Over the centuries, it became the axis around which both ecclesial structure and political aspiration revolved. The symbolic and doctrinal weight of Peter's mandate underpinned the rise of the papacy as a juridical and eventually geopolitical institution. What began as spiritual stewardship within the early Church gradually expanded into claims of temporal jurisdiction, enabling popes to intervene in imperial succession, arbitrate territorial disputes, and shape the contours of history.

In its early centuries, the Roman Church claimed spiritual authority but enjoyed limited political power. That began to change in the fourth century when Emperor Constantine legalised Christianity. The construction of St Peter's Basilica as a central shrine of Christendom marked the beginning of the Church's ascendancy in the political realm (Whalen 2014). Over the next two centuries, as imperial authority shifted eastward to Constantinople, a city established by Constantine himself, Rome began to decline. The weakening of imperial structures in the West, combined with repeated invasions by northern tribes, left a vacuum that the Church increasingly stepped in to fill.

The fifth and early sixth centuries were thus marked by existential anxiety for the city of Rome (Sessa 2012; Demacopoulos 2013). As the Western Roman Empire crumbled, the papacy assumed greater responsibility. Popes such as Leo the Great (440–461) served not only as spiritual leaders but also as effective civic authorities, overseeing the administration of Church lands, mediating local disputes, and engaging in diplomatic negotiations with foreign powers. These expansion of duties led to a substantial accumulation of land and influence, effectively laying the foundations for what would become papal diplomacy.

Pope Leo the Great (440–461) proved a capable and pragmatic leader in a time of crisis, as Roman wealth and power migrated east. Under his tenure, the papacy grew in both necessity and authority (Wessel 2008). Through successive upheavals, the papacy became a consistent institutional presence. Over time, it acquired temporal dimensions that extended far beyond ecclesiastical priorities. By the medieval period, it had emerged as one of Europe's most powerful political forces.

During this era, the scope of papal authority expanded significantly. Pope Innocent III (1198–1216) elevated the office to its zenith, asserting that the pope held authority even above that of kings and emperors. He consolidated earlier developments and insinuated the notion of the pope as an absolute monarch. Though Pope Francis frequently attempted to temper this image, the modern papacy remains, in legal and ecclesial terms, an absolute monarchy and sovereign head of state (Burns 2018). This model of authority remains embedded in the papal office.

To this day, the pope is in principle an absolute monarch, acknowledged by both supporters and critics alike. Despite its emphasis on collegiality, the Second Vatican Council's *Dogmatic Constitution Lumen Gentium* nonetheless affirms the supreme authority of the pope: "The Roman Pontiff, by reason of his office as Vicar of Christ... has full, supreme, and universal power over the whole Church. And he is always free to exercise this power." (Pope Paul VI 1964). Yet this teaching exists in tension with newer models of leadership that reflect a greater emphasis upon humility, service, and the collegiality promoted by the Council. Pope Francis made intentional efforts to decentralise papal authority, but the institutional structure positioned him as supreme leader of the Church, in both religious and legal terms.

From Exile to Empire: The Vatican Reborn in 1929

Papal diplomacy has long been shaped by conflict and crisis. The Protestant Reformation shattered the religious unity of Europe, resulting in major losses for the Catholic Church. Centuries later, Napoleon Bonaparte humiliated the Church by imprisoning popes and seizing papal lands. Yet perhaps the most defining rupture came in the 19th century with the rise of Italian nationalism and the establishment of the Italian state in 1870.

When modern Italy was unified, it annexed the Papal States, stripping the pope of his territorial holdings and reducing him, symbolically and physically, to what many described as a 'prisoner of the Vatican.' In response to this unprecedented loss of temporal power, the First Vatican Council (1869–70) proclaimed the doctrine of papal infallibility, largely to reinforce the pope's spiritual authority as his political authority waned (Washburn 2016).

The papacy faced an existential crisis and a diplomatic stalemate with the Italian state. This impasse continued until 1929, when the Lateran Treaty resolved the so-called 'Roman Question.' In this landmark agreement between the Holy See and Mussolini's fascist government, the Vatican was recognized as an independent sovereign entity, and the Holy See as a distinct international legal personality, separate from and not dependent upon Vatican City territory. This created a *sui generis* status for the papacy, whose sovereignty rested not on land or military power, but on religious authority and institutional continuity.

The treaty also included significant financial compensation for the loss of the Papal States, which had once spanned large parts of Italy. The Italian government provided a substantial cash payment and Italian government bonds, restoring the papacy's financial independence and enabling the modern expansion of Vatican institutions (Martens 2006).

The Lateran Treaty, however, did more than resolve a longstanding territorial and political dispute; it established the constitutional and legal foundations for the Holy See's unique status in international relations. It initiated the modern transformation of the Office from a position of resistance to one of redefined international engagement.

By formalising a new model of sovereignty grounded in religious authority and historical legacy, the treaty set a lasting precedent. This *sui generis* form of sovereignty became a defining feature of modern papal diplomacy. In exchange, the papacy pledged international neutrality. Armed with secure legal standing and vast financial resources, the Holy See re-entered global politics as an unconventional actor.

Crucial in the provisions of the Lateran Treaty, was a clear legal distinction between the Vatican City State (as physical territory) and the Holy See (as the juridical and diplomatic representation of the papacy). This hallmark enshrined a functional, non-territorial model of sovereignty (Murphy 1974). The term 'Holy See' referred to the See of Saint Peter and its sovereign incumbent, the pope, as Peter's successor. In international law and diplomacy, the Holy See, not Vatican City, is the recognised subject. It is the Holy See that formulates policy, appoints papal nuncios (envoys), and receives foreign ambassadors (Kent 1981). The treaty thus enabled the development of a diplomatic infrastructure more attuned to the complexity of modern global politics.

Through these structures, the Holy See maintains formal diplomatic relations with over 180 states. It also participates in a wide range of international organizations, including the African Union, the Council of Europe, and the European Union. It is a member of the International Atomic Energy Agency and the Organization for Security and Cooperation in Europe, and it holds permanent observer status at the United Nations, UNESCO, the United Nations Conference on Trade and Development, and the World Trade Organization. Additionally, it enjoys special membership status in the Arab League.

From Fortress to Forum: Vatican II and the Transformation of Papal Diplomacy

It was not until the Second Vatican Council (1962–1965) that the legal sovereignty established by the Lateran Treaty was matched by a renewed vision of the Church's place in the world. While the treaty had resolved the 'Roman Question' and secured the Holy See's international recognition, it left open the deeper question of how the papacy would engage a rapidly changing global order. The most consequential transformation in modern papal diplomacy thus came not from legal accords but from conciliar renewal. Vatican II redefined the Church's relationship with the modern world by opening it to ecumenical outreach, a commitment to social justice, and an active engagement with global institutions.

While the First Vatican Council (1869–1870) had responded to the siege of modernity by affirming papal infallibility, Vatican II offered a more expansive, outward-facing vision. It sought to cultivate a globalised papacy that projected itself well beyond the borders of Catholicism and entered into dialogue with the complexities of pluralism, secularism, and post-colonial international politics (Ferrarotti 1990).

If the Lateran Treaty provided diplomatic scaffolding for a sovereign Holy See, Vatican II supplied the theological and institutional imagination for its global mission. The Council invited the Church to speak not only to the Catholic faithful, but also to non-Christian religions, secular institutions, and international civil society. Ferrarotti (1990) held the view that Vatican II marked the emergence of a papacy no longer confined to Latin Christendom but initiated a complete reorientation toward active participation in a pluralistic world.

Though a later chapter will explore the full implications of Vatican II for contemporary diplomacy, some observations are necessary here to establish the historical continuity this chapter seeks to highlight.

Vatican II, the largest ecclesial gathering in Church history, brought together bishops from across the globe, reflecting the growing diversity and decentralisation of Catholicism. Unlike previous councils, it did not define new dogmas; rather, it reoriented the Church's self-understanding and missionary posture. Convened at the height of the Cold War, amid nuclear threat and ideological division, the Council addressed not only internal ecclesial concerns but also global anxieties.

Drawing on currents in contemporary humanist thought, including the evolutionary theology of Pierre Teilhard de Chardin, the Council developed a theological anthropology responsive to historical change and human development. Traditionally, Catholic theology had relied on static metaphysical categories often ill-suited to the dynamism of modernity. Stephen Schloesser described this older posture as one of "supernaturalist eternalism," in which tradition risked appearing disconnected from the flow of history (Schloesser 2006, 307). Bernard Lonergan interpreted Vatican II's intervention as a shift from "classical" to "historical-mindedness," repositioning the Church within the unfolding of human experience (Lonergan 2016, 1–10). Earlier approaches had often regarded modernity with suspicion; Vatican II instead encouraged engagement within it.

This institutional and pastoral reorientation had profound diplomatic implications. Papal diplomacy began to evolve in both scope and tone. No longer confined to internal Church affairs or state concordats, it emerged as a vehicle for humanitarianism, peacebuilding, and multilateral dialogue. The Church moved from a defensive position of confrontation to one of critical engagement, from viewing the world as adversary to encountering it as interlocutor. This shift became especially visible in the pontificates of John XXIII, Paul VI, John Paul II, Benedict XVI, and Pope Francis, all of whom drew deeply from the well of Vatican II's theological anthropology and global sensibility. Francis, in particular, would boldly adopt this legacy in his diplomatic vision.

Vatican II was thus less a doctrinal watershed than a diplomatic re-foundation. It liberated the papacy from outdated institutional models and enabled new forms of ecclesial statesmanship proving more agile, inclusive, and globally engaged. The modern papacy, with its emphasis on cultural dialogue, moral advocacy, and universal solidarity, stands on the structural and spiritual foundations laid by the Council. Understanding Pope Francis's international diplomacy, his messaging, his multilateral outreach, and his critique of systemic injustice, requires recognising the conciliar roots from which it draws.

This conciliar turn toward universalism fundamentally reshaped the diplomatic ethos of the Holy See. Papal diplomats were no longer merely emissaries to episcopal conferences and foreign ministries; they became participants in broader global conversations about human rights, economic development, environmental justice, and disarmament. The papacy positioned itself as a voice of conscience within the moral governance of international affairs, exercising a unique form of 'soft power' grounded in religious legitimacy, ethical continuity, and historical memory.

From the mid-twentieth century onwards, successive popes adopted and adapted this expanded vision. Each brought a distinct tone and emphasis, but all wrestled with the same enduring tension: how to reconcile the Church's spiritual vocation with the demands of contemporary international politics. This unresolved dynamic between faith and diplomacy, between transcendence and immanence, remains the fulcrum of papal diplomacy today.

The post–Vatican II papacy embraced its new diplomatic identity not as a vestige of lost empire but as the head of a moral and spiritual polity without borders. Freed from the burdens of territorial sovereignty, popes re-emerged as global actors whose authority was exercised through persuasion, presence, and witness rather than coercion or command. José Casanova observed that the very loss of territorial empire paradoxically enhanced the Church's influence in a newly emerging world (Casanova 1997).

Far from retreating into irrelevance, the papacy reconstituted its temporal role through non-material means. It participated in global institutions, mediated conflicts, and advocated for the marginalised. Its power now lies not in armies or borders, but in its capacity to shape ethical discourse and project moral diplomacy.

In sum, the twentieth century witnessed a decisive reimagining of papal diplomacy. From the legal recognition secured by the Lateran Treaty to the theological and institutional renewal of Vatican II, the papacy transitioned from a territorial power to a global moral presence. This transformation remains central to the Holy See's unique role in international affairs today—a presence no longer defined by empire, but by conscience.

The bold reorientation of papal diplomacy inaugurated by Vatican II did not however, emerge in a vacuum. It was the fruit of a renewed vision of the papacy found in the person and pontificate of Pope John XXIII. Far from being a mere transitional figure, John embodied the pastoral, open, and globally attuned spirit that would come to define the Council he convened. His election saw a turning point in both tone and substance. To understand the Council's diplomatic legacy, one must examine the pope who dared to open the Church's windows to the modern age, and in doing so, set the papacy on a new course toward global engagement.

Opening the Gates of the Vatican: John XXIII's Global Imagination

The evolution of modern papal diplomacy cannot be fully understood without examining the pivotal role of Pope John XXIII. His pontificate shaped a decisive transition. Building on a distinguished career in Vatican diplomacy, Angelo Giuseppe Roncalli, elected pope in 1958, brought to Rome a profound understanding of international politics, human suffering, and the moral demands of leadership in a post-war, ideologically divided, and rapidly decolonising world.

Before his election, Roncalli served with distinction as a senior Vatican diplomat. His assignments took him to some of the most geopolitically complex regions of the 20th century, including the Balkans, Greece, and Turkey. During World War II, as Nazi deportations extended into Greece, Archbishop Roncalli intervened, alerting Vatican authorities to the unfolding atrocities and undertaking personal efforts to assist Jewish communities in escaping persecution (Hoffmann 1989). After the war, he was appointed papal nuncio to France, an especially delicate posting given French resentment over the Vatican's perceived silence during the war. With personal warmth and diplomatic skill, Roncalli helped restore much of the Holy See's credibility in postwar France.

Understanding the legacy of John XXIII is essential to appreciating the reforms and global ethos later embodied by Pope Francis. Comparisons between the two pontiffs are common. Both shared a pastoral sensibility and a very particular vision for the Church. They championed inter-religious dialogue, cultural engagement, and attentiveness to the contemporary world (Borelli 2013). Church historian Massimo Faggioli noted that John XXIII is "the key to understanding the Church of today, especially after the election of Pope Francis... Both Roncalli and Bergoglio brought with them to the Vatican an idea of the Vatican that is more global and more historical than it was before their times" (Faggioli 2014, 137).

The most revolutionary act of John XXIII's papacy was his decision to convene the Second Vatican Council. The announcement astonished many within the Roman Curia, not least because the pope insisted that the Council proceed without a predetermined agenda. His vision was for a pastoral, rather than dogmatic, gathering that could speak to the spiritual and social anxieties of the modern world (Childs and Forell 2012). In a bid to control the Council's direction, Curia officials prepared over seventy draft documents. John XXIII rejected them, urging instead that the global episcopate, immersed in the lived realities of the faithful, take the lead in shaping the Council's agenda (O'Malley 2010).

This act of ecclesial decentralisation reflected the pope's diplomatic instincts and triggered a formative moment for Catholicism. The Council itself unfolded within a volatile international context. Just days after it opened, the Cuban Missile Crisis erupted (October 16, 1962), bringing the world to the brink of nuclear war. John XXIII quietly engaged in backchannel diplomacy, offering mediation that contributed to a peaceful resolution. Though often overlooked in diplomatic histories, the crisis deeply impacted the pope and directly influenced the composition of *Pacem in Terris* (1963), his landmark encyclical on peace, written during the Council (Rychlak 2011).

John XXIII's approach to the Cold War also marked a shift. Unlike his predecessor, Pius XII, who had framed the Church as an ideological bulwark against communism, John XXIII opted for engagement over open confrontation. He initiated channels of dialogue with the Eastern Bloc and avoided demonising the Soviet Union, positioning the Holy See in a more neutral disposition amid global ideological polarisation (Phayer 2008). In doing so, he distanced the papacy from geopolitical partisanship and advanced a new diplomatic style grounded in openness and reconciliation.

Although he did not live to see the conclusion of the Council (he died in June 1963) John XXIII had already established its tone and trajectory. He moderated authoritarian ecclesial leadership models, renewed the Church's relationship with modernity, and inspired a generation of leaders. His guiding vision of *aggiornamento*—meaning "bringing up to date"—came to define Vatican II. It symbolised reform, renewal, and a Church prepared to engage rather than retreat.

John XXIII envisioned a Council that would modernise not doctrine, but tone, method, and orientation. As Peter Hebblethwaite observed, the effect of this *aggiornamento* was far-reaching: it reshaped global perceptions of the papacy and helped restore its moral stature on the world stage (Hebblethwaite 1984). In a powerful shift, the image of the pope as a distant 'Italian prince' gave way to that of a 'Universal Pastor' (Corkery and Worcester 2010).

John XXIII's pontificate thus marked an inflection point in the history of papal diplomacy. By combining diplomatic experience with spiritual openness, he recalibrated the Church's global profile. His legacy endures not only in the conciliar texts of Vatican II but in the very architecture of a modern papal diplomacy capable of speaking to an increasingly pluralistic world.

This new diplomatic model would be institutionalised and expanded under his successor, Pope Paul VI, who steered the Council to its conclusion and translated its principles into a global strategy. Paul VI's tenure fortified the Holy See's engagement with multilateral institutions, advanced the Church's presence in the Global South, and introduced the image of the globe-trotting pope, culminating in his historic address to the United Nations in 1965. Decades later, this vision of a globally engaged papacy would find new expression in later popes including Francis.

The Seeds and the Harvest: John XXIII and Paul VI in Continuity

If Pope John XXIII initiated the a*ggiornamento* of the Catholic Church, it was his successor, Pope Paul VI, who guided it through turbulent waters and embedded its spirit in both ecclesial life and global diplomacy. Giovanni Battista Montini, elected pope in 1963 shortly after John XXIII's death, inherited the monumental task of bringing the Second Vatican Council to completion and translating its vision into concrete reality.

A man of refined intellect, cautious temperament, and seasoned diplomatic skill, Paul VI emerged as a transitional figure rooted in tradition yet unmistakably modern. Before ascending to the papacy, Montini had developed a formidable reputation within the Vatican Secretariat of State, where he served for decades as a senior diplomat and administrator. His tenure as Archbishop of Milan, one of Italy's most populous and socially complex dioceses, further sharpened his political insight and pastoral sensibility. In Paul VI, the Holy See found a pontiff capable of navigating the volatile intersections of post-conciliar reform, Cold War geopolitics, and the Church's expanding global mission.

Despite, one of Paul VI's most consequential achievements being the overseeing, conclusion, and implementation of the Council, his contributions went beyond theological reform. As the first pope in modern history to travel extensively outside Italy, Paul VI broke centuries of precedent. His pilgrimages, to the Holy Land (1964), the United Nations (1965), India (1964), Africa (1969), and elsewhere, were not merely symbolic. They signalled a different tact: the pope was no longer a secluded sovereign confined to the Vatican, but a visible global envoy for peace, justice, and human solidarity.

Paul VI went on to restructure the institutional architecture of Vatican diplomacy. He reorganised the Secretariat of State, professionalised the diplomatic corps, and expanded his global network of apostolic nuncios. Under his leadership, the Holy See established and enhanced relations with numerous states, including newly independent nations in the post-colonial Global South. He was also the first pope to engage seriously with the Soviet bloc, initiating a policy of *Ostpolitik*, a controversial yet pragmatic approach to establishing communication with communist regimes. Spearheaded by Cardinal Agostino Casaroli, this strategy sought compromise and dialogue to ensure the survival of Catholic communities behind the Iron Curtain. The results were mixed (Kramer 1980; Dunn 1982a):

critics decried it as appeasement, while supporters viewed it as strategic realism.

By the time of Paul VI's passing in 1978, the Church had undergone momentous transformation. The image of the pope as a distant, monarchic figure had been replaced by that of a global shepherd. In this respect, Paul VI did not merely continue the legacy of John XXIII; he institutionalised it and cemented the centrality of Vatican II for the papacy's future evolution.

Between Memory and Mission: The Diplomatic Legacy of John Paul II and Benedict XVI

The reign of John Paul I was tragically brief, lasting only thirty-three days. Yet even in this short time, his papacy signalled continuity with the pastoral openness of John XXIII and Paul VI. Committed to peace, dialogue, and social justice, John Paul I offered a vision of papal diplomacy that, had he lived longer, may have advanced a gentle and personal style of global engagement (Norwich 2012).

With the election of John Paul II in 1978, the papacy entered an era of unprecedented global visibility and assertiveness. Karol Wojtyła, the first non-Italian pope in over four centuries, brought with him an intimate and first-hand experience of totalitarianism, having lived under both Nazi occupation and Communist rule in Poland. This shaped his resolute defence of human freedom and dignity. A natural communicator and skilled political strategist, John Paul II understood the power of media and the symbolism of papal travel (Duffy 2011, 128–136). His commanding presence and globe-spanning visits elevated papal presence to an extraordinary diplomatic scale.

John Paul II used this global platform to advocate for human rights, economic justice, and religious liberty. His staunch opposition to communism proved central to his geopolitical vision. Nowhere was this clearer than in his support for the Solidarity movement in Poland, which played a crucial role in undermining the Communist Party's hold on power (Kengor 2017). His informal alliance with United States President Ronald Reagan in pressuring the Soviet bloc has been well documented (Gayte 2011).

Yet John Paul II's critique was not limited to the East. He also challenged aspects of the militarism of American hegemony and global neoliberal capitalism, warning against dehumanising materialism and the erosion of moral values (Gaeton 2021). His diplomatic legacy, while expansive and multifaceted, was anchored in a consistent assertion of moral authority over ideological power, and in a readiness to confront forces that he perceived as undermining human dignity.

Pope Benedict XVI (2005–2013) inherited the legacy of John Paul II but subtly recalibrated its emphasis. Whereas his predecessor had been a charismatic statesman, Benedict's strengths lay in academic theology and doctrinal clarity. He was less politically assertive and more focused on safeguarding Christian identity in the face of an increasingly secular and relativistic Europe. His diplomacy remained rooted in the post–Vatican II framework but focused on theological precision rather than broad political strategy. While he addressed major international issues such as climate change and the Middle East, his interventions lacked the symbolic resonance and global presence of both his predecessor and successor (Formicola 2006; Allen 2006).

Benedict's diplomatic efforts produced mixed results. He succeeded in establishing full diplomatic relations with the Russian Federation but faced significant challenges in engaging China, where his tone met with resistance (Wiest 2005, 40–43). The most serious misstep of his pontificate occurred in 2006, when his Regensburg address included a controversial quotation from a medieval emperor linking Islam with violence. The resulting backlash across the Muslim world revealed the high stakes of papal diplomacy in a global media environment, where gestures and words are amplified and easily misread (Soage 2007).

Despite these challenges, both John Paul II and Benedict XVI maintained a diplomatic vision that combined Vatican II's pastoral orientation with firm moral messaging. It would fall to Pope Francis however, to integrate this legacy into a new era marked by multipolarity, rising populism, and urgent global crises. His papacy was to reinforce the papal role as that of a bridge-builder in a fragmented world. Rooted in the conciliar tradition and informed by the pastoral tone of his predecessors, Francis leveraged the Holy See's role not simply as a moral witness but as a high-profile critic, reinvigorating the Church's voice toward new and sometimes controversial horizons.

Pope Francis and the Politics of Pastoral Presence
The resignation of Benedict XVI in 2013 signified the end of one era and the beginning of another. His successor, Pope Francis, brought a strikingly different approach, shaped not only by his Jesuit identity but by his intellectual formation in post-conciliar Latin America. Emerging from the theological and pastoral currents of CELAM (*the Latin American Episcopal Council*), Francis absorbed a reading of Vatican II grounded in liberation, dialogue, and justice (Luciani 2017). These commitments would fundamentally shape his diplomatic outlook.

From the outset, Francis departed from convention. He regularly declined the use of the bulletproof Popemobile, walking among crowds to the consternation of security officials (Smith-Spark 2014). In 2014, he knelt and asked for the blessing of Orthodox Patriarch Bartholomew, an act without precedent in papal history (la Stampa 2014). He was named among the Centre for Public Diplomacy's Top Ten Global Public Diplomacy Actors in 2013 and 2014 (Amiri 2015). These and other moments demonstrated the fashion in which Francis employed dramatic symbolism to sharpen his diplomatic messaging (Massaro 2021).

Francis consistently framed his pontificate around what he called a *'culture of encounter.'* His diplomacy was not defined by dogmatic assertion but by gestures of humility, solidarity, and inclusion. In 2013, he led a prayer vigil in St Peter's Square to oppose Western military intervention in Syria, curiously positioning the Vatican alongside Moscow and Beijing on the issue (Pope Francis 2013c). The following year, he hosted Israeli and Palestinian leaders at the Vatican, praying with them in a vivid public appeal for peace (Allen 2015b).

Not without controversy, Francis' diplomatic outreach included overtures toward Russia and China, motivated partly by pastoral concern for local Catholic communities, but also by a broader multipolar vision of international relations. In his dialogue with Patriarch Kirill of Moscow, Francis acknowledged a shared moral agenda with Russia, suggesting it filled a vacuum left by a secularised West (Poggioli 2016). His approach unsettled Western assumptions about the papacy's geopolitical alignments.

Central to Francis' diplomatic method was the revival of symbolic gesture. He prayed at politically charged sites such as the Israeli separation wall (Beaumont 2014), reflecting John Paull II's belief in the transformative power of papal presence. These acts embodied his outward-facing vision, and some scholars, including Massimo Faggioli, interpreted Francis as restoring the legacy of *Gaudium et Spes*, Vatican II's most socially engaged document which had been long sidelined by more conservative currents.

For Francis, reactivating that vision meant not only engaging the world, but reshaping the Church's diplomatic presence within it even when that entailed ambiguity and risk. The pope did not constrain his efforts within the boundaries of conventional statecraft. Although not in command of armies or vast territories, Francis never accepted the absence of hard power for an absence of influence. His understanding of power lay in presence and persuasion.

Francis presided over a Catholic population of 1.4 billion — around 18 percent of the world's people. More than a religious community, this is a transnational constituency embedded in the fabric of countless societies. The Church spans boundaries: religious and secular, local and global, pastoral and political. As of 2023, the Catholic Church operated 74,368 kindergartens, 100,939 primary schools, 49,868 secondary schools, 1,358 universities, 5,405 hospitals, and 15,276 care homes for the elderly, chronically ill, or disabled (Vatican News 2023a). This vast infrastructure enables the Holy See to reach millions daily in fields from education to health care.

The Church also coordinates numerous global networks, particularly in the Global South. The Community of Sant'Egidio — a lay movement favoured by Francis — exemplifies faith-based diplomacy committed to interreligious reconciliation. Other major institutions like Caritas International and the Jesuits extend the Church's reach through humanitarian work, education, and advocacy for social justice. Though the Church's financial assets are difficult to quantify, its operational influence is undeniable. In many states with limited welfare systems, Catholic institutions serve as crucial partners in delivering care to vulnerable populations. Francis actively leveraged this scope.

Francis relied on the legacy of diplomatic neutrality that enabled him to act as a rare intermediary in international relations. Even in countries like China or Russia, where suspicion of Catholicism persisted and Catholic populations were small, Francis understood the Vatican's symbolic power was sometimes courted for the moral legitimacy of state interests. This form of influence, non-coercive yet frequently significant, constitutes a kind of moral soft power for the pope that Francis leveraged. Governments may dismiss ecclesial authority rhetorically, but few ignore the Church's practical impact, especially among the poor, displaced, or marginalised.

Francis stepped into this tradition with a vision both continuous and reformative. His diplomacy drew upon Catholic Social Teaching, but also reflected his own spontaneity, pastoral sensibility, and personal charisma. He resisted institutional insularity and brought the papacy closer to the people through language, action, and presence. Rooted in Jesuit formation, the pope took a pragmatic and improvisational approach to diplomacy. He made strategic use of modern communications, symbolic capital, and the Vatican's unique international standing. In doing so, he embodied a form of papal diplomacy that was deeply personal, relational, and attuned to complexity.

He assumed the papacy during a time of dramatic geopolitical change: the rise of populism, a disruptive Trump presidency, an assertive China, and a revisionist Russia. He described the moment not as "an era of change," but as "a change of era" (Gibson 2018). The phrase captured a fundamental shift and a corresponding opportunity for the Church to reimagine its role on the global stage.

In tracing the historical and theological contours of papal diplomacy, it becomes clear that this tradition is both resilient and adaptable. Francis inherited its foundations, but he also reinterpreted them for an increasingly fractured world. To fully understand his distinctive diplomatic approach, we must now turn to the forces that shaped him — his Jesuit vocation, the spirit of Vatican II, the impact of key theological and philosophical thinkers, his upbringing in Argentina and his experiences amid political upheaval and social inequality. The following chapters explore these formative influences and the emergence of a pope whose diplomacy would echo across continents.

Chapter Two: Between Rome and the World An Introduction to Mapping the Diplomatic Legacy of Pope Francis

The transition from Pope Francis to his successor, Leo XIV, represented a critical juncture in the ongoing development of the modern papacy's diplomatic and pastoral identity. As Francis' tenure ended, his diplomatic legacy laid a complex foundation for Leo XIV. The election of Pope Leo XIV was not merely administrative; it represented a shift that compels us to assess the legacy of Francis as a new pontificate takes shape.

Popes labour at the intersection of a universal religious mission and the realities of a secular global order. Christianity, with its absolutist tendencies, has long seen itself, particularly within Catholicism, as the custodian of ultimate truth. This perception raises a compelling question: how does the pope, as both spiritual leader and the symbol of unity for the Catholic Church, engage meaningfully with a world that is largely non-Christian and non-Catholic?

Within the sphere of international diplomacy, Francis had no religious counterparts operating at a comparable level. He functioned as a hybrid global actor, operating transnationally as an unrivalled religious leader while simultaneously enjoying sovereign legal personality. This dual identity enables every modern pontiff to participate fully in formal diplomacy and Francis did so with vigour (McLarren and Stahl 2020). In addition to his diplomatic role, the pope's authority over the global Catholic hierarchy bestowed upon him an uncommon form of domestic influence in countries with significant Catholic populations, allowing him to participate in both religious and, at times, political discourse within and between national contexts.

While operating within common broad themes expected from each pope, Francis chartered his own path, advancing unique goals with individual strategies. He pushed boundaries and redefined priorities in ways that set him apart. His pontificate's approach was less defined than John Paul II's, who aligned with the West against the Soviet bloc, and more global in scope than Benedict XVI's, which heavily focused on reminding Europe of its Christian roots.

Pope Francis was singularly equipped to navigate complexity, moving between the secular and the sacred, bridging divides between Christianity and other faiths, and reaching across the spectrum of Christian traditions. Ensuing chapters of this book will explore the influences that shaped his ability to do so, and examine, by way of example, how this was expressed in his diplomacy with three non-Catholic states, one avowedly atheist (China), one predominantly Orthodox Christian (Russia), and one that has traditionally led the global order, the United States.

Mapping the terrain of Francis' diplomatic approach requires an appreciation of the distinctive spiritual, intellectual, and cultural traditions that shaped his vision. Central among these was the Ignatian Jesuit tradition, which offered him distinct frameworks for discernment and decision-making. Rooted in a spirituality that values slow, process-oriented dialogue and reflection, this tradition emphasises personal encounter over ideological confrontation. It stands in stark contrast to zero-sum models of diplomacy, favouring patient, open-ended engagement. Furthermore, though aligned with his predecessors in devotion to the vision of Vatican II, Francis was particular in demanding its complete and unyielding realisation.

Another key influence was the thought of Catholic philosopher Romano Guardini, whose writings Francis studied in postgraduate work. Guardini approached opposing positions not as problems to be synthesised, but as tensions to be held in creative, often unresolved, dialogue. Rather than seeking premature resolution, his paradigms allowed for complexity, ambiguity, and the slow emergence of direction over time, a rhythm resonating deeply with the Jesuit ethos of cyclical reflection.

Francis' formation was also indirectly (some would argue, directly) shaped by the Perónist political culture, and the Latin American schools of liberation theology that characterised mid-20th-century Argentina. Liberation theology and Francis' adjustment of its more Marxist interpretations took the form of a bottom-up approach to socio-religious engagement. Perónism, though often an unclear political ideology, did nonetheless, harbour a wariness of rigid bipolarity during the cold-war, and an even greater suspicion of global unipolarity. Its instinct was to move beyond global camps, and instead to seek pluralistic, multipolar forms of engagement in Argentina's national interests.

Pope Francis was therefore, shaped by a rich interplay of intellectual, spiritual, and political traditions, each leaving a distinct imprint on his international diplomacy. Together, these influences formed the unique contours of his style and the substance of his outreach.

In highlighting how Francis diverged from the caution of his predecessors, veteran Vatican commentator and editor of Crux, John Allen Jr., emphasized the pope's unconventional style. "In all honesty," Allen wrote, "the unofficial anthem of this papacy probably ought to be Frank Sinatra's 'My Way.' This is a papacy, after all, for which bucking tradition and courting confusion in the name of evangelical authenticity is essentially its modus operandi" (Allen 2022). True to this observation, Francis proved frequently ambiguous, off-script, and sometimes impulsive in his public statements. He was often difficult to anticipate.

While maintaining clear and consistent stances on issues such as environmental stewardship, the plight of migrants and refugees, and his critique of neoliberal global structures, his positions became less predictable when addressing more politically sensitive matters. In areas where he sought ongoing engagement with certain powerful state actors, Francis repeatedly compromised, and his responses at times appeared inconsistent, particularly when entangled with complex geopolitical dynamics. His handling of Russia's war in Ukraine and China's actions in Hong Kong serve as notable examples of his strategic ambiguity.

To illustrate, in an unprecedented departure from diplomatic protocol, Francis made an unannounced visit to the Russian Embassy to the Holy See on 25 February 2022, just one day after Russia launched its full-scale invasion of Ukraine (White 2022a). Traditionally, popes do not visit embassies. Instead, protocol dictates that they summon foreign envoys through the Vatican's Secretariat of State, receiving them in formal audiences at the Vatican. No previous pope is known to have made such a gesture (Pullella 2022). Yet while his visit to the Russian embassy conveyed a sense of urgency and pastoral concern, he notably refrained from directly condemning President Vladimir Putin. Instead, he pointed a critical finger at the West, suggesting NATO had provoked Moscow's aggression. In a subsequent interview with Corriere della Sera, Francis accused the alliance of "barking at Russia's door," implying that its eastward expansion had contributed to the crisis (Harlan and Pitrelli 2022). Less than three weeks later, in a Zoom meeting with Patriarch Kirill of Moscow, Francis again changed tack. He sharply rebuked the Russian Orthodox leader for aligning the Church too closely with

Putin's war, warning: "The Patriarch cannot transform himself into Putin's altar boy" (Bella and Westfall 2022).

This sequence of events highlights the often-perplexing nature that was Francis' diplomacy. Within the span of a few weeks, the pope shifted from placating Moscow to protesting its aggression in an unconventional visit to its embassy; from suggesting NATO bore some blame for the conflict, to publicly rebuking the head of the Russian Orthodox Church, all without explicitly naming or shaming Putin. Were these moves part of a carefully calibrated diplomatic strategy, or did they reflect a more improvised mix of moral concern, political caution, and pastoral impulse? His actions in this regard have been variously interpreted as naïve appeasement, impulsive protest, strategic ambiguity, or principled opposition.

The pontiff's approach to China followed a similarly enigmatic pattern. In what was framed as an attempt to unify the Catholic communities in China, in 2018 the Vatican signed a Provisional Agreement with Beijing concerning the appointment of bishops. This arrangement was renewed annually but consistently met with scorn by critics who highlighted the dangers of compromise with the Chinese Communist Party amid growing repression of religious minorities (Leung 2020). Yet Francis remained unmoved by these concerns, even in the face of strong opposition from within the Church, which included among others, the outspoken 90-year-old Cardinal Joseph Zen of Hong Kong. Despite escalating clampdowns on religious freedom, the pope continued to prioritise engagement with Beijing, choosing what he viewed as discretion over confrontation.

At other key moments in his papacy, Francis did not hesitate to undertake bold and controversial gestures that carried both symbolic and diplomatic weight through his papal presence. In 2013, early in his pontificate, he travelled to the Italian island of Lampedusa, where he offered a striking rebuke of global indifference toward asylum seekers, refugees, and migrants. Many had perished attempting to cross the Mediterranean (White 2023). The following year, during a visit to the Middle East, he made an unplanned, yet emblematic and highly provocative stop to pray at the separation wall constructed by Israel in the West Bank. By chance (or perhaps not), he was accompanied by a young Palestinian girl holding her national flag (Beaumont 2014). In 2015, Francis entered an active conflict zone (a papal first) when he visited Bangui, the capital of the Central African Republic. There he met with internally displaced persons, celebrated Mass in a war-torn city, and called for peace and reconciliation between warring Christian and Muslim militias (Stein and Sengupta 2015).

In 2016, he achieved another historic milestone when he became the first pope in history to meet with the head of the Russian Orthodox Church. Their encounter took place at José Martí International Airport in Havana, Cuba, chosen as 'neutral ground' for a delicate and long-awaited encounter at the highest religious level between Catholicism and Russian Orthodoxy (Gallaher 2019). Their joint statement, however, was replete with platitudes and didn't address elephants in the room such as the plight of Catholics in Ukraine or the 2014 Russian annexation of sovereign Ukrainian territory.

These powerful acts, rooted in presence, solidarity, and implicit defiance, were not merely spontaneous; they reflected deeper layers of Francis' identity. They were consistent with Jesuit traditions of frontline encounter and risk-taking discernment. They also echoed the religious, political and cultural outlook of his formative years in Argentina, a worldview shaped by suspicion of hegemonic power.

In navigating the complex landscapes of China, Russia, and the United States Pope Francis attuned to a shifting world order. His diplomacy embraced a multipolar, relational approach embedded in cultural encounter and long-term relationship-building. With authoritarian regimes, he favoured incremental rapprochement above open confrontation, while with Western powers like the United States he expressed both cooperation and critique. In this he projected a papacy shaped by the interplay of Jesuit discernment, Latin American political consciousness, and a commitment to Vatican II. His diplomacy was at once spiritual and strategic, seeking to hold tensions creatively, and often ambiguously, in a quest for a more inclusive and reconciled global order.

From all this, Pope Francis emerged a complex and unconventional figure, at once spiritual leader, political actor, and dialogue partner in an increasingly fragmented and evolving world. His papacy reflected not only the enduring institutional weight of the Holy See, but also the deeply personal imprint of a man formed by Jesuit spirituality, particular schools of religious-philosophical thought, Argentine political culture, and the project of Vatican II.

Francis' diplomatic posture was neither doctrinaire nor aloof; he combined conviction with relational engagement. In the realm of multilateral diplomacy, he consistently promoted cooperation. Rather than asserting rigid positions or remaining a distant observer, the pope positioned the Holy See as an active participant in global conversations. His method favoured sustained dialogue and connection among nations to address complex, and at times, insurmountable transnational challenges.

In sum, the pontificate of Francis demonstrated a clear commitment to strengthening multilateral frameworks as vital instruments for global stability and shared responsibility. The pope's distinctive *modus operandi* reflected a careful balance between engagement and flexibility, avoiding rigidity while maintaining a fluid and active global presence. By questioning dominant geopolitical paradigms and embracing new modes of dialogue and collaboration, he asserted the role of the papacy in contemporary international relations. This orientation exposed both the possibilities and limitations of papal diplomacy in an era characterised by contested truths and the resurgence of authoritarianism. It underscored how the Vatican, through Francis, remained a relevant actor amidst shifting power dynamics and complex global challenges.

To grasp the foundations of this diplomatic vision, one must explore the development of Francis' worldview, how his personal background, theological and philosophical influences, and his political and pastoral experiences collectively shaped his view for the Church's international role. His early life in Argentina, marked by encounters with social injustice and political turmoil, as well as his Jesuit formation, provide a crucial context. This backdrop laid the foundations for a diplomatic style that was relationally orientated and attuned to the nuances of international politics.

The following chapter delves into some of these formative influences, tracing the intellectual and experiential trajectory that informed Francis' international outlook. Through an exploration of his theological and philosophical inheritance, in tandem with his life experiences, we can more fully grasp how his idiosyncratic diplomatic vision took shape in a determination to connect disparate actors, facilitate multilateral efforts, and articulate an exceptional presence within international affairs.

Chapter Three: The Diplomatic Imagination of Pope Francis

Unlike previous pontiffs, Pope Francis emerged from a markedly different background, one shaped by experiences and traditions often distinct from those of a European papacy. He was not burdened by the historical legacies that weighed heavily on his European counterparts. Moreover, Francis was the first pope to have had no direct involvement in the Second Vatican Council, yet the Council's spirit and tradition remained deeply embedded in him.

The pontiff advanced perspectives on globalisation that opposed both the standardisation imposed by neoliberal agendas and the fragmentation encouraged by nationalist withdrawal. His leadership style had clear implications, and this chapter offers a detailed exploration of the evolution of Pope Francis' political worldview by delving into the varied intellectual and cultural traditions that shaped his thinking and diplomacy.

It opens with a concise biographical overview, highlighting the formative experiences and early influences that laid the groundwork for his later perspectives. The analysis then shifts to examine his significant intellectual engagement with Latin American theology, most notably liberation theology. The presence of Perónism is also given consideration, not as a direct political allegiance but rather as a non-conformist ideology that contributed to the pope's worldview. His formation within the Jesuit tradition is central, as it instilled a spirituality reflecting a specific type of discernment, contemplation, and pragmatic, context-sensitive modes of decision-making. These diverse foundations collectively gave rise to what became Francis' hallmark diplomatic style: the promotion of a *'culture of encounter'* and *'outer dialogue'*. Given their critical importance, this chapter offers an overview of these elements, while more comprehensive discussions of his Jesuit formation and the transformative influence of the Second Vatican Council are reserved for dedicated chapters later in this book.

Before the Keys: The Story of Jorge Mario Bergoglio
Bergoglio was born on 17 December 1936 in Buenos Aires, Argentina, the eldest of five children to Italian immigrants Mario Bergoglio and Regina Sivori. Before entering the priesthood, he trained and worked as a chemical technician. At the age of 21, he suffered a severe bout of pneumonia that led to the removal of part of his right lung, an early physical affliction that would later add to the distinctiveness of his persona.

Bergoglio entered the Society of Jesus in 1958. He undertook studies in the humanities in Santiago, Chile, and later earned a Master of Philosophy in Buenos Aires. He went on to teach literature to high school students, a vocation that reflected his early dedication to both education and pastoral care.

Upon the completion of theological studies, he was ordained a priest in 1969 by Archbishop Ramón José Castellano. Francis had studied theology through the Faculty of Philosophy and Theology at the San Miguel Seminary, after which, he was appointed as master of novices while lecturing there. Following further study at the University of Alcalá de Henares in Spain, Bergoglio professed his final vows as a Jesuit on 22 April 1973. Profession of his vows signified the culmination of his Jesuit formation. Just a few months later, on July 31, 1973, Bergoglio was appointed Provincial Superior of the Jesuits in Argentina, a role he held until 1979. He had ascended swiftly through the ranks.

Leadership as Provincial Superior unfolded during a turbulent chapter in Argentina's modern history. Following the death of Juan Perón in July 1974, his widow Isabel assumed power amid growing social unrest. Political violence soon escalated, leading to a military coup launched by Lieutenant General Jorge Rafaél Videla in March 1976. The ensuing dictatorship set in motion the so-called "Dirty War," during which an estimated 10,000 to 30,000 people disappeared under the guise of anti-insurgency operations (Morello 2015).

The events of this period placed Bergoglio in an immensely difficult position. In May 1976, two Jesuit priests under his supervision, Orlando Yorio and Franz Jalics, were kidnapped and tortured by the regime. Although both were eventually released after five months, the episode sparked debate over whether the Provincial Superior had done enough to protect them. Francis later maintained that he was actively engaged in covert negotiations to secure their release (Reese 2013). However, some question whether his actions were sufficient, as both priests initially believed he had denounced them to the regime. Over time, Franz Jalics clarified that he did not hold Bergoglio responsible. The incident, nonetheless, remained a controversial episode in the pope's ecclesiastical career.

Commentators did not shy away from critiquing his actions during this time. Andrew Sullivan, for instance, argued that this was not a period in which Bergoglio displayed his best qualities. Sullivan references a candid interview Francis gave to *America Magazine*, in which he reflected upon the faults of his early leadership: "My style of government in the beginning had many faults… My authoritarian and quick manner of making decisions led me to have serious problems and to be accused of being ultraconservative" (Spadaro 2013a).

After completing his term as Provincial Superior (1973–1980), Bergoglio was appointed rector of the San

Miguel Faculty of Philosophy and Theology, a role he held until 1986. In March of that year, he travelled to Germany in pursuit of doctoral studies. His academic focus centred on the thought of Romano Guardini, a prominent Catholic theologian whose ideas come to heavily influence Francis' spiritual and intellectual outlook (Borghesi and Hudock 2018a). Although he did not complete his doctorate, Bergoglio devoted himself intensively to study during this time. In the words of Alejandro Bermudez, he remained "a Jesuit of the old school" (Harris 2018).

As a bishop, Bergoglio became widely known for his humility and solidarity with the poor. He opted for public transport, chose to live modestly, and championed the rights of the marginalised. His involvement in the Latin American Episcopal Conferences further penetrated his theological and pastoral mindset. Notably, he had played a key role in drafting foundational documents at the 2007 Aparecida Conference, texts that projected a renewed emphasis on the Church's *'preferential option for the poor'* and which reinterpreted aspects of Liberation Theology through a pastoral, rather than Marxist ideological lens (Crosthwaite 2019). These reworked Marxist expressions of Liberation Theology supported the Church's renewed emphasis on the preferential treatment of the poor and were deeply influential for Bergoglio.

Contours of Thought: The Intellectual Formation of Pope Francis

Pope Francis' intellectual identity defied easy categorisation. Biographer Austen Ivereigh noted that while Bergoglio was not a systematic theologian in the academic sense, he possessed a penetrating intellect informed by a deep familiarity with key Catholic thinkers. His affinity for Latin American theological currents was clear, yet he resisted being pinned to any single school of thought (Ivereigh 2014).

Coupled with Latin American theological trends, the Jesuit tradition furnished Francis with noteworthy processes for diplomacy, highlighting the role of gradual discernment through attentiveness to the esoteric world and its connection with an ever-changing external one. This emphasis upon the inner life and its response to the external world does not lend itself to dogmatism and partly explains Francis' preference for relational experience over dogmatic proclamation. In his native Latin America where social injustice and poverty were rife, abstract theology mattered less than it did for the European branch of the Church. This further explains his stress upon pragmatism.

Antonio Spadaro, in his interview with Francis in 2013, wrote: "The key to understanding his thought and his action can be sought and found in the Ignatian spiritual tradition. His Latin American experience is incorporated into this spirituality and must be read in its light if one is to avoid interpreting Francis by falling into stereotypes. His own episcopal ministry, his style of acting and thinking are shaped by the Ignatian *vision*, by the antinomian tension to be always and everywhere *contemplativus in actione*" (Borghesi and Hudock 2018a, xxvii). This fundamental dialectic, an enduring tension between opposites, is a key element for understanding his papal legacy.

Francis nurtured his worldview by drawing upon several thinkers. An analysis of his intellectual formation is challenging for Western commentators, as his sources of inspiration were generally non-European and non-Western in both origin, outlook, and tradition. Borghesi's account of Francis' thinking presented a man unable to submit himself to forms of zero-sum diplomacy. Francis did not view opposite positions in Hegelian dialectic terms where two rival ideas generate a third superseding synthesis, but in terms of a reconciled diversity submitting to a transcendental co-existence of opposites. This is a very particular understanding of diversity (Borghesi and Hudock 2018a).

The structure of international politics that began in the twentieth century as a multipolar system, morphed into a bipolar one following World War II. After the formal demise of the Soviet Union in 1991, the United States led a unipolar structure under its own hegemony. As China slowly began reasserting itself, the structure of international politics entered a new phase of either an emerging bipolarity according to some, or multipolarity according to others (Chitadze 2021; Chu and Zheng 2020; Rapanyane 2021). Francis was at ease with the uncertainty of a new emerging global order.

The Jesuit pope brought with him his religious Order's capacity to sit with unresolved tension for extended periods. It is a capacity that Massimo Borghesi described as *"coincidentia oppositorum,"* a 'unity of opposites,' and finds support among thinkers that were dear to Francis like Romano Guardini (Borghesi and Hudock 2018a). In addition to Guardini, Gaston Fessard and Henri du Lubac echoed this approach. Francis was influenced by them and other intellectuals like Argentine philosopher Amelia Podetti and Uruguayan historian Alberto Methol Ferré (Borghesi 2018; Rourke 2016).

Ferré's understanding of Latin America's place in the contemporary world formed a further basis for Francis' discernment of modernity. From Fessard, Bergoglio gained a paradigm of dialectical thought central to his thinking and, by extension, to his diplomacy. But it is perhaps Romano Guardini, who bestowed the deepest influence (Borghesi 2019; Borghesi and Hudock 2018b).

As noted, Francis had commenced a doctoral thesis on Guardini's thought but did not submit his doctorate. He examined Romano Guardini's ideas about holding opposite positions in tension. The unpublished thesis was entitled *"Polar Opposition as Structure of Daily Thought and of Christian Proclamation"* (Borghesi 2019). The thesis intended to provide an examination of Guardini's philosophical anthropology about the evident polarities in life, through an examination of his 1925 book, *Der Gegensatz* (*'Contrasts'*). The book became a dominant force in both Francis' leadership and diplomacy. Its most visible expression is found in the four principles of Francis' 2013 apostolic exhortation *Evangelii Gaudium* (nos. 217–37), which constituted his criteria for discernment in navigating the polarity of positions.

This particular dialectical tradition of thought, which started with a reflection on the tension between grace and freedom in Ignatius' *Exercises*, took on the characteristics of a philosophy aimed at unifying the hard contrasts of history and global relations. Francis' pontificate witnessed increased fragmentation of the global system, and the absorption of Guardini's thought was evident in Francis' paradigm for managing this. He applied Romano Guardini's thought to politics, wherein reality is superior to ideas, and in circular fashion, any way forward must avoid abstraction and return to pragmatism. These were evident in Francis' methodology and remained consistent with his stress upon *'encounter and time'* as essential dimensions of diplomacy (Borghesi 2019; Borghesi and Hudock 2018b).

Guardini frequently addressed the political issues of his own time and reflected upon the extremes of fascism and Marxism. Francis studied Romano Guardini's ideas of holding conflicting positions in tension, applying them tactfully within a pluralist world. The latter had proposed the possibility of respect for *'polar tensions'* without negating or reducing them to a higher synthesis in Hegelian terms.

Guardini thus, rejected Hegel's dialectic of linear history. On Guardini and his views on the relationship between faith and culture, Arno Schilson wrote: "He did not approach the contemporary world in a judgemental or patronizing manner… he sought to bring about an encounter that was neither rushed nor marked by arrogance so that the Christian faith and its theological reflection would emerge in dialogue with culture. It was with a remarkable openness, inquisitiveness, and readiness to learn that Guardini made the effort to comprehend varied cultural forms" (Schilson 1995).

Massimo Franco, while analysing Vatican relations with the United States, described Francis as: "A man of reconciliation in South America's divisive and at times tragic stories. The global equivalent of the reforms he has undertaken within the Vatican, which have met with both controversy and opposition, is the destruction and removal of all the ideological debris and waste left behind after the Cold War" (Franco and Flamini 2008, xxiii). In his earlier life, the pope had struggled with the opposites that divided Latin America. His overarching aim was not a mere synthesis, nor a centrist solution, but a pragmatic experiment proposing an antinomian unity, where opposites co-exist in relationship and encounter. For Bergoglio, this encompassed a dialectical view in which reconciliation is not entrusted, as in Hegel, to intellectual speculation seeking a synthesis, but to some higher force.

Another influence upon Pope Francis, by way of both example and thought, was the early Jesuit, Peter Faber. Firmly rooted in the early Ignatian tradition Faber lived in the 16th century (1506–1546). He was a companion of Ignatius. In a 2013 interview with Spadaro, Francis spoke of his admiration for Faber's "dialogue with all, even the most remote and even with his opponents; his simple piety, a certain naïveté perhaps, his being available straight away, his careful interior discernment, the fact that he was a man capable of great and strong decisions but also capable of being so gentle and loving" (Spadaro and Whiteside 2013, 27). On Faber, Massimo Borghesi elaborated: "In a divided Europe, Faber put himself at the service of reunification: An agent of conciliation and entrusted with pontifical missions into these enemy countries, he proceeded thoughtfully in a humanly hopeless enterprise, at a time when the unhinging of Christendom marked the birth of modern Europe. His 'universal spirit' put him on the path of ecumenism; he united in his own prayer those who led this divided Europe: the pope, the emperor, the king of France, the sultan, Luther, and Calvin" (Borghesi and Hudock 2018a, 241).

Like Faber, Francis similarly promoted himself as a bridge-builder, a mediator, an agent of change, and an interlocutor for vast and diverse international actors. In this sense, he aimed to reflect the papal title of *Pontifex Maximus*, which means *'great priest,'* though also understood as *'great bridge builder.'*

The influence of Faber was evident in much of Francis' diplomatic technique. In an address prior to his papal election, Bergoglio stated in a pastoral letter, "One of the most powerful impressions in recent decades has been the experience of finding closed doors." This letter, penned in October 2012, merged several themes evident in his later writings. Central among them, was the *'encountering'* of the *'other'*, adopting risk in opening pathways for dialogue, reaching toward new frontiers, and overcoming barriers (Bergoglio 2013).

Bergoglio, consequently, held that members of diverse societies were inherently obliged to court risk, discomfort, and the danger of crossing thresholds toward encounter with the other. He emphasised these same points in his 2013 Apostolic Exhortation, *Evangelii Gaudium*, in which he contemplated transformative encounters between diverse peoples, cultures, and languages (Pope Francis 2013d).

      The Jesuit pope preferred dialogue over coercion. His era was one marked by internal divisions within the Church and external tensions in throughout the world. His strategy aimed to understand and manage polarities without prioritising one over another (Borghesi and Hudock 2018a). His spiritual and intellectual framework as a consequence, accepted the inevitable incompleteness of relations and, in turn, favoured cyclical processes of dialogue. Open-ended thinking and persistent reflection took precedence. His approach was innately open ended.

      Insisting that realities are more important than ideas (Pope Francis 2013e, §231), the pope urged new paths, creating and allowing tension between polarised parties. There were of course, risks associated with this path, especially when other players remained intent on exploiting papal prestige for their own interest and when that same prestige was regarded as naïve.

Faith from Below: Latin America's Theological Legacy in Francis

      Latin American Catholicism has long been associated with the emergence and development of liberation theology, which aspired toward a theological synthesis of Christian doctrine with elements of Marxist analysis. Liberation theology aimed to address the political and economic plight of oppressed and impoverished populations throughout Latin America. Foundational figures of the movement included Gustavo Gutiérrez, Leonardo Boff, Juan Luis Segundo, and Jon Sobrino, who collectively advocated for a bottom-up ecclesial and social structure. Their approach elicited significant opposition from Rome, especially during the pontificates of John Paul II and Benedict XVI, both of whom viewed the movement's Marxist undercurrents with deep suspicion.

Maria Clara Bingemer identified the origins of liberation theology not solely with Gutiérrez and those mentioned above, but also with the *'Pact of the Catacombs'* — a largely overlooked document emerging near the close of the Second Vatican Council. Signed by a group of Latin American bishops, the pact committed its signatories to a Church of the poor, and in doing so, laid a conceptual pillar for liberationist thinking in the region (Bingemer and Lucchetti 2016).

The conciliar constitution *Gaudium et Spes* (1965) nourished this theological trajectory by emphasising the Church's responsibility to engage with the modern world. Soon after, Pope Paul VI's encyclical *Populorum Progressio* (1967) explicitly addressed global inequality, aligning closely with the concerns animating Latin American theology. During his attendance at the Second General Conference of Latin American Bishops in Medellín (1968), Paul VI gave legitimacy to themes of poverty and liberation, albeit without endorsing Marxist frameworks.

A more distinctly Argentinian theological current, developed however, and is critical in understanding the worldview of Francis. While liberation theology predominated in many parts of Latin America, Argentina developed a related but particular strand known as *teología del pueblo* (theology of the people). Rooted in the cultural and spiritual realities of the common people, this framework eschewed imported political ideologies, particularly Marxist ones, viewing them as yet another form of European cultural imperialism. *Teología del pueblo* instead prioritised local traditions and cultural contexts as vehicles for political and spiritual transformation. Jorge Mario Bergoglio aligned himself with this approach early, interpreting it through the historical lens of Jesuit missions in Latin America (Luciani 2017).

The distinction between these two theological movements became pronounced at the Third General Conference of Latin American Bishops held in Puebla in 1979. While the conference acknowledged the legacy of liberation theology, it simultaneously redirected the Church's attention toward culture and not class struggle as a principal agent of social change. The Fifth General Conference, convened in Aparecida, Brazil in 2007, further refined this emphasis.

Cardinal Bergoglio played a pivotal role in editing the Aparecida Document, which distanced itself from left-wing utopianism, revolutionary violence, and political messianism. The document articulated a theology deeply rooted in Latin American experience, one that confronted dominant European models and charted a different theological course for the region (Pope Benedict XVI 2007b). *Teología del pueblo,* while emerging from the liberationist tradition, offered a more contextually attuned and culturally sensitive framework for understanding the Church's social mission in Latin America. Its influence on Pope Francis was evident throughout his papacy, particularly in his encyclical *Evangelii Gaudium* (Scannone 2016).

Where early versions of liberation theology had interpreted 'the people' through the lens of Marxist class struggle, *teología del pueblo* rejected this approach, viewing it as an Enlightenment project at odds with Latin American identity. Echoing at some point, the ideological ambitions of Perónism, the theology sought to transcend traditional left-right dichotomies. Its intellectual and theological architecture helps illuminate Francis' conscious distancing from Euro-centric categories in both theology and politics. His diplomatic gestures and language reflected the relational ethos intrinsic to *teología del pueblo*, which placed cultural context and encounter at the centre of both theological reflection and practical engagement.

One of the movement's most influential thinkers, Juan Carlos Scannone, consistently emphasized a *'culture of encounter'* as central to Christian social thought. This *'culture of encounter'* rejected isolationism, championed engagement, and favoured the primacy of time (understood as process and discernment) over space (as a definition associated with static control and rigid interests) (Regan 2019). These frameworks directly shaped Francis' prioritisation of dialogue, cultural humility, and openness in the face of complexity. In this respect, his papacy extended the vision of Latin American theology, particularly in its critique of Eurocentric ideologies and its emphasis on listening and accompaniment.

Francis' *'diplomacy of encounter'* nonetheless, was not without its limitations. The praxis of dialogue met serious challenges when dealing with authoritarian regimes or political actors uninterested in mutual engagement. The real-world application of this theological vision was often fraught, and Francis' interactions on the global stage reflected the tensions inherent in attempting to apply a 'theology of the people' within the frameworks of international diplomacy.

Politics of the Pueblo: Francis and the Legacy of Perónism

Pope Francis grew up within the politically charged and cultural milieu of Perónist Argentina. While it would be inaccurate to classify Francis as an ideological Perónist, notable parallels existed between his political demeanour and numerous features of Perónism. Central to Perón's ideology was the rejection of European political models, a pronounced emphasis on national independence, and a populist tendency that prioritises connecting with the ordinary citizen. Although Perónism's objectives have been primarily domestic, its spirit can be discerned in Francis: his resistance to hegemonic power, his cautious distance from the United States, his leaning toward populism, and his intentional outreach to multiple centres of power in the pursuit of broader interests.

Juan Domingo Perón articulated his political philosophy in terms that were both humanist and emotive. In a 1948 address to the Argentine Congress, he declared: "Perónism is humanism in action; Perónism is a new political doctrine, which rejects all the ills of the politics of previous times… Perónism is a question of the heart rather than of the head. Fortunately, I am not one of those Presidents who live a life apart, but on the contrary, I live among my people" (Perón 1952). Perónism, in this formulation, rejected both capitalism and communism in their classical European expressions. Instead, it envisioned an alternative politics, committed to political sovereignty and emotional proximity to the people. It is this *'third way'* that perhaps resonated with Francis as he searched for alternative forms of global engagement.

Perónism also typically revolved around the presence of charismatic leaders. From Perón himself to more recent figures such as Néstor and Cristina Kirchner, Argentine Perónist presidents invested heavily in cultivating personal legitimacy through public devotion. This populist dimension is a key characteristic of the tradition (Andrews-Lee 2021). Perónist movements consequently, often framed politics as a contrast between 'the people' and a 'privileged elite'. In Argentina, this engendered suspicion toward employers, financial institutions, and others who were perceived in alignment with Western liberal ideology (Karush 2010). This dynamic was frequently nurtured by a dualistic political narrative: workers versus elites, trade unions versus business self-interests, Argentines versus foreign influence.

Pope Francis displayed a certain affinity with this style particularly in his conviction that both politics and diplomacy must embody the aspirations of the excluded (Gregg 2017). Like Perónist presidents, Francis was a charismatic figure who appealed directly to the disenfranchised, even as he accepted the inevitable opposition of elites. His leadership evoked sharp polarisation, compelling both allies and critics to define their stance in binary terms, either for or against him (Remeseira 2015).

To outsiders, Perónism may appear opaque, with its internal contradictions and populist instincts difficult to decode. The same may be said of *teología del pueblo*, the distinctively Argentine expression of liberation theology that shaped Bergoglio's theological imagination. Unlike traditional liberation theology, which framed "the people" within Marxist paradigms of class struggle, *teología del pueblo* viewed ordinary people not as a revolutionary class but as a culturally rich and spiritually dignified collective seeking greater inclusion. Bergoglio was openly critical of those who, in his view, spoke *about* the people while remaining detached 'from the people'. He summed up this critique with the phrase: "All for the people but nothing with the people" (Ivereigh 2014).

This core principle carried over into Francis' diplomacy, which sought to include often-overlooked actors such as the Orthodox Christian world and the diverse religious traditions of Africa and Asia. For this, he drew criticism, particularly from analysts and commentators in the United States, who accused the pope of political naïveté. These critiques were especially pronounced in response to his positions on China, Russia, and the United States itself. Agostino Giovagnoli, for instance, wrote critically about

Francis' goals as "far from Western" in their orientation (Giovagnoli 2019).

The debates surrounding these geopolitical stances will be explored later in the book. For now, it is sufficient to note that a Perónist lens offers some interpretive value in understanding Francis in diplomacy. It helps explain his navigation of international affairs as stemming from non-Western narratives that challenged Euro-American categories and drew, at least in part, upon an Argentine tradition that is both populist and postcolonial in instincts.

A Papacy Unbound: Francis and the De-Westernisation of Vatican Diplomacy

Unlike John Paul II, whose worldview was shaped by Cold War binaries, Pope Francis inherited a diplomatic landscape marked not by ideological dualism but by multipolar uncertainty. The global arena was becoming increasingly unpredictable, defined by emerging powers, eroding alliances, and shifting political terrain. Within this evolving world order, the inevitable challenge Francis faced was how to maintain the Holy See's credibility while engaging with regimes that operated in contradiction to its ethical teachings. During his papacy, global leaders were increasingly reactive, responding to crises rather than proactive in shaping outcomes to protect existing global norms (Mladenov 2021).

Francis was equipped in a unique way to respond to this new reality. His approach was both intellectually and theologically armed with an emphasis upon periphery over centre. From the start he reframed the Holy See's international relations by privileging perspectives arising from beyond the traditional centre of power of United States hegemony. This shift disrupted established diplomatic models. While his predecessors showed themselves largely at ease with Western ideological alignments, Francis promoted what might be termed a diplomacy 'from the ground up.' Jodok Troy observed that such peripheral rhetoric represented a reimagining of global politics that conceptualised world order from outside its dominant centre of power (Troy 2021, 9). In this light, Francis' strategy was deliberately to subvert conventional expectations in an effort to reshape papal diplomacy with new, and often, controversial narratives (Troy 2017).

This provided a counterweight to the asymmetries of Western liberal globalisation. It introduced space for alternative voices and expanded the scope of international engagement beyond established norms. To this end Francis highlighted the importance of inter-civilisational and inter-religious dialogue as playing formative roles (Smart 2003). In this emerging paradigm, politics was not only about state interests or geopolitical calculus, but also about the moral and spiritual dimensions of global life. This model enabled him to engage with non-religious authoritarian states like China on inter-civilisational terms, and with regimes that politicised religion, such as Russia, on both inter-religious and inter-civilisational grounds.

Unity Without Uniformity: Francis' Polyhedral Imagination

Pope Francis regarded contemporary globalisation not as a neutral process of interconnection, but as a force tending toward cultural homogenisation and the erosion of meaningful diversity. At the heart of his critique rested a contention that liberal market systems have been responsible for the progressive flattening of humanity into a mass of indistinguishable consumers and by extension, identities. According to his view cultural identities were diminishing under the weight of consumerist uniformity. The consequence, Francis argued, was a global culture lacking diverse compasses and incapable of articulating, let alone upholding, coherent principles to guide international relations (Rourke 2016). This type of globalisation, in his view, fostered a kind of indifference that privileged formalities over lived realities, allowing both market forces and national interests to dominate at the expense of the common good (O'Connell 2016).

Against such a backdrop, Francis proposed radically different models for international engagement. His vision invited interaction between plural cultures, not for the sake of synthesis or compromise, but for mutual enrichment. He believed that divergent cultures brought their own historical values into conversations, defending and adjusting them as needed, without dissolving into an undifferentiated global mass. In this regard, Francis rejected superficial syncretism. To illustrate this ideal, he invoked the image of a polyhedron, a shape in which distinct facets coexist, converge, and contribute to a unified whole without surrendering their uniqueness. This image encapsulated a diplomatic conviction: that authentic transformation of the world order must be inclusively constructed (Vourvoulias 2015).

With this goal in mind, Francis relied upon a method of political discernment that maintained creative tensions between unity and diversity. He accepted this as a form of human craftsmanship inevitably immersed in ambiguity, echoing Guardini, who, writing during the upheavals of his era, was deeply concerned by the dehumanising effects of technological and economic globalisation. Guardini resisted ideological categories. His *'incarnational'* approach to global events maintained a sense of realism that affirmed the Church's responsibility to remain engaged with political life. In this way, his thought offered Francis both a theological and practical basis for critiquing global systems that alienate people from each other in the name of uniform progress (Guardini 2001).

Alberto Methol Ferré, the Uruguayan philosopher and an ardent Perónist, similarly viewed modern globalisation as possessing a latent logic of political integration disguised as progress, but susceptible to cultural and economic imperialism (Díaz and Podetti 2017). Like Guardini, Ferré rejected the bipolar ideologies of the mid twentieth century. He denounced Marxism as atheistic messianism, and capitalism as a form of libertine materialism that eroded moral values. For Ferré, unrestrained consumerism led inevitably to the loss of transcendence, leaving behind only the pursuit of power as a guiding principle. In such a world, global politics is stripped of ethical foundations.

These critiques were not abstract notions to Francis. They formed a core for his political theology and provided an alternate way of proceeding in international affairs, one aimed at transcending the traditional language of power and rigidity. Drawing from this tradition, Francis advocated for a global political culture animated by solidarity, cultural rootedness, and the pursuit of a common good through the very prism of encounter (Borghesi and Hudock 2018a). In doing so, he imagined diplomacy not as a contest between strategic interests, but as a polyhedron space for dialogue, global encounter, and the preservation of diversity.

The Art of Encounter: Relational Diplomacy
Pope Francis' signature approach, what may be called *encounter diplomacy*, framed much of his global engagement. Though difficult to define in immutable terms, encounter diplomacy operates across multiple registers: spiritual, cultural, and political. Its core lies in prioritising dialogue over doctrine, relationship over control, and engagement over confrontation. Its posture under Francis' leadership, enabled the Holy See to open conversations not only with traditional allies but also with historically mistrusted actors. Francis approached Russia and China for example, not

through the lens of politics and ideology, but as custodians of significant civilisational heritages. For him, diplomacy started not with negotiation, but with relationship-building. This differed significantly from traditional statecraft.

Francis linked encounter diplomacy closely with the theological virtues of solidarity and charity, presenting it as a viable path toward conflict resolution. He frequently referred to this as *caminar juntos*— "journeying together" — which he framed as a vision for international coexistence (Auza 2016).

Following the Cold War and the ensuing unipolarity of United States hegemony, Vatican diplomacy had entered a period of inertia, appearing adrift without a compelling global purpose. Francis revitalised it, in large part through the force of his personality and the depth of his vision, which inherently carried with it relational encounter. His model flowed from spiritual foundations that emphasised listening, patience, and mutual respect. Whether this approach could yield tangible geopolitical results remained an open question, but under Francis it articulated the tone and arc of papal engagement.

Encounter was not simply a 'method of diplomacy' for Francis. He believed it was a way to safeguard human integrity. In a 2010 conversation with Rabbi Abraham Skorka, Bergoglio expressed his critique of globalisation as "essentially imperialist and instrumentally liberal, but not human," adding that it ultimately functioned as "a way of enslaving people" (Bergoglio and Skorka 2014, 150). In his estimation, contemporary globalisation prioritised ideas, technologies, and markets over human need, creating in the process, cultural and spiritual voids. These voids, he contended, could only be filled through alternative forms of knowledge rooted in the world's diverse socio-cultural traditions (Pope Francis 2015, §110).

For this reason, Francis offered a piercing critique of the prevailing logic of global politics. He contended that the erosion of human integrity, understood as a deeper commitment to moral order, had been supplanted by a cold calculus of utility. In such a landscape, decisions were no longer anchored in justice but swayed by the volatile currents of political convenience. As he put it: "With the loss of a sense of an objective moral order, and a corresponding demotion of reason as no longer capable of truly distinguishing right from wrong, what replaces properly moral reasoning is the mere calculation of advantages and disadvantages and the reign of a levelling consensus based on ever-shifting public opinion" (Pope Francis in Rourke 2016, 127).

This critique underscored an overarching orientation: to stand apart from prevailing narratives and instead promote what might be termed *outer dialogue*, a form of engagement with non-Catholic, often non-Western, political and religious blocs. Francis' desire was to build bridges across multiple horizons.

Outer-Dialogue as Diplomacy: Pope Francis and the Global Other

China presented the potential of an immense missionary field, Russia offered religious synergy on moral issues and Christian unity, while the United States remained the hegemonic power of a democratic West which traditionally promoted similar values of freedom and democracy attuned with Catholic Social Teaching. All three powers were important for Pope Francis' diplomacy but required a finely balanced approach. The Holy See's relationship with each constituted what Boris Vukicevic termed *outer dialogue*, diplomatic engagement with non-Catholic states (Vukicevic 2015).

While each relationship served different goals for the Vatican, two shared certain characteristics: China and Russia were and continue to be, authoritarian regimes with small or marginalised Catholic populations. The United States on the other hand, is formally a liberal democracy with a significant, though in places, polarised Catholic minority.

As Catholicism in the Western world declines, the Vatican has sought new avenues for relevance, presence, and influence. For his part, Benedict XVI left a complicated legacy, particularly regarding relations with Islam after his controversial Regensburg address (Pope Benedict XVI 2006). More broadly, between John Paul II and Francis, the papacy had entered a period of diplomatic inertia.

Notably, nearly all European countries that had never hosted a papal visit were predominantly Orthodox, underscoring historical tensions with the Orthodox world, particularly among Slavic populations where anti-Catholic sentiment runs high and requires delicate management by Orthodox ecclesial leadership. By example, diplomatic relations between the Holy See and Russia were not formally established until 2009, partly due to the reticence of the Russian Orthodox Church. Francis, with his non-European and non-Eastern-European background, enjoyed greater diplomatic flexibility in this regard. The historic meeting between Francis and Patriarch Kirill in Havana in 2016 was unprecedented, despite the fact that the prospect of a papal visit to Russia remained elusive (Alfeyev 2018).

Francis persisted in recalibrating inter-religious and inter-civilisational engagement with 'outer-dialogue' by capitalising on his global appeal and openness. The Vatican occupies a singular position in global affairs, unique among religions, in possessing a sovereign head of state. Under Francis, it strategically harnessed this status to amplify its voice on the world stage. This conferred upon Pope Francis a unique quasi-representative status effectively allowing him to serve as a symbolic voice for religion *per se*, thus strengthening his capacity for outer dialogue, and especially with non-majority Catholic states.

The Second Vatican Council's *Gaudium et Spes* had affirmed the Church's role as a moral conscience and compass in global affairs. Francis passionately revived this vision. Vatican II reoriented the Church's focus outward, away from ecclesiasticism and toward global politics. This will be examined in greater detail later in this book, but suffice to say Francis nurtured this impulse by positioning his pontificate as a voice within global civil society, not above it.

As previously discussed, encounter diplomacy and outer dialogue, however, remained fraught with symbolic and practical risks. In 2014, when Francis released two white doves as a sign of peace for Ukraine, the birds were attacked by a crow and a seagull, interpreted by some as an ominous symbol of the fragility of peace (BBC 2014). His intervention in Syria failed to alter the course of a war defined by sectarian and geopolitical rivalries.

If John Paul II was a pope of grand gesture in an ideologically divided world, Francis gestured more modestly at the intersection of culture, faith, and civilisational narrative. David Ignatius described Francis' diplomacy as deriving strength from a judicious use of perceived weakness (Ignatius 2015). John Paul II mastered the art of dramatic symbolism in the age of television; Francis operated by magnifying the voice of vulnerability. His *Urbi et Orbi* blessing during the Covid-19 pandemic, delivered alone in a rain-swept and empty St Peter's Square on 27 March 2020, was a striking example of papal diplomacy through performative humility. It resonated globally during a time of collective insecurity (Salai 2021).

Francis himself remained the focal point of outer-dialogue for Catholic diplomacy.

Francis positioned the Holy See as a 'religious coordinator' for global diplomacy. His tactic was savvy. Like John Paul II before him, Francis comprehended the papacy's capacity to project an image on its own terms. While differing in ideology, both popes recognised the potential of 'staging' in shaping global influence: John Paul II, as the first Polish pope, commanded moral authority against communism; Francis, as the first Latin American pope, enjoyed popularity beyond Europe (Faggioli 2020a).

Francis was an effective diplomatic duo with Secretary of State Cardinal Parolin: the charismatic, prophetic pope and the cautious, strategic diplomat. In a spirit to enhance diverse input, together they created a council of nine cardinals (known as the C9) representing the global Church and which could both inform and advise the pope in his quest for broader engagement. Parolin embraced his pope's paradigm and worked hard in giving flesh to a culture of encounter and direct it into the waters of outer-dialogue.

The Architecture of Thought: Four Dimensions Shaping Francis' Diplomacy
Francis risked his moral credibility on numerous occasions. He was accused of complicity through engagement with regimes whose agendas starkly conflicted with the moral objectives of the Catholic Church. Four key pillars of his thought, however, go far in helping explain how he attempted to manage complexity and risk:
1. Time is greater than space.
2. Unity prevails over conflict.
3. Realities are more important than ideas.
4. The whole is greater than the part.

These principles, rooted in Jesuit spirituality and in the thought of Romano Guardini, upheld Francis's conviction that "it is more important to start processes than to dominate spaces" (Magister 2016). The notion that *'time is greater than space'* featured prominently in Francis's writings. He first introduced the idea in *Lumen Fidei* (Pope Francis 2013a, §57), expanded it alongside the other three dimensions in *Evangelii Gaudium* (§§222–225), included it in *Laudato Si'* (§178), and reiterated it in *Amoris Laetitia* (§§3, 261).

In *Evangelii Gaudium*, referring to this concept of *time over space*, Francis elaborated: "This principle enables us to work slowly but surely, without being obsessed with immediate results... Giving priority to space means madly attempting to keep everything together in the present... Giving priority to time means being concerned about initiating processes rather than possessing spaces" (Pope Francis 2013c, §223). In a 2013 interview with Antonio Spadaro, Francis (then Bergoglio) affirmed this outlook: "We must not focus on occupying the spaces where power is exercised, but rather on starting long-run historical processes" (Spadaro 2013b).

The second recurring motif in Francis's thought was that of *'unity prevailing over conflict'* or *'reconciled diversity'*, which he explored in §§226–230 of *Evangelii Gaudium*. Here, Francis adopted a dialectical stance of sorts, viewing conflict and diversity not as obstacles but as openings. His polyhedral metaphor for globalisation illustrated this as a unity that preserved difference without flattening it. He rejected both the paralysis of perpetual conflict and the illusion of seamless harmony. Instead, he promoted another way, which he describes as "a willingness to face conflict head on, to resolve it and to make it a link in the chain of a new process" (Pope Francis 2013c, §227).

These were the terms of reference within which he initiated inter-religious and inter-cultural dialogue. His conviction of *'unity prevailing over conflict'* promoted a solidarity based upon the allowance for tensions to generate "a diversified and life-giving unity," where no side is subsumed by the other (Pope Francis 2013c, §228).

Francis' third pillar guides his views on the relationship between *ideas and reality*. Francis consistently privileged the latter. For him, ideas often simply evolved into ideologies. These systems subsequently imposed abstract principles at the expense of contextual reality. Ideologies, whether communist, capitalist, or other, in his view, obscured truth and inhibited pragmatic responses. In asserting that *'realities are more important than ideas,'* Francis invited engagement with lived experience over intellectual abstraction. While not anti-intellectual, he insisted that ideas serve communication, understanding, and praxis, but not domination. "Ideas disconnected from realities generate unhelpful idealism that can stifle constructive action" (Pope Francis 2013c, §232).

The final principle, *'the whole is greater than the part'*, informed Francis's macro-strategic thinking. It was an essential dimension, proposing that while each part of a whole (e.g. local context, cultural identity) must retain its integrity, the common good must guide the whole. The polyhedral model reappears here: local distinctiveness must not be sacrificed to global uniformity, yet the local must contribute to the global good.

Francis incorporated elaborated his political theology with four additional but related key themes:

1.   Politics is a form of service, not an end in itself or a tool for domination.

2. Politics must aim at harmonising diverse interests through commitment to objective truth.
3. Politics should express solidarity, accommodating pluralism within unity.
4. All nations possess cultural identities that should shape national goals.

Pope Francis envisioned a political culture that refused both the illusions of naïve optimism and the paralysis of cynical despair. In their place, he proposed a paradigm grounded in pragmatic hope, tempered by patience and nourished by the wisdom of the world's spiritual traditions. For Francis, these traditions offered fertile ground for cultivating unity amid diversity. Rather than relegating religion to the private sphere or stripping it of public relevance, he affirmed its enduring role in animating political life with moral depth and transcendent purpose.

Though critics might point to religion's misuse in fomenting conflict, Francis drew attention to its deeper, often overlooked vocation: to infuse politics with meaning and to orient power toward the common good. In this vision, he echoed a warning voiced by Rourke: "Just as the Jesuit mission had to be destroyed so the imperial projects from Europe could live, so does contemporary globalisation need to privatize religion and increasingly reduce its influence over political life" (Rourke 2016, 161).

Drawing the Threads Together
Pope Francis' worldview resists easy classification both within ecclesial contexts and in the realm of international diplomacy. His background and perspective shaped him into a global actor who privileged pragmatism over intellectual abstraction. Rather than maintaining the status quo, his worldview pursued transformation. While consistently constructing global challenges in moral terms,

he was not above strategic compromise. This resulted in a widely respected, globally popular leader who enjoyed varied success in building relationships, even with regimes typically alienated in the past from papal diplomacy (Lyon et al. 2018).

Despite his unconventional approach, Francis's diplomatic priorities drew heavily from several intellectual sources of religious and political thought. His encyclical *Evangelii Gaudium* articulated much of this. *Teología del pueblo*, which emerged as a distinctive response to Vatican II, especially *Gaudium et Spes*, represented Argentina's tempered version of liberation theology. While Latin American liberation theology took a more radical stance on political engagement, Argentinian Catholicism developed a more pastoral, culturally embedded alternative (Luciani 2017). Francis embraced *teología del pueblo* in his early ministry, and its influence was visible throughout *Evangelii Gaudium* (Ivereigh 2014).

At the heart of Francis' vision lay a form of globalism rooted in inclusive engagement. This vision featured prominently in the fourth chapter of *Evangelii Gaudium* (Pope Francis 2013d; Scannone 2016). The confluence of Latin American pastoral theology, Jesuit spirituality, and some Peronist sensibilities shaped Francis, as he dismissed hegemonic ideologies, challenged Euro-centric narratives, affirmed the primacy of local cultures, and willingly took diplomatic risks in pursuit of deeper relations with difficult secular power.

The Jesuit tradition served as a unifying core of these influences, grounding his vision in a spirituality that blended contemplation with action. Jesuit spirituality constituted an essential framework of Francis's diplomatic persona both in substance and style (Massaro 2018). He himself repeatedly affirmed his Jesuit identity (Piqué 2014).

Consequently, his pontificate's international diplomacy was characterised by a dual focus on interior discernment and outward effectiveness, both a reflection of the Jesuit ideal (Massaro 2018). This perspective animated his dedication to inter-religious and inter-cultural dialogue and is the focus of this book's next chapter.

Chapter Four: Jesuit Spirituality as Diplomatic Formation and the Inner Life of a Global Actor

Pope Francis was profoundly shaped by the Jesuit tradition. The affiliation was symbolically evident in his papal coat of arms, prominently featuring the Jesuit seal. Upon his election in 2013, one of his first gestures was to contact the Jesuit headquarters in Rome and speak with the Superior General of the Society. Shortly thereafter, he shared a meal with members of the Jesuit curia. One of his most extensive interviews, conducted in August 2013, was granted to Jesuit Antonio Spadaro, Editor-in-Chief of *La Civiltà Cattolica*. A Jesuit publication of considerable influence and closely aligned with the Holy See, its articles are always reviewed by the Vatican Secretariat of State before publication. Because of this, the publication is typically seen as reflecting the thinking of the papacy, and therefore at the time, that of Pope Francis. (for access to the full interview see Spadaro 2013b).

Later, in October 2017, Francis addressed the thirty-sixth General Congregation of the Society of Jesus, affirming his enduring connection to the Order (Pope Francis 2016b). Then in 2019, on the occasion of the fiftieth anniversary of his ordination, the pope delivered a lecture honouring his Jesuit spiritual mentor, Father Miguel Ángel Fiorito. A master of Ignatian wisdom, the Argentine Jesuit Miguel Ángel Fiorito profoundly shaped Bergoglio's interior life, sharpening his discernment, and deepening his pastoral gaze. The pope began his address by expressing gratitude for all the Society had given him. In remembering Fiorito, the pontiff highlighted the priest's capacity to transcend ideological boundaries, cultivate dialogue, and practise deep listening, qualities that were to become central to Francis' own ethos (O'Connell 2019).

These personal gestures echoed throughout Francis' public discourse, particularly in recurring themes: outreach to the peripheries, discernment, patient decision-making, and an emphasis upon open encounter and outer dialogue. His fraternal relationship with Arturo Sosa, who was appointed the 31st Superior General of the Jesuits in October 2016, was further testament to these ties. Notably, Sosa, like Francis, hailed from Latin America (Venezuela) and was the first Latin American to lead the Order (O'Malley 2014). They connected seamlessly; both having inherited the milieu of liberation theology while both having rejected its more Marxist elements in favour of the pastoral and pragmatic applications of its principles. Both held non-Eurocentric world-views. Their shared advocacy for a decentralised Church, that emphasised global multipolarity, cultural diversity, and inter-cultural dialogue, served to reinforce each other's vision and efforts.

This chapter offers an overview of the Jesuit Order, tracing its historical development, theological foundations, philosophical perspectives, and distinctive spiritual tradition. Special attention is given to the Jesuit strategies of adaptation, accommodation, and inculturation. These form core principles of the Society's engagement with diverse contexts. They provide methods that form a foundational lens for understanding the diplomatic flexibility and responsiveness that defined Pope Francis' style of diplomacy. The chapter also explores Ignatian methods of discernment, especially as they pertain to decision-making, and considers how these spiritual practices shaped Francis in his international diplomacy.

The Jesuits have a long and complex history of political involvement and controversy. It is not uncommon for Jesuit strategy to employ deliberate provocation. This helps us in understanding the broader context of Pope Francis' public actions. This legacy of activism, especially in the realms of social justice and political critique, underscores the inherent political orientation of the Society and, by extension, of the first Jesuit pope. This is not to say that the Jesuit Order is monolithic; it encompasses a broad spectrum of views and internal dissent. That said however, what does constitute the unifying force among Jesuits is not ideological uniformity but a definitively singular process of thinking, decision-making, and engagement. Understanding diplomacy through an *'Ignatian lens'* enables a deeper insight into what Thomas Massaro had termed the "Jesuit layer" of Pope Francis' diplomacy (Massaro 2018, 41–57).

Born for the Frontiers: The Jesuit Order Takes Shape
The Jesuits are unlike any other Order of the Catholic Church. The Society of Jesus was formed during the Renaissance period, itself characterised by a spirit of humanism. Jesuits remain the largest male religious Order of the Catholic Church. Their pioneering frameworks abandoned medieval schemas of monasticism, refusing to wear religious habits or form traditional monastic communities. Furthermore, neither were they interested in following monastic liturgical rites. From its start, the Order set out to be active in civic life, particularly in the areas of education, missionary endeavour, and charitable work.

Often regarded as a counter-reformation Order, the Jesuits were founded by Ignatius of Loyola and his companions in the 16th century. Ignatius, a Basque from northern Spain, enjoyed a life of nobility having served as Paige to the Treasurer of the Kingdom of Castile, before subsequently entering military service under the Duke of Najera and Viceroy of Navarre, Antonio Manrique de Lara. In 1517, he became a knight, giving him diplomatic experience while serving de Lara. Common for his class, Ignatius was reared to be a courtier and diplomat in royal service. In his early life, he was purportedly prone to vanity and lax morality.

In 1521, Ignatius sustained extensive injuries during a battle defending Pamplona. The event proved pivotal in a spiritual awakening which unfolded during lengthy periods of convalescence. In 1522, he transitioned from military to spiritual life. By 1523, he undertook a pilgrimage to Jerusalem, after which he began his studies.

Ignatius' style of thinking generated suspicion from the Spanish Inquisition. Distrusted by the local ecclesiastical hierarchy for his maverick style, Ignatius was interrogated and imprisoned on numerous occasions. Despite being repeatedly exonerated, he deemed it safer to leave Spain and avoid further provocation.. Ultimately, his journey led him to the University of Paris, where he pursued studies between 1526 and 1535 (Maryks 2014). The curriculum at the University of Paris, shaped by the intellectual currents of the French Renaissance, included grammar, linguistics, and the humanities, alongside studies in science, philosophy, and theology. Ignatius successfully earned a master's degree, but was denied entry into doctoral studies due to his advanced age of 44. (Bangert 1986).

During his time at the University of Paris, Ignatius formed a group of companions who together envisioned the *Societas Iesu* (Society of Jesus) in 1535. By 1539 the group had established a stable and structured community. Pope Paul III approved the new order in 1540.

Over the course of several years, Ignatius of Loyola meticulously developed his *Spiritual Exercises*, a foundational text that would receive papal approbation in 1548. The Ignatian exercises introduced a dynamic and reflective spirituality. They were unafraid to engage the human imagination as a vital tool for spiritual experience, an approach that contrasted with much of the medieval tradition, which had largely dismissed or distrusted imaginative faculties in the context of inner spiritual life. In contrast, Ignatius regarded the human imagination as a vital resource and a key element for his model of 'contemplation in action'.

All the founding members of the Society held tertiary degrees, thereby laying the foundation for the Jesuits' enduring commitment to higher education and intellectual formation. From the outset, academic rigour was a defining feature of Jesuit identity. (Fabre 2019, 3–22). Among its noteworthy earliest members were Peter Faber and Francis Xavier. Faber worked extensively in Italy and Germany. He was also appointed by Pope Paul III to act as an expert at the Counter-Reformation Council of Trent (1545–1563). Faber was known as a gentle spirit, avoiding dogmatism in favour of personal spiritual experience (Padberg 2006; Purcell 2014). Francis Xavier began his missionary work in Goa, India, before embarking on extensive evangelisation efforts across Asia, including in Japan and Borneo. Though he aspired to establish a mission in China, he died in 1552 before this ambition could be realised (Schurhammer and Costelloe 1973).

The governance structure of the Society of Jesus vested considerable authority in its Superior General, informally known as the 'Black Pope'. This nickname, which arose in 17th-century Rome, reflected the perception of the Jesuit leader's considerable influence, exercised from the Order's Roman headquarters. In Catholic parlance, the term 'Black Pope' referred to the Superior General's prominent role in ecclesial and political affairs, often seen as a counterpart to the white-robed Bishop of Rome, though without his formal ecclesiastical rank.

The foundational documents of the Society included the *Formula Vivendi* (also known as the *Formula of the Institute*) and the *Constitutions*, both of which articulated a centralised model of governance and a prominent emphasis on obedience to the pope, particularly in missionary contexts. Among the Society's defining features was this vow of special obedience to the pope regarding mission fields, a commitment often referred to as the unique 'fourth vow' not found in other Catholic religious orders. Missionary outreach lay at the heart of Jesuit identity and activity, and under this guiding principle, the Order swiftly established a far-reaching global network (Friedrich 2019, 44–74).

As Ignatius' Order expanded, it came to demonstrate an unparalleled capacity within Catholicism in forming, nurturing, and maintaining a global organisation. Ignatius was known for a firm but flexible approach, encouraging initiative among members. These traits served the Society well (Gonçalves da Câmara, Eaglestone, and Munitiz 2004, xxii–252), and Jesuits penetrated divergent cultures and distinct political landscapes. Some historians identify the Society as the world's first truly global religious Order. Luke Clossey, in his extensive study of early Jesuit missions, maintained that: "Early globalisation colours so many of the historically important facets of the early-modern world, and the missions of the Society of Jesus were the globalising institution par excellence" (Clossey 2008, 257).

Early Jesuit activity coincided and connected with the expansion of 16th century globalisation. Colonisation presented the Order with many opportunities, and it found itself in unlikely contexts. Jesuits cultivated a flexible method of global engagement that affirmed cultural distinctiveness while remaining rooted in their religious mission. Scholars of Jesuit history, Banchoff and Casanova noted that: "In the early modern phase of globalisation, into the eighteenth century, no other group contributed so much to global connectivity and, through their correspondence and cultural and political influence, to a global consciousness linking the four quadrants of the world" (Banchoff and Casanova 2016, 1).

As a genuinely transnational order, the Society infused its global missions and schools with a form of 'Christian humanism' that embraced intellectual inquiry and cultural dialogue. Nowhere was this synthesis more evident than in its scientific contributions, including the leadership of Jesuit astronomers at the Imperial Bureau in Beijing during the seventeenth and eighteenth centuries. José Casanova aptly described the Society as the first historical body to operate with a truly global consciousness (Casanova 2016, 261). This global posture was sustained by a vision of inter-religious and inter-cultural engagement that propelled the Church beyond its inherited socio-cultural confines.

The Soul of Reform: Erasmus and Renaissance Christian Humanism

Ignatius of Loyola and the nascent Society of Jesus emerged during a period of transformation for European history. The waning of medieval structures and worldviews coincided with the rise of both the Protestant Reformation and the Renaissance, movements that ushered in new and humanist paradigms to which Ignatius and his companions were notably receptive.

The Society of Jesus took shape as European exploration expanded, ancient classical texts were rediscovered, and scientific paradigms shifted. Renaissance culture flourished through figures like da Vinci, Michelangelo, and Erasmus. The early Jesuits readily engaged this intellectual resurgence, embracing rhetorical, philosophical, and scientific traditions. The rigid scholasticism of medieval theology surrendered to a more liberal and dynamic intellectual ethos in which the Jesuits revelled.

Jesuit expressions of humanism initially encountered little resistance from the institutional Church. On the contrary, Renaissance popes often embraced the movement, commissioning and celebrating many of its most iconic artists. Popes like Nicholas V (1447–1455), Julius II (1503–1513), and Leo X (1513–1521) commissioned grand artistic and architectural projects in Rome, transforming the city into a Renaissance capital. Infused with a renewed confidence in human potential, the Renaissance offered an anthropological optimism and creative vitality that diverged from the rigid world of medieval Christendom.

While intellectually fruitful, the more liberal strands of Renaissance humanism paradoxically laid the groundwork for challenges to ecclesial authority. Martin Luther, who had been formed within the humanist tradition, applied its emphasis on returning *ad fontes* (to original sources) to engage critically with Scripture and early Church texts. Armed with these tools, he exposed perceived abuses within Roman ecclesial practice and advanced a vision of faith that was more directly accessible to the laity, thereby diminishing the traditional reliance on clerical mediation.

Christian humanism, of which, as noted, the early Jesuits were willing inheritors, represented a renewed emphasis on human nature, interpreted through the lens of humanist Christian theology. Its leading figures upheld the value of reason, personal development, and individual conscience, stressing the harmony between classical learning and Christian revelation (Modras 2004).

It is important, however, to distinguish between humanists who were Christian merely by historical circumstance and those 'Christian humanists' who deliberately integrated humanist ideals within a theological framework. Thomas More exemplified the latter, ultimately sacrificing his life in defence of both Catholic orthodoxy and

Christian humanist principles. His enduring friendship with Erasmus was grounded in their mutual commitment to reform, moderation, and tolerance (Baker-Smith 2010).

Christian humanists sought both personal transformation and institutional reform by drawing on classical philosophy and early Christian patristic thought (Nauert 2006b; Zimmermann 2012). Among them, Erasmus stands out as one of the most influential of Catholic humanists, leaving a lasting imprint on the intellectual climate that helped shape Ignatius of Loyola. The early collaboration between Erasmus and Martin Luther in advocating reform ultimately gave way to theological divergence, placing the Jesuits in the crossfire of Reformation polemics. While Erasmus remained loyal to the Catholic Church, Luther's decisive break with Rome created a rupture that neither thinker could fully bridge (O'Malley 1974). In the long arc of history, Erasmus' legacy proved decisive; modern scholarship has largely affirmed both his Catholic identity and his intellectual foresight (Rummel 1989; O'Malley 2013).

The Jesuits echoed the spirit of Erasmus in important ways, his aptitude for navigating ambiguity, maintaining critical distance, and resisting rigidity. The *Spiritual Exercises* embody key themes consistent with his thought. Jesuits like Jerónimo Nadal explicitly rejected speculative scholasticism in favour of practical engagement (Gray 1963). Jesuit rhetorical styles drew inspiration from classical orators like Cicero, blending Christian piety with an emphasis on personal conversion and transformative experience (O'Malley 2000).

Humanism, and Christian humanism in particular, also promoted an internationalist ideal, albeit within the cultural and political constraints of its time. Latin, serving as the lingua franca of the educated elite, facilitated the transmission of ideas across Europe and helped forge a transnational intellectual community. Education, central to both Erasmus and the Jesuit project, became the linchpin of a shared vision for renewal. Jesuit institutions sought to shape the minds of future leaders, with the explicit aim of fostering social and political transformation grounded in intellectual moral and spiritual formation. Erasmus, foreseeing the eventual fragmentation of Protestantism, championed a vision of unity and dialogue, an aspiration that aligned closely with Jesuit ambitions for a reconciled and intellectually engaged Christendom (Enenkel 2013).

Pope Francis, like the early Jesuits, resonated with the 'Erasmian' ideal of privileging conscience and practice over dogmatic inflexibility. Both Erasmus and Pope Francis attracted criticism from conservative quarters within the Church, who accused them of excessive leniency and of pushing reforms that unsettled traditional boundaries. In his *Enchiridion Militis Christiani*, Erasmus prioritised inner virtue and tangible acts of compassion above ritual observance (Erasmus 1963, trans. R. Himelick). His candid rejection of dogmatism and his insistence on personal transformation as the heart of Christian life prefigured key elements of Francis' vision, especially his focus on mercy, pastoral care, and personal spiritual authenticity.

Jesuit Strategies of Encounter: Adaptation, Accommodation, and Inculturation

Jesuits did not originate the notion of 'the common good,' (it originated in the ancient political philosophy of Aristotle) but they significantly developed and advanced it, particularly within the context of early Catholic social thought, education, and global mission. While the Jesuits inherited the concept, they pioneered new applications of it, especially in the wake of European global expansion. They did so through adaptation, accommodation, and inculturation.

Inculturation is a process through which Christian faith is afforded expression within, and adapted to, a particular culture, allowing that culture's values, symbols, and traditions to shape how the faith is lived and understood. Inherently, it calls for a posture of accommodation that embraces diversity rather than resisting it. Jesuit missionaries in China, India, and Latin America were early practitioners of inculturation, shaping faith through cultural encounter. Jesuit missionaries adopted local dress, learned native languages, and incorporated indigenous symbols and customs into Christian worship — early expressions of inculturation that reflected a deep respect for cultural difference. In the modern era, Pope Francis has reaffirmed the importance of inculturation for a truly global Church, one that transcends Eurocentric frameworks. He has consistently argued that Christianity should not impose itself as a colonising force, but should instead take root in the local soil, giving rise to diverse cultural expressions of the same faith.

With a spirit of adaptation, accommodation, and inculturation, some Jesuits became early critics of colonial abuse. In Paraguay, between the early 16th and the mid-17th centuries, they helped establish semi-autonomous communities among the Guaraní that protected indigenous people from colonial exploitation. These 'Jesuit Reductions' as they become known, represented early models of social justice and indigenous advocacy within frameworks of the Order's mission work. The 'Reductions' were guided by principles of solidarity, communal ownership, and mutual responsibility.

Needless to say, in some places this led the Order on a collision course with imperial authorities who responded with force. In 1767, Jesuits were expelled from Latin American Spanish territories effectively ending the reductions. With the expulsion of the Jesuits, the indigenous communities nurtured through the Reductions soon succumbed to the encroaching forces of colonisation (Sarreal 2014). On his 2015 visit to Paraguay, Pope Francis lauded the Reductions as a luminous chapter in Church history—an embodiment of inculturation and social justice where the Gospel was sown not in conquest, but in cultural communion (Pope Francis 2015c).

Revealing an ethos both inclusive and responsive, the Jesuit approach was marked by a rare adaptability. John O'Malley has noted that such flexibility became a defining feature of Jesuit practice (O'Malley 2016, 5). Though their *Constitutions* laid out structured goals, they were imbued with a dynamic principle: to adapt in light of time, place, and circumstance. In this spirit, John Bossy wryly observed that 'Few religious superiors can have told members of their order so firmly to forget the rules and do what they thought best' (Evennett and Bossy 1970, 130).

The Society enacted new perspectives that wouldn't be fully embraced by the wider Church until the 20th century. The Jesuits favoured engagement with the real world, drawing meaning from experience, reason, and shared human values. Strategy focused on persuasion and dialogue. The *Spiritual Exercises* themselves aligned closely with humanist ideals of the self-aware leader and the Order expected this from its members themselves (O'Malley 2000).

Renaissance Christian humanism heavily influenced the Jesuits' approach to missionary work, equipping them to engage more deeply with local cultures. Jesuit missions thus developed along religious, cultural, and inter-civilisational lines (Maryks 2016). One example is Alessandro Valignano (1539–1606), who helped lead Jesuit missions to East Asia. He advocated for incorporating local customs into Catholicism and for developing indigenous clergy. Another example is Matteo Ricci (1552–1610), perhaps the most famous of Jesuit missionaries in China, who fully immersed himself in Chinese language and culture, to the point of dressing as a Confucian scholar. His deep cultural accommodation and his strategy of inculturation stirred controversy but nonetheless steered him to becoming the first European to enjoy the Emperor's patronage in the royal court of China and enter the Forbidden City of Beijing in 1601.

This principle of accommodation (adjusting one's approach to meet people where they were) became increasingly embedded in early Jesuit practice. Ignatius' letters reveal a spirit of accommodation and discernment; he would propose a course of action, yet regularly temper it with the caveat, 'unless you think some other course would be more effective', a telling mark of Jesuit flexibility (O'Malley 2013).

Not everyone approved of the Jesuit strategy of accommodation. In the 17th century, Blaise Pascal sharply criticised a policy of accommodation, accusing Jesuits of 'casuistry' by adapting moral principles too freely. Casuistry is a method of moral reasoning that deals with the contextual dimensions of a given reality. Instead of starting with broad rules and deducing solutions, casuistry begins with specific, often complex, real-life situations and seeks to determine a pragmatic course of action. Pascal claimed that bending Christianity to suit different cultures compromised its integrity. Others like Bishop Pero Fernandes Sardinha in Brazil concurred, and objected to the incorporation of native rituals (Shapiro 1987; Wright 2004). But O'Malley (1993) argued that accommodation was a cornerstone of Jesuit anthropology, a bold and radical approach, laying the groundwork for modern Catholic openness and especially visible in the character that was Pope Francis (Prieto 2017).

Jesuits like Francis, believe that people should be convinced, not compelled. Consequently, both casuistry and rhetoric became central elements of the Jesuit paradigm, conveying primacy to conscience, conversation, and encounter. Cultural integration, or *'inculturation'*, as it became known, continues to guide Jesuit action and clearly found a place in the thought of Pope Francis. The Society's Complementary Norms affirm the importance of this: "Our formation must be such that a Jesuit can be one with the people to whom he is sent, capable of communicating with them. He must be able to share their convictions and values, their history, their experience, and aspirations; at the same time, he must be open to the convictions and values of other peoples, traditions, and cultures" (Padberg 1996, 156). Pope Francis wove this framework into the very fabric of his diplomacy.

From Power to Persecution: The Suppression of the Society of Jesus

Despite some moral failures, most notably, their involvement with slaveholding in Maryland, the Jesuits generally aligned themselves with the victims of colonial power. From the Guaraní missions in Paraguay to the defence of Tamil and Chinese Christians in Asia, they frequently clashed with colonial regimes, other Catholic Orders, and at times, invited the suspicion of the Roman Curia. Their often-controversial stance led to multiple expulsions across European territories in the 18th century, culminating in the suppression of the entire Order by Pope Clement XIV in 1773.

The pressure came not from theological disagreement per se, although their use of inculturation drew theological criticism, but from powerful Catholic monarchs. Portugal, France, and Spain, all successfully lobbied the papacy to suppress the Society. Many Jesuits were forced to renounce their vows or go into exile. Unlike other Catholic Orders, the Jesuits' distinctive character provoked consistent backlash.

Jesuit popularity at royal courts aroused clerical jealousy, while their success in education antagonised universities. In Roehner's words, "whether we consider the state, the Parliament, the church, or the universities, their reaction toward the Jesuits are quite revealing of their respective goals and ambitions" (Roehner 1997, 165). The Society's global scope, and their defence of local populations contributed to their precarious political standing. Portugal had expelled them in 1759, long before papal suppression. France followed in 1764, and Spain and Sicily soon after in 1767. This widespread opposition derailed the Order's rapid expansion, which had flourished from 1550 to 1730. The suppression lasted over forty years and dealt a blow to morale, numbers, and influence.

Paradoxically, it was Orthodox Russia that offered refuge. Catherine the Great, unimpeded by the papal bull, allowed Jesuits to continue operating. Despite resistance from the Russian Orthodox Church, she valued their educational contribution and a capacity to secure Polish loyalty. The Russian mission became a vital conduit for the Order's eventual restoration, later helping it regroup in Western Europe, Britain, and the United States.

Formal reinstatement came in 1814 under Pope Pius VII with the bull *Sollicitudo Omnium Ecclesiarum*. Occurring alongside the Congress of Vienna and the aftermath of the Napoleonic Wars, the restoration marked a new chapter, though it omitted any mention of Jesuit achievements in science, education, or missions (Worcester 2014). The Society, nonetheless, re-emerged, albeit in a weakened state. Its members number fewer than 600 but were ready to resume activity in 1814 (Shore 2020, 77).

The Order's revival involved cautious rebuilding rather than bold expansion. The Society shifted away from scientific and theological experimentation and focused instead on institution-building. Resources were limited and opportunities to re-establish elite European colleges had diminished, pushing Jesuit initiatives once again, increasingly toward non-European centres (Grendler 2018). Over time, the Society regained its footing. New opportunities arose, especially in the Global South. By the mid-20th century, the Society had undergone a major transformation. It became defined not by proximity to royal courts or European elites, but by a renewed focus on the poor, the marginalised, and the socially excluded (Shore 2020, 91).

The long ordeal of suppression and recovery sparked a fundamental rethinking of identity and mission. The restored Order was not always united in vision or method, but the seeds of Ignatian spirituality adapted and flourished in unexpected places. From these new conditions emerged renewed movements of inculturation theology in South Asia and liberation theology in Latin America, both rooted in contextualised socio-political engagement (Friedrich and Dillon 2022).

At its heart, the Society has always been outward-facing and heuristic, an approach to problem-solving that employs a practical, experience-based method that is not guaranteed to be optimal or perfectly rational, but is nevertheless regarded as 'good enough' for an immediate purpose. The heuristic model sat well with the Society's motto of *'contemplation in action'*. Jerónimo Nadal, one of Ignatius' closest collaborators, put it simply: "We are not monks. The world is our house" (O'Malley 1984, 14).

The Jesuit journey, of which Francis was a part, reflects that sentiment in striking ways. Members of the

Order served as astronomers to Chinese emperors, introduced Western sciences to Asian courts, owned plantations in the Americas, and cultivated vineyards in Australia. Their schools educated a striking range of figures—from Voltaire and René Descartes to Fidel Castro, Alfred Hitchcock, and Bill Clinton (Höpfl 2004).

Interior Freedom and Apostolic Fire: The Foundations of Jesuit Spirituality

At the heart of Ignatian *'contemplation in action'* is discernment, the capacity to make considered decisions that align with long-term goals, especially those that serve the spiritual and secular mission of the Church. Ignatian discernment involves a reflective process that includes spirituality, information gathering, contemplation, decision, and action, all within a continuous feedback loop. This approach acknowledges and does not shy away from complexity, uncertainty, and ambiguity, especially in the context of politics and global affairs (Nullens 2019).

Ignatius believed that divine presence permeates every aspect of life. His teachings emphasised finding the Divine in daily activities and using that awareness to inform action. This spirituality prioritises emotional intelligence, imagination, and inner exploration, dimensions that are central to making wise and creative decisions. A key objective of Jesuit spirituality thus involves a process of achieving inner freedom from attachments, biases, and predetermined goals with the aim of openness to influences from various contexts. This outlook intrinsically values adaptability over rigid prescription. The *'Daily Examen'*, a core Jesuit practice, fosters continual reflection and alignment with reality. Both the Exercises and the Examen encourage openness to all possibilities, detachment from personal preferences, and clarity in purpose.

The '*First Principle and Foundation*' calls practitioners to discern their vocation with integrity and freedom. Several other distinctive traits also define praxis. Firstly, the idea of 'finding God in all things' cultivates an inclusive, globally-minded spirituality. This anchored Francis's diplomatic engagement. Secondly, Jesuits are *'contemplatives in action,'* and by extension, deeply involved in secular affairs as an expression of their spirituality. Thirdly, flexibility is a key virtue; Jesuit responses are context-specific and adaptive. Lastly, Jesuits are trained for patience and long-term engagement, believing that meaningful change more often than not, unfolds slowly.

Francis's diplomatic strategy exemplified all these traits (Brackley 2004; Molina 2013). Jesuit formation, by its very nature, cultivates independent thinking. Yet, this means members frequently navigate a tension between obedience and creative autonomy. Zupanov highlighted this paradox, observing that Jesuits, through their long formation, learn to both obey and resist, to be purposely provocative if needed, and to be at ease with ambiguity if necessary (Zupanov 2019, 5).

Membership of the Order requires extensive formation, beginning with a two-year novitiate, including a thirty-day silent retreat. This is followed by philosophical and theological studies, practical ministry, another retreat, and often postgraduate education. Education remains a critical part of formation and mission.

The Society emphasises learning across disciplines: the social sciences, history, and culture, alongside the physical sciences, to better understand and influence the world. Final vows may take up to twenty years to attain.

Discerning the World: Jesuit Intelligence Behind Francis' Global Strategy

Pope Francis simply put, had a Jesuit DNA. He displayed caution in not necessarily seeking predetermined outcomes preferring instead to cultivate an openness for all possibilities. He engaged forms of discernment that required constant evaluation and re-evaluation. To onlookers this made him sometimes appear inconsistent, but in his diplomacy, this translated into imaginatively envisioning all concrete choices and long-term outcomes. Communication, both with others and within oneself, was a vital element of his Ignatian method, where decisions are not solely rational; rather, they make room for intuition, imagination, and affective insight.

The Ignatian approach to decision-making, whether personal or for Francis' diplomacy, follows these steps:

1. Identify the decision or issue at hand. It should be practical—focused on taking or refraining from action.
2. Formulate the issue as a concrete, specific proposal. Frame it positively (what, where, when).
3. Acknowledge any biases, emotional obstacles, or underlying feelings influencing the decision.
4. Collect all relevant information necessary to understand processes and outcomes.
5. Identify the pros and cons for each available option.
6. Evaluate these pros and cons through the lens of both logic and spiritual insight.
7. Sit with the decision in silence and assess it through reflective and spiritual discernment (O'Sullivan 1990).

An example of this methodology's relevance can be found in the overlap between Ignatian spirituality and the principles of just peacemaking theory. Both emphasise discernment before action, the use of imagination to explore alternatives, and respect for all parties. In international affairs, decisions are often made hastily, without deep contemplation of long-term consequences. The U.S. invasion of Iraq, for instance, illustrated a failure to imagine the post-conflict scenario, a shortcoming that Ignatian discernment would have resisted (Menkhaus 2009).

Borghesi and Hudock (2018a, 60) describe the Ignatian vision as one of 'harmonizing opposites' by bringing seemingly irreconcilable perspectives into dialogue, aiming not for compromise but for an often-long-term process-orientated outcome. In this sense, Francis typically approached political engagement in non-linear terms, emphasising instead, relational and cyclical reflection, shaped by encounter and revisitation. He tended toward an avoidance of *either/or* thinking and was comfortable in embracing paradox and tension as spaces for growth and transformation. It reflected his deep commitment to process-oriented dialogue, even if on occasion, at the cost of papal prestige. Critics, particularly from *realist* traditions of international relations, viewed this as naive, yet it reflected a spiritual logic where engagement itself is sometimes the main priority and value. A spiritual capacity to hold and navigate tension equipped Francis with a unique aptitude for global diplomacy, in which the process of encounter took precedence over immediate results.

From Altar to Assembly: The Jesuit Tradition of Political Engagement

Political engagement runs deep for Jesuits whose tradition maintains that contemplation must lead to action. The Ignatian *'way of proceeding'* is rooted, as already discussed, in discernment, but it demands responsiveness to political and social realities. In turn Jesuits are expected to engage directly with public life, diplomacy, and even conflict. This commitment to civic engagement is reflected explicitly in the Order's rules: "Any realistic desire to engage in the promotion of justice in our mission will mean some kind of involvement in civic activity" (Padberg 1996, 279).

Another rule states: "All our members, but especially those who belong to the affluent world, should endeavour to work as much as is appropriate with those who form public opinion, as well as with international organizations, to promote justice more effectively among all peoples" (Padberg 1996, 280).

In the introduction to the Jesuit Conference of Canada and the United States' 2020 guide to civic engagement, President Timothy Kesicki affirmed this vision: "As we respond to the call to be agents of change in society inspired by God's special love for those on the margins, we will inevitably be led into the public square to participate in the messy, urgent work of politics. Through political and civic engagement, we can use our voices to advocate for the transformation of social structures that are marred by sins like racism, sexism, nativism, economic inequality, environmental degradation, the targeting of human life and dignity at every stage, and so many others" (Jesuit Conference of Canada and the United States 2020). In this vision, political engagement is not optional but central. It is 'contemplation in action'—transformative, responsive, and grounded in justice.

Pope Francis embraced direct political action, and was not averse to promoting its more radical expressions. In a significantly symbolic act, he canonised Salvadorian Archbishop Óscar Romero, once dismissed as Marxist by conservatives. Óscar Romero, the Archbishop of San Salvador from 1977 until his assassination in 1980, played a pivotal role in defending human rights and speaking out against political violence and injustice during a period of intense civil unrest in El Salvador. He appealed to international audiences, including writing to United States President Jimmy Carter, urging him to stop sending military aid to the Salvadoran government, as it was being used to repress the population. The ultra right-wing government, controlled by a military dictatorship allied with a small, wealthy oligarchy enjoyed support from Washington. Political power was concentrated in the hands of elites who opposed any redistribution of land or wealth. Efforts to canonise him were resisted by conservative elements within the Church. While Romero was not a Jesuit, he was deeply influenced by Jesuit theology and spirituality, particularly through his friendship with Jesuit priest Rutilio Grande, whose assassination in 1977 marked a turning point in Romero's ministry. Francis defended his position on Romero and also highlighted several other specifically Latin American Jesuits at the forefront of social justice (Wooden 2019b).

Promoting Accommodation: Jesuit Spirituality and the Diplomatic Ethos of Pope Francis

Because discernment stands at the core of Ignatian spirituality, it is by its very nature complemented by the central role of imagination and reflection. Integral to the *Spiritual Exercises*, these principles inform a diplomatic method that values imagination and the patient development of relationships. Historically, Jesuit strategy emphasised the rhetoric of accommodation, as demonstrated by Matteo Ricci's *True Meaning of the Lord of Heaven* (1603), which sought to synthesise Chinese and Catholic worldviews. Toulmin (1992) noted this Jesuit openness to contextual integration as a precursor to both modernity and post-modernism. Ricci's approach ultimately failed due to the Catholic Church's preference at the time for universal axioms over contextual flexibility, a preference in part created in response to the turmoil of the Reformation and subsequent religious wars in Europe.

John O'Malley's seminal work on the Jesuits identified accommodation as a key principle rooted in Renaissance humanism. As already mentioned, accommodation emphasised adaptation to time, place, and person (O'Malley 1993, 255). Inevitably, accommodation requires holding tensions in a reflective fashion and moving forward in incremental fashion. This Ignatian *'way of proceeding,'* grounded in the logic of accommodation, informed Francis' profoundly.

Jesuit missionaries brought Catholicism to a variety of cultural contexts, requiring nuanced epistemological and hermeneutical methods. Importantly however, accommodation should not be confused with syncretism or superficial acculturation; instead, it involved complex and multidimensional engagement where universal truths and local realities interacted. Schloesser (2014, 358) reflected that Jesuits operate within a binary of flexibility versus rigidity. Practical wisdom and good judgment require great flexibility, avoiding a rigid imposition of norms. Francis Xavier, writing from India, requested Jesuits who were "*amabilem*" (gentle and loving) rather than rigid and authoritarian.

Catholicism itself, has now evolved through a dialectical and cyclical dialogue with diverse religious and cultural traditions, giving rise to a richly textured, multifaceted identity. This approach, neither purely universalist nor relativist, allows contemporary Jesuits, like Francis was, to inhabit the tensions between the global and the local, making them particularly adept at diplomacy and inter-cultural negotiation (Tutino 2019).

The Interior Compass of a Global Pope
Jesuit tradition laid essential foundations for modern Catholicism by providing a framework rooted in Christian humanism. While this humanism may no longer dominate contemporary thought, it provides modern popes with a language and vision conducive to engagement with modernity.

Ignatian spirituality, grounded in a particular practice of discernment, and emphasising the realities of ambiguity finds its driving force through the Society's motto 'contemplation in action.' The *Spiritual Exercises* are structured around a 'both/and' logic, which forms a foundation for engagement in complex political realities. Rather than seeking binary solutions, Jesuit thought values process-orientated methods that evolve and mature through time. This ethos privileges encounter over ideological conflict and dialogue over dialectic. In the diplomatic realm, it promotes a method that is relational, attentive to contextual awareness, and comfortable with risk if required. This makes for a slow diplomacy, often ambiguous, yet couched in a relational space.

Francis' Jesuit formation deeply informed his pontificate and diplomacy. His priorities reflected Jesuit principles. His leadership exemplified a Jesuit legacy committed to dialogue (Pavone 2016, 125–126). Francis himself repeatedly affirmed his Jesuit background.

Having explored the diverse intellectual currents, political contexts, and theological debates that shaped Jorge Mario Bergoglio's early formation, it becomes evident that these influences did not operate in isolation. Rather, they were deeply intertwined with, and often mediated through, his identity as a Jesuit.

The Society of Jesus not only provided the institutional and spiritual framework within which Francis discerned his vocation but also offered a distinctive set of values, discipline, and global perspectives that would come to define his diplomatic vision. The Jesuit ethos shaped not only the Society's historic missions but also the personal spirituality of Pope Francis. Values such as dialogue, cultural discernment, and openness to difference, resonated in the *aggiornamento* spirit of the Second Vatican Council. These currents converged in Francis, framing a Church more attuned to the complexities and pluralisms of the modern world.

The Second Vatican Council provided the institutional and theological scaffolding through which Francis' Jesuit instincts matured into a coherent global strategy. Vatican II redefined the Church's role in the international order, not as a moral judge above nations but as an actor partner within and between them. Its emphasis on inter-religious and intercultural dialogue, and the Church's shared responsibility for the fate of humanity resonated deeply with Francis. Under his leadership, Vatican diplomacy would echo the Council's call for solidarity and encounter, seeking not hegemony but harmony amid global fragmentation. The next chapter examines how the Council's reforms, far from being merely theological, offered Francis a diplomatic template for navigating the complexities of contemporary international relations.

Chapter Five: The Legacy of Vatican II in the Francis Pontificate

The Second Vatican Council, held from October 1962 to December 1965, marked a decisive shift in the Catholic Church's engagement with the world. Longstanding positions and traditions were re-evaluated, questioned, and reoriented in a comprehensive effort to reshape the Church's relationship with contemporary society. The Council brought together nearly 2,500 Catholic bishops, along with thousands of observers, auditors, and lay participants. Its scale and significance are difficult to overstate. The Council was convened by Pope John XXIII, who passed away during its course, and was brought to completion by his successor, Pope Paul VI.

This chapter offers a brief contextual history of the Council but not a detailed account of internal proceedings. Rather, it examines key documents pertaining to critical shifts that shaped the Church's global posture, and in particular, that of Pope Francis. Given the elemental role Vatican II played in influencing Francis, this chapter also explores the Council's legacy, its reception, and the frameworks it offered for his diplomacy. It shows that Francis drew deeply upon the Council's paradigms to promote cultural diversity, pluralism, and his 'encounter diplomacy' (Christiansen 2017, 203–227). It also anchored his willingness to engage with complex and often controversial global actors.

Francis was still a seminarian when the Council took place and was in the process of forming his own theological and pastoral outlook. The debates and resolutions of Vatican II, nonetheless, were to have a significant impact on his intellectual, spiritual, and political evolution. Francis displayed unwavering commitment to advancing the vision and full implementation of Vatican II. His support for the

Council was unmistakable. This was particularly evident in *Evangelii Gaudium*, which Massimo Faggioli interpreted as a clear expression of Francis' wholehearted embrace of the Council's legacy (Faggioli 2017b, 38–54). His fidelity to the spirit of Vatican II was consistently reaffirmed (Wooden 2021).

The Road to Renewal: Prelude to Vatican II
The Second Vatican Council was the Catholic Church's long-delayed engagement with modernity. Pope John XXIII (1958–1963) announced the convocation of the Council on 25 January 1959, just three months after his election. The announcement shocked much of the Catholic world and ultimately altered the trajectory of Catholicism.

Although it was John XXIII who initiated the Council, the idea had received earlier consideration by his predecessor, Pope Pius XII (1939–1958), primarily as a means of completing the unfinished work of the First Vatican Council (1870). The Council had been suspended due to the political and military upheaval caused by the Franco-Prussian War and the annexation of Rome by the Kingdom of Italy on 20 September 1870. The annexation effectively ending the temporal power of the pope and incorporated Rome into the Italian Kingdom. Pope Pius IX suspended the Council indefinitely on 20 October 1870. It was never formally closed, but it never reconvened.

Pontiffs had approached modernity in varied ways. Pope Pius IX (1846–1878) responded forcefully, issuing a sweeping condemnation of modernist ideas in *Errorum Modernorum*, appended to his 1864 encyclical *Quanta Cura* (Pope Pius IX 1864). His successor, Pope Leo XIII (1878–1903), took a more measured approach with his encyclical *Rerum Novarum* (Pope Leo XIII 1891). *Rerum Novarum* was a landmark encyclical that defended workers' rights, upheld private property, criticised both socialism and unregulated capitalism, and called for state and Church responsibility in promoting justice. It laid the foundation for much subsequent Catholic Social Teaching.

Leo XIII's relative openness was reversed under Pope Pius X (1903–1914), with his encyclical *Pascendi Dominici Gregis* (Pope Pius X 1907). *Pascendi Dominici Gregis* was a definitive anti-modernist encyclical that condemned attempts to reinterpret Catholic doctrine in light of modern philosophy, history, and science. It reinforced papal authority, traditional dogma, and led to a period of intense suspicion and surveillance in Catholic theological circles. Although some theologians and scholars sought to reconcile Catholicism with emerging intellectual developments (such as archaeology, historical criticism, and modern philosophy) their efforts were frequently met with resistance from the papacy. While these initiatives often aimed to strengthen the tradition through contemporary methods (M. O'Connell 1994), Catholic thinkers associated with modernism remained under suspicion for decades, receiving broader vindication only with the reforms of the Second Vatican Council (Mettepenningen 2010).

Pius XII (1939-1958), however, was compelled to respond to the turmoil of his time through a strategy of principled restraint, balancing public caution with discreet diplomacy, and defending doctrinal orthodoxy while cautiously engaging with modern developments. He was spurred by war, ideological conflict, scientific change, and theological unrest, and his pontificate reflected both the constraints of his era and the seeds of future reform that Vatican II would later cultivate.

During his papacy, Pius XII witnessed the destructive potential of science, especially during, and in the aftermath of global conflict. His tenure faced rising totalitarianism and increasing secularisation, with the waning public influence of traditional religion. These socio-political conditions necessitated a response. Although Pius XII considered convening a Council after World War II, he ultimately refrained, despite his attentiveness to global challenges. The Council that eventually took place under his successor, Pope John XXIII, drew from Pius XII's theological reflections (Ventresca 2013). Pius XII, while acknowledging the difficulties of calling a Council, nevertheless did authorise secret preparatory research through the Holy Office to identify key themes and select potential contributors (Komonchak 2011, 7).

Pius XII undertook some internal reform, particularly in the structure of the Roman Curia, laying groundwork for the eventual globalisation of the papacy. He adapted some aspects of the codification of Canon Law first initiated by Benedict XV in 1917, thus creating a juridical framework that facilitated, albeit incrementally, a more universal vision of Church administration. These reforms would later serve Paul VI well for restructuring and re-orientating the Curia more globally after Vatican II. Despite the burdens Pius XII faced during both World War II and the early Cold War period, in his later years, he increasingly focused upon expanding the international dimension of papal diplomacy.

Pius XII's preparatory work came to cessation in 1951. The documentation from these early stages was archived until 1959, when John XXIII authorised the Ante-Preparatory Commission of Vatican II to revisit and utilise them. Komonchak's research showed that Vatican II's genesis was neither as sudden nor as unplanned as it is sometimes portrayed. The postwar geopolitical and cultural upheavals created an undeniable imperative for the Church to engage in global affairs if it wished to retain relevance (Komonchak 2011). Karim Schelkens similarly situated the Council within the broader arc of these epochal changes: two world wars, the Great Depression, the rise of totalitarianism, and the spread of secular ideologies (Schelkens 2020).

Unlike previous councils, Vatican II was not convened to resolve doctrinal disputes but to address pastoral concerns and re-evaluate the Church's role in a rapidly changing world. Pope John XXIII imagined a Church renewed through reform and open to global dialogue. His vision faced resistance from within the Vatican bureaucracy. The Curia's conservative elements made the preparatory phase particularly contentious, producing rigid and retrograde draft documents that would later provoke heated debate among the Council's participants (Wilde 2020).

Pressing forward, John XXIII championed *aggiornamento*, the call to 'bring up to date' a Church he perceived as outdated. *Aggiornamento* became a central theme for the Council and embodied the desire for a Church that was both contemporary and relevant (White 2017). It called for attentiveness to the 'signs of the times', a process of listening, interpreting, and engaging with the realities of the modern life. The pope promoted a shift toward greater cultural and inter-religious dialogue, not as a strategy to proselytise, but as an encounter rooted in mutual respect. It marked a departure from the Church's prior defensiveness and proselytising posture, and aimed to move it toward increased openness and engagement.

Although born of humble peasant stock, John XXIII brought considerable diplomatic experience to his leadership. He had served in various contexts where Catholics were a minority, Turkey, Bulgaria, and Greece for example. These were regions historically marginal to the Vatican's Western focus. His assignments shaped a particular vision of diplomacy for the Church. His final posting, in France, came under difficult circumstances. He succeeded the Papal Nuncio Cardinal Valerio Valeri, and was tasked with restoring Vatican credibility in a post-liberation France suspicious of the Holy See's wartime caution. His effectiveness in this role affirmed his prowess and informed the diplomatic and pastoral outlook that he would bring to Vatican II (Hebblethwaite and Hebblethwaite 2000).

The Council in Motion: Texts, Turning Points, and Transformation

Among the documents produced by the Second Vatican Council, four stand out as especially influential for international papal diplomacy. *Gaudium et Spes* addressed the Church's relationship with the modern world (Second Vatican Council, 1965a). *Nostra Aetate* (Second Vatican Council, 1965b) marked a turning point by recognising the value of non-Christian religions, thus laying the groundwork for modern inter-religious diplomacy. Alongside these were *Dei Verbum*, which clarified the Church's understanding of divine revelation and its mission in the world (Second Vatican Council, 1965c), and *Lumen Gentium*, which explored the Church's identity and role from a renewed ecclesiological perspective (Second Vatican Council, 1964).

As earlier mentioned, historically Church councils typically convened to identify and correct doctrinal errors, pronounce anathemas, and introduce canonical reforms. The Second Vatican Council, however, represented a profound departure: it condemned no errors, issued no anathemas. Instead, it embraced a conciliatory tone with a multi-religious and multi-cultural world. Its spirit was one of receptiveness and responsiveness to an expanding world of secularism and decolonisation. The Council increased the Church's willingness to engage with non-Christian traditions. The Church had become restrained by outdated structures and an outlook rooted in waning models of church-state symbiosis. For the first time, the Council considered history itself, positioning the Church not as a timeless fortress, but as a participant in the evolving human story.

The urgency of renewal was underscored by the immediate global context in which the Council opened. The Cuban Missile Crisis coincided with the Council's first session, leaving a palpable sense of anxiety among the bishops. It was in this context that John XXIII emerged as a subtle but influential mediator. Though the Vatican had no formal ties with either the United States or the Soviet Union, the pope's appeal for peace on 25 October 1962 became a hallmark of ecclesial diplomacy. Speaking in general terms, but understood by all as referencing the crisis, he called on world leaders to "do everything in their power to save peace" (Fogarty, 2017, 36).

A few months later, John XXIII issued *Pacem in Terris*, an encyclical that spoke not only to Catholics, but to "all people of good will" (Pope John XXIII, 1963). The document marked another pivotal turn in diplomatic language: it opened the Church to dialogue with hostile regimes, including the Soviet bloc, and reframed diplomacy in terms of universal peacebuilding [Hebblethwaite, 1985]. In so doing, the pope advanced a model of neutrality that would guide future pontiffs, including Francis. His diplomatic mediation in the missile crisis became possible precisely because of this principle of neutrality, one that was institutionalised in Vatican diplomacy after the Lateran Treaty but given new moral and theological legitimacy by John XXIII [Murphy, 1974].

Gaudium et Spes, promulgated by Pope Paul VI on 7 December 1965, was perhaps the Council's most ambitious document. As the *Pastoral Constitution on the Church in the Modern World*, it represented a bold attempt to integrate Christian anthropology with the ideals of a more secular humanism. Its tone was one of solidarity, affirming human dignity while engaging the existential, philosophical and political vocabulary of the era. It posited a "dynamic, open ontology," calling the Church not only to self-renewal but also to engage with global socio-political systems (Hanvey, 2013, 47–52).

Gaudium et Spes however, also raised questions. The document stated that political communities derive their legitimacy from a pursuit of the common good (Second Vatican Council, 1965a, §74) and affirmed the Church's institutional independence from any political system (Second Vatican Council, 1965a, §76). Yet, it left only partly resolved, a key diplomatic question: how should the Church engage regimes that do not share its commitment to human rights or religious liberty?

While Gaudium et Spes did not explicitly name authoritarian regimes, it unequivocally articulated moral principles that stood in direct opposition to political authoritarianism. Despite its pastoral tone, the constitution created a framework that legitimised strategic engagement with authoritarian regimes, one that Pope Francis would later draw upon. By prioritising dialogue even in contexts where freedom was absent, *Gaudium et Spes* provided the Vatican's diplomacy with a rationale for entering into conversation with all political systems, not to endorse them, but to promote peace, safeguard the faithful, and uphold its mission under constrained conditions (Second Vatican Council, 1965a, §92). This engagement with Marxist or authoritarian governments was not presented as a compromise, but rather as an expression of the Church's character. Implicitly, the document acknowledged that cooperation with imperfect regimes is simply necessary to achieve limited but meaningful progress (Second Vatican Council, 1965a, §81–83). This went far in laying the groundwork for the *Ostpolitik* of Pope Paul VI and Cardinal Agostino Casaroli during the Cold War, as the Vatican sought *quiet diplomacy* with Eastern Bloc regimes to secure space for the Church to function, even under repression.

Dignitatis Humanae (Second Vatican Council, 1965d), the Council's *Declaration on Religious Freedom*, was adopted on its final day. The principal writer composing the document was Jesuit theologian John Courtney Murray, a specialist on the relationship between Church and state. His ideas were crucial in shaping the document's central affirmation: that religious freedom is a right grounded in the dignity of the human person, not a concession by the state. Murray articulated a coherent vision that reconciled traditional Catholic teaching with a modern understanding of freedom of conscience and religious pluralism.

The document departed from centuries of Catholic teaching that upheld state support for Catholicism and, in doing so, had permitted on occasion, coercive measures against other religions. Whereas 19th-century popes like Gregory XVI and Pius IX had condemned 'religious liberty' and the 'separation of church and state' (Pope Gregory XVI, 1832; Pope Pius IX, 1864; O'Malley, 2010, 59), Vatican II enshrined freedom of conscience as a central principle. This shift enabled a broader and more inclusive diplomacy that no longer privileged Catholic regimes but opened space for cooperation with pluralistic and even non-religious states.

The new approach seeded the ground for a reimagining of papal diplomacy. Previously, the Church had relied predominantly on concordats (formal agreements with states) to ensure protection and influence. These were particularly common in Catholic-majority nations, as in Spain under Franco in 1953. But *Dignitatis Humanae* broke from this tradition, prioritising individual liberty over state-enforced religiosity and aligning Catholic diplomacy more closely with universal human rights [O'Malley, 2010, 212].

Pope Paul VI gave this new diplomatic posture public expression in his historic address to the United Nations in 1965, the first by any pope. In it, he affirmed the role of the United Nations in safeguarding peace and human rights. Drawing directly from *Dignitatis Humanae*, he underscored religious liberty as foundational to peace and dignity. "What you are proclaiming here are the basic rights and duties of man, his dignity, his liberty and above all his religious liberty," he declared [Pope Paul VI, 1965a].

Together, *Dignitatis Humanae*, *Pacem in Terris*, *Gaudium et Spes*, and *Nostra Aetate* established the theological and rhetorical foundations of modern papal diplomacy. These documents, both in substance and style, adopted a more existential and dialogical language that moved beyond scholastic formulations, favouring instead a tone of empathy, encounter, and moral persuasion. This transformation in tone and method enabled subsequent popes, most notably Francis, to pursue a diplomacy grounded in affective engagement and relational presence.

Between Vision and Reality: The Afterlife of the Council
Every post-conciliar pope has been tasked with interpreting and enacting the legacy of the Second Vatican Council. Both Pope John Paul II and Pope Benedict XVI consistently framed the Council as a reforming event that remained in organic continuity with the Church's enduring tradition. While each resisted ultra-traditionalist repudiations of Vatican II, they were equally cautious of radically progressive readings that, in their view, risked distorting its theological and ecclesial intent. By contrast, Pope Francis interpreted the Council as a moment of profound movement, an epochal turning point rather than a mere *aggiornamento*. Speaking to the Plenary Assembly of the Pontifical Council for Promoting the New Evangelization in 2013, he affirmed: "As children of the Church, we must continue on the path of Vatican Council II, stripping

ourselves of useless and harmful things, of false worldly securities which weigh down the Church and damage her true face" (Pope Francis 2013c).

Debate over the meaning and legacy of Vatican II has been vigorous and, at times, divisive. Competing interpretations of the 'spirit' of the Council have been mobilised by various ecclesial and theological camps in response to contemporary challenges (Faggioli 2012). Massimo Faggioli stated on this point: "The event of Vatican II is still having consequences, sometimes at a deep level. The discontinuities introduced by the Council still emerge, not only regarding the Church of the early twentieth century, but also concerning the epochal consequences of the Council for the global Church. In the history of the Catholic Church, incidents are many, but events charged with consequences such as Vatican II are few. Vatican II is certainly a uniquely consequential event in the last four centuries of the Church's history" (Faggioli 2015a, 10).

Given the centralised and traditionally monarchical structure of the Vatican, initial expectations for reform were modest. However, to the surprise of many within the Curia, the Council quickly gained momentum. A spirit of dialogue emerged, with strong support for progressive positions on the role of the laity, freedom of conscience, inter-religious respect, global solidarity, and structural shifts in ecclesial authority. This unexpected openness gave rise to creative and visionary outcomes with developments that few early observers could have foreseen.

Stephen Schloesser situated Vatican II within the broader context of twentieth-century upheaval. Many bishops had come of age during World War II and now confronted Cold War tensions, nuclear threat, decolonisation, and the waning of European global dominance (Schloesser 2006). These global realities, combined with the emergence of post-modernist paradigms, rendered older modes of triumphalism untenable. The Council thus represented a dramatic shift away from the posture of a Church perceiving itself as above the secular world to one called to action within it. Schloesser noted this transformation was so profound that "a mere two decades later, it had become impossible to imagine what had existed before" (Schloesser 2006, 289).

Two principal hermeneutics have evolved to interpret the Council's significance. The first sees Vatican II as a rupture, emphasising discontinuity with the past. The second embraces a hermeneutics of reform, highlighting continuity with Catholic tradition. In matters of papal diplomacy, the former interpretation came to hold greater sway. As Pope John XXIII made clear in the Council's opening address: "Our duty is not only to guard this precious treasure, as if it were concerned only with antiquity, but to dedicate ourselves with an earnest will and without fear to that work which our era demands of us…" (Pope John XXIII 1962, §6).

In many respects, Vatican II enabled the papacy to emerge as a more pertinent actor on the global stage, a modern moral voice and diplomatic presence (Murray 1966). Even in the twenty-first century, the Council remains a work in progress. Its legacy continues to provoke polarisation between progressive and conservative interpretations. Nonetheless, its influence surpasses these binaries. Faggioli says: "The history of Vatican II and of the post-conciliar debates is important because it gives us the coordinates of deep ecclesial rifts, of powerful long-term movements, and of specific Catholic geopolitics that becomes visible only in conciliar-synodal moments" (Faggioli 2015a, 331–332).

The Diplomatic Imagination of the Council

Pope Paul VI penned *Ecclesiam Suam* during the Council (Pope Paul VI, 1964). The most distinctive contribution of *Ecclesiam Suam* is its development of the idea of dialogue as the Church's mode of engagement with the world. Paul VI outlined four concentric circles of dialogue:

1. With all humanity – including atheists, agnostics, and those of no religion [§96–101].
2. With other religions – interreligious dialogue grounded in mutual respect [§102–107].
3. With other Christians – ecumenical engagement to foster unity [§108–112].
4. Within the Catholic Church – communion and charity among members [§113–121].

These concentric points begin in dialogue with humanity at large, moving to dialogue with non-Christian religions, then to relations with other Christian faiths, and, finally, to dialogue within Catholicism itself. Paul VI introduced the fundamental concept of dialogue to Catholic and papal discourse.

Dialogue became a hallmark of subsequent papal diplomacy, utilised by John Paul II, sometimes ambiguously by Benedict XVI, and reaching a new crescendo with Francis. Gerald O'Collins describes the shift in Vatican thinking as ground-breaking for the global relations of the Catholic Church. In terms of inter-religious dialogue, he writes, "Vatican II brought such a remarkable change in teaching about other religions and in subsequent church practice that it represents considerable discontinuity, if not reversal" (O'Collins 2015, 197).

The Council acted in response to monumental geopolitical changes. As Faggioli argues: "At the end of the fifties, the choice of putting behind the "age of Constantine" was a turning point germinated in the biography of Angelo Giuseppe Roncalli (Pope John XXIII), and this shift was brought to maturity in the years of the Second Vatican Council. During Vatican II, the universal, or Catholic, identity of the church was a prerequisite to the culture of dialogue and dialogue between cultures and political ideologies. It was a theological choice acquired at the centre of the Catholic church in Rome, which found, in its political and diplomatic dimensions, some clear limits (like in the council debates dealing with communism) due to the tensions of the Cold War" (Faggioli 2015a, 158).

Global actors gradually adjusted to a constitutional core of papal diplomacy. This included a preference for democracy, individual rights, and the value of human conscience. To these, one could add John XXIII's renewed insistence upon Vatican neutrality. The Council took note of social change and new post-Second World War international relations. Furthermore, it expressed a new preference for collaboration over earlier models of its own authoritarianism. In turn, this nurtured the evolution of fresh approaches to diplomacy and a greater willingness for multilateral effort with non-Catholic parties.

The post-Vatican II papacy consequently inherited a capacity to converse with all parties, maintaining the integrity of its own institution while engaging within and beyond traditional boundaries. This provided a level of justification for engagement with authoritarian states.

Engagement with all actors increasingly became part of the Catholic conception of peace. The Holy See's promotion of global order began to stem from a new view of the necessary unity of humanity coupled with the Church's communitarian vocation. The result was a diplomacy heavily committed to international institutions, civic movements, and relations with all states where possible (Christiansen 2006).

The Second Vatican Council thus espoused a tight connection between geopolitics and the socio-political agenda of the Vatican. Moreover, the 'global agenda' of the Church set in motion a dynamic that would gradually move it away from Euro-American hegemony. The *Ostpolitik* of John XXIII and Paul VI during and after Vatican II for example, advertently or inadvertently generated a new type of global independence for the papacy.

This geopolitically re-orientated papal foreign policy. In this sense, the Second Vatican Council was as important for its global outlook as it was for the internal workings of the Catholic Church. Faggioli's commentary is especially relevant to Francis' approach: "The 'communist threat' represented an opportunity to rescind geopolitical alliances that have previously bound together the political and cultural destinies of the Catholic Church and the West. This major geopolitical shift in the agenda of the Catholic Church would not have been possible without the cultural and theological changes that blossomed in post–World War II Catholicism and that changed the language of Catholicism in the decade called the sixties" (Faggioli 2015a, 301). While John Paul II definitively positioned himself in a Western camp of geopolitics, and Benedict XVI focused upon a de-Christianising Europe, Francis, in the spirit of Vatican II openness, was intent on forming relations with non-Western global actors.

The Council chose not to retreat from the outside world with hostility (as it did in the 'anti-modernism struggle' at the turn of the 20th century). Instead, it aimed to project Catholicism as a global church for the world. Through the Council, the Church expressed its own plurality and its own process of becoming a global society.

Concordats between the Holy See and important states, for example, Italy in 1929 and Germany in 1933, were not conspicuously abrogated, but fresh modes of international relations for the Holy See gradually formed.

O'Malley draws attention to the monumental shift in how authority, and by extension the papacy, is now better furnished for modernity. The Council introduced unprecedented language and furnished Francis with more existential concepts. In comparison to previous Councils held by the Church, O'Malley emphasises the profound difference between Vatican II and its predecessors as being so extraordinary that it rendered itself a different kind of entity. He writes, "The most obvious characteristic is of course the Council's massive proportions, its remarkable international breadth, and the scope and variety of the issues it addressed" (O'Malley 2010, 33). A different vision of Catholicism emerged. Insularity was replaced by an outward-looking vision.

The Echo of the Council in the Voice of Francis

Emerging scientific knowledge, modernist approaches to socio-religious issues, and the parallel rise of multiple forms of secularism presented formidable challenges to an ancient institution like the Catholic Church. These were compounded by the resurgence of authoritarian regimes and the looming threat of global warfare, developments that highlighted the urgent need for the Church to respond.

The last major ecumenical council prior to these upheavals (the Council of Trent) had concluded in the sixteenth century, long before the onset of the modernist project. By the twentieth century, Catholic leaders were compelled to articulate a theological and diplomatic posture capable of addressing a new global complexity. The Second Vatican Council became the primary mechanism through which they sought to do so, and Pope Francis appeared to absorb and embody its legacy in distinctive ways (Bourg 2015).

Francis did not entertain polarised or revisionist narratives concerning Vatican II. For him, the Council was a *fait accompli*, a sacred and unnegotiable part of Catholic identity. Speaking to catechists in Italy, he declared: "You can be with the Church and therefore follow the Council, or you can not follow the Council or interpret it in your own way, as you want, and you are not with the Church... On this point we must be demanding, severe. The Council cannot be negotiated" (McElwee 2021).

The parallels between John XXIII and Francis are striking. Both men emerged from humble origins, both embraced the necessity of ecclesial reform, and both emphasised inter-religious encounter as a pastoral priority. John XXIII unsettled conservatives in his time, as did Francis during his papacy. He was remembered by family as "slow to judge or condemn. He considered all the aspects of an issue, reflected, and then it seems, reflected some more" (O'Malley 2010, 107).

Francis engaged with authoritarian regimes even while championing democracy and human rights, an approach shaped significantly by the post-Vatican II emphasis again, on ecumenism, inter-religious dialogue, and openness. The Council, initiated by John XXIII and embraced by Francis, remained an indispensable theological and diplomatic foundation.

For Francis, Vatican II served as an organic source of diplomatic and ecclesial vision. He rose through the ecclesiastical ranks in the decades following the Council and was actively involved with CELAM, the Latin American Episcopal Council, during its crucial period of interpreting Vatican II through a Latin American lens. This regional interpretation left a deep imprint on Francis' papal vision. In *Evangelii Gaudium*, his 2013 Apostolic Exhortation, he repeatedly referenced major teachings of Vatican II, especially its call for a renewed relationships (Pope Francis, 2013: § §16, 25, 84, 239). Notably, his election coincided with Jubilee celebrations of the Council, reinforcing his identity as a pope deeply immersed in its legacy.

Evangelii Gaudium functioned as a manifesto for Francis' pontificate. It drew heavily from the insights of *Gaudium et Spes* (1965), quoting Vatican II documents at least twenty times (Faggioli 2017). Francis explicitly recalled Pope John XXIII's opening speech at the Council, which called for discernment in the face of cultural change. Francis echoed this theme, asserting that providence is "leading us to a new order of human relations" (Pope Francis 2013, §84).

To understand Francis' reception of Vatican II is to understand the trajectory of his papacy and its theological, diplomatic, and pastoral emphases. In contrast to his immediate predecessors, who at times felt compelled to define or qualify their relationship to the Council, Francis accepted it in full, without reservation or reinterpretation (Faggioli 2017). Unlike Benedict XVI, Francis did not focus upon a 'correct hermeneutic' or interpretation of the Council. He regarded Vatican II as a complete and authoritative event to be implemented, not debated. He was neither a Council theologian nor a participant, but rather its first unencumbered papal heir. In this sense, Francis was the first fully post-conciliar pope. He represented the culmination of a Church envisioned by the Council, a global Church with a global pope (Faggioli 2015b). Accordingly, *Evangelii Gaudium* advocated for a Church that transcends a Roman centre, Europe, and the West, promoting instead a Catholicism enculturated across diverse contexts.

This vision aligned closely with Pope John XXIII's encyclical *Pacem in Terris* (1963), in which he sought to disengage Catholic diplomacy from Cold War alignments. Francis extended this legacy, advancing the global vision first articulated by Jesuit theologian Karl Rahner, who described the emergence of a "world Church." Rahner viewed this as a natural theological progression: from Judaic roots to Greek and Latin cultural forms, and finally to a truly global Church embodied in a multiplicity of cultures (Rahner 1981).

The implications of this evolution for papal diplomacy were profound. If Vatican II was foundational in defining the Church as global, and if John XXIII was its first global pope in intention, then Francis was the first pope to truly emerge in an unencumbered fashion within the global Church that the Council anticipated.

Final Reflections on Francis and the Second Vatican Council

Pope Francis carried forward the vision of Pope John XXIII with the Second Vatican Council serving as his vital reference point. John XXIII inaugurated Vatican II with the aim of modernising the Church to respond effectively to new and emerging realities. He described his vision as *aggiornamento*—a "bringing up to date" (Schelkens et al. 2013). In both thought and action, Francis reflected this legacy. His canonisation of John XXIII in 2014 displayed the profound influence of that pope's vision on his own pontificate.

Like John XXIII, Francis remained deeply committed to dialogue, ecumenism, and inclusiveness, hallmark features of the Vatican II tradition. Unlike his immediate predecessors, who often preferred hierarchical, centralised decision-making, Francis conspicuously promoted a model of Church and diplomacy shaped by conciliar principles. He drew not from the centre of ecclesiastical power but from the 'periphery,' a concept that has both theological and geopolitical resonance. This approach mirrored the example of St. Ignatius of Loyola, the founder of the Jesuits, who was himself scrutinised by the Spanish Inquisition for unconventional methods. The Second Vatican Council laid the groundwork for a more open and engaged Church, one capable of bridging the distance between centre and periphery. Francis chose to walk that path.

Earlier ecclesiastical traditions had often pursued change through top-down strategies. Vatican II marked a departure from this paradigm. It rejected the prevailing model of authoritative imposition and instead sought to reposition the Church toward more constructive and dialogical relationships. This marked a necessary break from the Church's nineteenth-century anti-liberal posture, which had alienated it from modern culture. By the mid-twentieth century, international institutions and post-war governance structures were evolving in ways that left the Church increasingly marginalised. Vatican II responded by crafting a new theological and diplomatic tradition, one that remained central to Pope Francis' global outlook (Oftestad 2018).

This conciliar heritage was not merely a backdrop to Francis' diplomacy; it was its living framework. Through it, Francis advanced a form of Catholic engagement that remained rooted in the Council's call for *aggiornamento*, dialogue, and global solidarity.

The influence of Jesuit spirituality on Francis is unmistakable. Yet Jesuit formation alone does not fully account for the contours of his papal diplomacy. Francis is also a son of the Second Vatican Council, which informed his language and horizons. The following chapters explore how the spirit and documents of Vatican II not only informed Bergoglio's pastoral and theological imagination, but furthermore, found pragmatic expression in challenging relations.

Vatican II provided the theological and ecclesial framework that allowed Francis to speak across divides. This vision now takes shape in practice as we turn to three key case studies that reveal the concrete outworking of Francis' diplomacy. The following chapters examine his evolving relationship with the United States, where shared values clashed with political tensions; with Russia, where interreligious dialogue and geopolitical realism met on a tightrope of moral ambiguity; and with China, where an unprecedented and controversial agreement sought to reconcile ecclesial unity with state-imposed limitations. Together, these chapters illuminate the global reach, and the limits of Francis' encounter and outer-dialogue diplomacy in a fragmented world order.

PART II: Francis in the World: Relations with the United States, Russia, and China

Chapter Six: Francis and the American Imperium

This chapter examines Pope Francis' relationship with the United States, a global superpower that has played a decisive role in shaping the institutions and economic ideologies of modern global politics. From his early critiques of American-style capitalism to his unprecedented 2015 papal address to the United States Congress, Francis consistently positioned himself as both a challenger to and in conversation with, American political, cultural, and ecclesial power. He was among the few global leaders to articulate a forceful alternative to dominant narratives of globalisation promoted by the United States, showing no hesitation for example, in confronting Washington over a range of contentious issues.

To contextualise his engagement, the chapter draws upon the formative influence of Juan Perón's political tradition, which cast a shadow over Francis' youth in mid-century Argentina. A 1954 National Intelligence Estimate by Washington's Department of State described Argentina under Perón as a state lacking secure ties with major powers, pursuing a 'Third Position' strategy of non-alignment, marked by anti-capitalist, anti-communist, and anti-imperialist rhetoric and with an opportunistic foreign policy (Foreign Relations of the United States 1983).

While not asserting that Francis was a Perónist in any dogmatic sense, the ambiguities and populist appeal of that tradition were a presence in his formative years. These subtle influences help to explain Francis' diplomatic posture toward the United States, particularly his scepticism toward its hegemony and neoliberal capitalism. Early in his papacy Francis stated: "some people continue to defend trickle-down theories which assume that economic growth, encouraged by a free market, will inevitably succeed in bringing about greater justice and inclusiveness in the world. This opinion, which has never been confirmed by the facts, expresses a crude and naïve trust in the goodness of those wielding economic power and in the sacralized workings of the prevailing economic system" (Pope Francis 2013e, §54).

Combined with Francis' Jesuit tradition of 'speaking truth to power' this disposition predicated the pope's perception of the United States not only as a geopolitical power but as the guardian of an economic order he observed to be structurally unjust. His critiques made him a target for powerful conservative elements within the American Catholic Church, who challenged his moral positions on divorce, migration, and LGBTQ rights, in addition to his international stance with certain authoritarian states.

Subsequently, it is important to reflect upon Francis' relationship with the United States through a dual lens of his Jesuit identity and the influence of Argentina's Perónist legacy. Moreover, it considers a paradox at the heart of this relationship: that although the pope shared common ground with the United States on human rights, he concurrently opposed the global liberal economic model it advanced. The United States was both an ally and the locus of Francis' most vocal critics. His attempts at rapprochement with China and Russia generated unease in Washington.

Pope Francis walked a fine line in his relations with Washington. If too close to the United States, he risked complicity with its economic and global order. If he was too distant, he forfeited a potent platform for global advocacy. By tracing the development of United States–Vatican relations, Francis can be understood within the wider context of post–Cold War diplomacy. His approach was partly Latin American (shaped especially by Argentina's historical experience), partly Jesuit, and a critical departure from the Euro-centric worldviews of his predecessors.

Between Cross and Republic: The History of U.S.–Vatican Relations

Historically, the United States had periodically engaged with the Vatican to achieve various national interests, recognising the Holy See not only as a unique diplomatic actor but also as a rich source of intelligence and influence. As early as 1848, Senator Edward Hannegan referred to the Vatican as "the emporium of intelligence in Europe" (Franco 2004, 38), and more than a century later, United States Ambassador to the Holy See James Nicholson described it as a "beehive of ideas, information, conspiracies, collaboration and diplomatic manoeuvres" (Nicholson 2004, 9). President Franklin D. Roosevelt similarly viewed the Vatican as a strategic asset, particularly in the realm of foreign intelligence (Hastings 1958).

Despite this recognition, formal diplomatic relations between the two powers faced significant obstacles. In 1867, the United States Congress passed legislation prohibiting federally funded relations with the Vatican. This was driven to a degree by strong Protestant sentiment and concerns that such ties would violate the principle of church-state separation (Nicholson 2004). The fear that official recognition of the papacy would imply religious favouritism fed resistance to institutionalising a formal diplomatic relationship.

Several presidents, nevertheless, pursued informal channels of communication. During World War II, Roosevelt appointed Myron Taylor as his personal representative to the Holy See, circumventing the 1867 ban by making the role unsalaried. Taylor was tasked with intelligence gathering and coordinating initiatives that aligned with American interests (Flynn 1972). President Truman (1945-1953), seeing ideological alignment in the Vatican's anti-communist stance, attempted to formalise relations by nominating a full ambassador. His efforts however, met with congressional resistance (Gill 1987). Mounting pressure led to withdrawal of the initiative.

Successive administrations under Eisenhower (1953-1961), Kennedy (1961-1963), and Johnson (1963-1969) also failed to secure official representation (Formicola 1996). It was only during the Reagan presidency that significant progress was made. In 1984, Reagan succeeded in repealing the 1867 prohibition on funding a diplomatic mission to the Holy See, thereby paving a way for the establishment of full formal diplomatic relations that same year.

Sacred Strategy: John Paul II, Ronald Reagan, and the Cold War

Under the papacies of John XXIII and Paul VI, the Vatican had cautiously moderated its inherent alignment with the West, gradually adopting instead a strategy of re-alignment with Cold War-era superpowers. Despite this shift, the United States continued to view the Catholic Church as a potentially valuable ally, particularly in Latin America where Marxist movements were gaining momentum. Nelson Rockefeller, President Nixon's (1969-1974) adviser on Latin American affairs, identified the Catholic Church as an institution that would be useful for effecting meaningful influence in the region to safeguard the Unites States' political agenda (Rockefeller 1969). In the same report, Rockefeller had noted a rise in Latin American nationalism and intensifying anti-Washington sentiment that could perhaps be mitigated with the help of the Catholic hierarchy (Brennan 2019).

Concurrently, the United States had begun to sharpen its foreign policy rhetoric around the global promotion of human rights (Primus 1999). This generated common ground with papal declarations on similar themes, laying ground for closer collaboration. Ideologically, there was some notable agreement. Pope John Paul II's encyclical *Centesimus Annus* (Pope John Paul II 1991, § §46-47)) for instance, articulated a vision of democracy, human rights, and social justice that paralleled American political and economic values. The pope had though, tempered the encyclical by critiquing 'unrestrained' capitalism, rather than outright rejecting capitalism itself.

While Pope John XXIII endorsed democracy but maintained equal distance from both Cold War blocs, declining to explicitly condemn communism, John Paul II adopted a clearer and more ardent anti-communist stance (Kengor 2017). The imposition of martial law in Poland in 1981 propelled him into the global spotlight as an unambiguous critic of Soviet oppression thus amplifying the likelihood of an alliance with the United States. Both the pope and President Reagan shared a deep opposition to Soviet power.

President Reagan (1981-1989) capitalised on this calibration early in his presidency, reaching out to John Paul II in 1981 through a personal representative, William Wilson, who later became the first official United States Ambassador to the Holy See (Essig and Moore 2009; Kengor 2017). Reagan also benefited from the pope's firm stance against Latin American liberation theology and, by extension, the spread of Marxist ideology there (Quade 1982).

This partnership culminated with the establishment of formal diplomatic relations in 1984. For the remainder of his presidency, Reagan remained committed to securing papal support (or at least papal silence) for key elements of United States foreign policy. Vatican endorsement was on occasion, utilised to confer moral legitimacy on American interventions. As Gaetan (2009, 724) observed: "The need to secure Vatican support for key US foreign policy decisions is one factor that motivated the decision to establish diplomatic relations on January 10, 1984, when Reagan appointed Wilson as the first US ambassador to the Holy See." Reagan recognised the Vatican's considerable influence in Latin America as he feared the appeal of left-wing Catholic clergy in the region (Keeley 2020).

Despite his friendship with Reagan, Pope John Paul II did nonetheless, pursue his own agenda which was focused upon development in the global South, international peace, conflict resolution, and social justice. This sometimes clashed with Washington's priorities (Hehir 1990). During his 1998 visit to the United States, John Paul II opposed the United States' embargo on Cuba as oppressive and criticised the United States' tendency in connecting humanitarian aid to ideological and strategic interests (Schaller 1992).

Vatican foreign policy continued to be fundamentally multilateralist, and papal objection emerged from time to time, especially when the United States acted unilaterally with the use of military force (Franco 2004). While Vatican relations with Washington reached their zenith in the latter half of the 20th century under President Reagan and Pope John Paul II, the two continued to pursue their respective visions: Reagan through the East–West lens of Cold War rivalry, and John Paul II in continuity with the broader aims of John XXIII and Paul VI. Together nevertheless, they played pivotal roles in dismantling of the Soviet bloc.

Diplomatic Encounters: Pope Francis and the American Republic

While allies on some issues, the United States and the Holy See have had different visions of global socio-economic and political justice. This created an uneven progression for relations. Popes involved themselves in some matters of interest to the United States but opposed others.

After the Cold War, Holy See and United States interests began to sometimes diverge. Common projects were pursued, especially on issues of human trafficking, religious freedom, the protection of Christian minorities in the Middle East and, up until President Trump, the revival of Middle Eastern peace processes (Franco and Flamini 2008). But a grand common narrative, more evident under John Paul II and the presidency of Ronald Reagan lessened.

A diminishing of the common grand narrative between the Vatican and Washington did not mean that backdoor papal diplomacy was not useful for the United States. This was exemplified by the successful re-establishment of formal relations between Cuba and the United States in which the Vatican played no small part. Pope Francis had sent personal letters to both President Clinton (1993-2001) and President Raúl Castro (2008-2018) urging a reconciliation (Stafford 2016). His efforts were fruitful and led to a re-establishment of full diplomatic relations with the reopening of embassies in July 2015, marking a significant thaw after over five decades of estrangement. Soon after, on August 14, 2015, United States Secretary of State John Kerry visited Havana to preside over the formal flag-raising ceremony at America's Embassy, marking the first visit by a Secretary of State to Cuba in 70 years.

In 2015 Pope Francis took a papal apostolic journey to Cuba. His four-day visit between 19 and 22 September 2015 was purposely planned to take place immediately before his arrival in the United States (Dwight 2015). During his Cuban visit, the pontiff refrained from making provocative political statements. He requested freedom for the Catholic Church in the country "to carry out its mission", while praising the restoration of diplomatic relations between the two states (Pope Francis 2015a).

Both statements maintained a pastoral tone. He was received warmly by President Raúl Castro who personally greeted Pope Francis at the airport upon his arrival, a gesture of high protocol. The two held a private meeting at Havana's *Palacio de la Revolución* (Revolution Palace), where Castro expressed gratitude for the pope's role in facilitating the normalization of relations between Cuba and the United States (Kuivala 2017).

In his statements Francis said: "For some months now, we have witnessed an event which fills us with hope: the process of normalizing the relations between two peoples following years of estrangement. It is a process, a sign of the victory of the culture of encounter and dialogue, 'the systems of universal growth' over 'the forever-dead system of groups and dynasties' as José Martí said. I urge political leaders to persevere on this path and to develop all its potentialities as a proof of the high service which they are called to carry out on behalf of the peace and well-being of their people, of all America, and as an example of reconciliation for the entire world. The world needs reconciliation in this climate of a piecemeal third world in which we are living" (Pope Francis 2015a).

On other aspects of Washington's international strategy, Francis diverged, in part because of contrasting visions for global economics, climate change, refugee policy, immigration, and the ultra-conservative 'culture wars' from within conservative American politics. His chosen way forward with Russia and China also gave rise to disparity with United States foreign policy.

Although not ignoring relations with Western countries, Francis nevertheless avoided a Western-centric foreign policy. In so doing, he did not place the United States, and the so-called 'Anglosphere' at the centre of his vision. Instead, his focus was on redrawing the geopolitical map of Catholicism, with emphasis on new and emerging non-Western states (Giovagnoli 2019). For Catholicism, this meant predominantly Asia and Africa. For Inter-religious relations with Orthodox Christianity, it meant an eastward focus as well (notably with Russia), while those with Islam brought the pope's attention to North Africa and the Middle East. His Asian strategy necessarily included some form of engagement with China. All this represented a shift resulting in implications for his relationship with the United States.

A non-European pope directed perspectives away from the lens of American hegemony. While in general continuity with his predecessors' broad aims, Francis' non-Eurocentricity nonetheless was elevated to unprecedented levels. He was not a member of the "Eurocentric Roman ecosystem," to quote Jodok Troy, within which his predecessors felt more comfortable being ideologically aligned with the West (Troy 2021, 561). A map of papal journeys confirmed this change in Francis' geopolitics. He sought to open pathways for the de-Europeanisation and de-Westernisation of his church (Giovagnoli 2019). In May 2022 alone, he named 21 new Cardinals, many of whom were of non-European origin, and many from minority Catholic states (Gagliarducci 2022). By 2023, Pope Francis had appointed 83 of the 132 cardinal electors, amounting to approximately 63% of the total. His appointments significantly shifted the geographical composition of the College of Cardinals.

Without labouring the point too far, deciphering aspects of the Perónist philosophy goes some way in explaining Argentine sentiments toward the United States and, by extension, those of Francis. Argentinians have a history of antipathy toward the United States and the United States has had its own history of viewing Argentina with wariness.

Enduring attitudes about Washington's foreign policy in Latin American engendered considerable suspicion of its hegemony. During Argentina's financial crisis of 1999–2002, for example, when bank deposits were frozen, unemployment reached almost 40%, and the population endured the largest foreign debt default in world history, Argentines recalled little if any assistance from the United States (Nisley 2018). Bergoglio was witness to these events and how they contrasted with assistance (through the IMF) to Mexico (1994) and Brazil (1998) during their economic crises.

The sensibilities of Perónist ideology characterised at least some of Francis' reluctance to bow before American power. Bergoglio's rejection of neoliberal economics and Marxist alternatives placed him on a Perónist type of spectrum (Gregg 2017) which denounced both. Perónism espoused a form capitalism with limits, but perhaps more importantly, it refuted the might of a global hegemon which it perceived to have imperialist economic tendencies.

Francis and the Oval Office: Diplomacy Across Two Administrations

Popes and American presidents have had their ebb and flows, disagreements, and tensions in the past, but none as directly and openly as Pope Francis and President Trump (especially during the President's first term 2017-2021). The ascent of Pope Francis and the election of President Donald Trump brought several contentious issues into the fore and exacerbated the internal conflicts between conservative American Catholics and Francis' geopolitics. Opposing conceptualisations about numerous concerns exposed philosophical cleavages between the papacy and Washington.

Francis and Trump chose to highlight those differences. Their disagreements were on open display in 2016, during Trump's Presidential campaign when they exchanged taunts over immigration. Trump's plan to build a United States-Mexican Wall was labelled un-Christian by Francis; in return, Trump stated such a comment coming from a religious leader was disgraceful (Healy 2016). Disagreement over border policy continued until Biden's entry into the White House before resurfacing in November 2024 with Trump's re-election.

Francis was operating beyond bipolar frameworks, whether between the United States and Russia, or the United States and China. In his address to the diplomatic corps on 7 January 2019, the pope admonished isolationist policies and their potential to undermine the essential vocation of international organisations as settings for dialogue and encounter. He reiterated the centrality of multilateralism. In his speech, the pontiff echoed his oft-employed theme that politicians should not occupy spaces (meaning the protection their power) but initiate processes of dialogue (Pope Francis 2019). The speech was addressed to an international audience, but nevertheless implicitly conveyed displeasure with President Trump. Francis intuited a fragmenting world. Trump perceived a world in which America must look after its own (Giovagnoli 2019). The pontiff's emphasis upon the need for the active engagement of all states resulted in a chasm between him and Trump.

Relations remained strained for the whole period of Trump's first term and continued into his second term, shortly before Francis' passing. After barbed public exchanges in 2016 and an uneasy 2017 meeting in Rome, both largely ignored each other except in the pope's indirect taunt in the aforementioned 2019 speech.

Vastly different viewpoints on the future of a rapidly changing world created an almost untenable working relationship between the two. Ironically, in style both Trump and Francis were disrupters, frequently conducting themselves beyond their respective traditional structures and bureaucracies. Both aimed their appeal to the common people and those who felt marginalised by mainstream institutions (Deye and Fairhurst 2019).

There was some improvement under President Biden (2021-2025) who was historically the United States' second Catholic President. On the morning of his inauguration, Biden visited St Matthew's Catholic Cathedral in Washington; the following Sunday, he attended Mass at Holy Trinity Church in Georgetown, known for its Jesuit affiliation. Father Leo O'Donovan, a high-profile Jesuit, and former president of Georgetown University delivered the invocation at Biden's inauguration. President Biden enjoyed a personal and filial relationship with Francis.

By many accounts, Biden was a devout Catholic. He regularly attends Mass, often carries a rosary, and has publicly referenced Catholic Social Teaching as important for his political values (Faggioli 2021). Behind his Oval Office desk was a photo of him together with Pope Francis. The pope had extended significant pastoral support to Biden's family during his papal visit in 2015, offering comfort upon the loss of their son Beau.

Nonetheless, Biden's devotion to Catholicism came with caveats. Jack Jensen pointed out: "where Catholic morality rubs up against welfare or justice issues such as abortion and gay rights, Biden's understanding of his duty as a politician and a Catholic is clear: Decisions are to be informed by the faith he learned from nuns of his youth, not dictated by it" (Jensen 2020). Despite his personal relationship with the pontiff, President Biden did not kiss the papal ring, reflecting the posture of America's only previous Catholic President, John F. Kennedy. Kennedy had taken a cautious religious posture to balance the public perception of his Catholic faith with a secular presidency. Biden did not face the same anti-Catholic sentiments directed towards Kennedy but regardless, accepted that subtlety was sometimes required in his religious identity (Jaffe 2021).

President Biden had more commonalities with Francis than did President Trump. Both for example, were at odds with conservative bishops in the United States (Nicholas 2021). On key moral issues, Biden competed with Catholic conservatives. His stance on abortion for instance, remained firm. In response, Cardinal Raymond Burke was especially vocal on the issue, saying "that politicians who 'publicly and obstinately' support abortion are 'apostates' who should not only be barred from receiving communion but deserve excommunication" (Sherwood 2021). Francis did not supportive Biden's abortion stance but was subdued in his response. Cardinal Burke represented elements in American Catholicism, which hosted voices that were the most powerful source of opposition to Francis.

Pope and President aligned on multiple issues, but Biden's hard line on China, nevertheless, stood in contrast as the Holy See remained committed to its Provisional Agreements with Beijing (Hadro 2021). The pope's management of relations with Moscow also contrasted with Biden's foreign policy. In the final analysis, whereas President Trump brought a hiatus, Biden allowed renewed endeavours, re-pivoting Washington's foreign policy to more familiar themes.

The Pontiff and the Republic in a Fragmenting Global Order

America's grand narrative has generally centred upon the promotion and defence of a liberal international order. Donald Trump assailed its core values. His pronouncements on multilateralism stood not only in opposition to Francis' vision, but in tension with his own nation's long-term foreign policy as guarantor of the liberal international order (Ikenberry 2017). President Biden had attempted to rectify the damage rendered under President Trump and found himself largely in tandem with Francis on numerous global issues (Miller and Madhani 2021), only to witness another reversal with Trump's second term.

After the Cold War, the United States shaped its foreign policy in hegemonic terms, pursuing national interests but also promoting its version of a liberal international order, democracy, human rights, and individual freedom. This strategy has been a consistent feature of the United States' grand strategy, and is rooted in both *realist* and *idealist* internationalist traditions. With the collapse of the Soviet Union, Washington focused on maintaining unipolarity and restraining the rise of rival power. It actively worked to dissuade, disrupt, or contain alliances that could undermine its position, a strategy observable in both its military alliances and economic diplomacy. Whether framed as preserving stability or projecting dominance, this has been a central feature of Washington's foreign policy.

In maintaining this outlook, and prevent alliances that could challenge it, Washington adopted a policy of containment in its strategy with both Russia and China. United States opposition to the China-Russia strategic alignment is a clear example. Military cooperation and shared critiques of American foreign policy by Russia and China have drawn sharp responses from Washington. The QUAD (U.S., Japan, India, Australia) and AUKUS (U.S., UK, Australia) serve as further examples of a strategy to restrain China's growing influence in the Indo-Pacific.

While China is an emerging regional power with aspirations for global influence, Russia acts like one. Russia is regionally aggressive, while China is globally assertive its interests. This poses problems for the United States and had complications for Francis, who wished for deeper relations with both. While the United States engages China and Russia with a policy of containment, the pope courted and compromised with them. In 2020, President Trump's Secretary of State Mike Pompeo publicly aligned with Francis's critics over his strategy on China (Horowitz and Jakes, 2021). Although Biden realigned the United States' foreign policy toward more predictable agendas, his administration nonetheless, had also continued to stand firm in tensions with Russia and China.

Francis' comments, in the early phase of Russia's invasion of Ukraine, about NATO "barking at Russia's door" neglected to recognise that NATO expansion occurred through the free choice of new members. It also largely ignored the reality of Russia's violation of another state's sovereign territory. This raised eyebrows in Washington and uncomfortable realities for Francis that will be discussed later in this book.

Russia has a will for global power, but lacks the economic and military strength to shape a post-West world order. China is another matter, and one that further distanced Francis from Washington. The pope typically glossed over China's human rights record or its abhorrent treatment of the Uyghur population (US State Department, 2021). Although China's ascendancy is a work in progress, by most accounts it will be deeply influential in re-shaping, at least to some extent, the future international order (Zhao 2019). United States–China strategic competition will affect the international system. The rise of China made it impossible for Francis to ignore Beijing, or in his chosen strategy, to openly oppose it.

Although not a formal military alliance, Russia and China are committed to a strategy of challenging the United States' hegemony. "For Beijing and Moscow, an ideal world order would be the democratisation of interstate relations in which multiple centres of different political, economic, and civilizational entities would co-exist" (Bin 2018, 123). Yu Bin's assessment reflected parallel sentiments held in Francis' conceptualisation of decentralised multilateralism reflective of his polyhedron view of the world discussed in a previous chapter. China and Russia perceive themselves as civilisational blocs with unique worldviews resisting Western values. In his rhetoric, the pope did not shy away from acknowledging the civilisational dimensions of Beijing's emerging power and Moscow's revisionist agenda (Vukicevic 2015; Allen 2022).

A challenge to Western cultural and economic dominance aligned, to some extent, with Francis' diplomatic vision of 'encounter' (Aguilar 2021). Unlike many Western diplomats, he did not view Russia and China primarily as threats. Instead, he placed his trust in broader civilisational frameworks, approaching both powers relationally and seeking to integrate their distinct cultural identities into the global order on their own terms (de Volder 2019).

But given the authoritarian nature of both regimes, Francis' approach was not without risk. Nor was it without criticism from Washington. He exercised caution in his engagement with the United States' adversaries, and likely maintained a degree of diplomatic distance from the United States to better position himself as a credible interlocutor with its rivals. Compared to his efforts with Russia and China, his relationship with the United States appeared less intensive and more effusive.

Some have argued that Francis was selective in the forms of imperialism he chose to critique. He avoided endorsing Ukraine's right to self-defence and exercised strategic restraint in publicly condemning Russian aggression (Dettmer 2022). His sustained engagement with Moscow, alongside perceived concessions to Beijing regarding episcopal appointments, reflected a papacy focused on cultivating adaptable relationships. With this orientation, the Vatican's long-standing cultural ally, the United States, was, to some extent, sidelined as Francis sought to reposition papal diplomacy.

Contesting the Pontiff: Ultra-Conservative Resistance in American Catholicism

The pontiff encountered strong resistance from a vocal conservative faction within the American Church. His emphasis on economic inequality and climate change, coupled with his reluctance to engage in culture war rhetoric, provoked criticism from conservative bishops and segments of the laity in the United States (Winters 2022). In the realm of international diplomacy, this resistance was particularly evident in their condemnation of his approach to China. While some offered tentative support for his engagement with Russia, it was often framed around a perceived alignment with President Putin on so-called 'Christian morality'—a position more accurately understood as an ideological convergence on anti-'woke' sentiment.

Conservative Catholic commentators pre-emptively attacked the Pope Francis at the first sign of his liberal outlook (Federico 2021). Papal adviser Cardinal Oscar Rodriguez Maradiaga singled out movements in the United States as the epicentre of the anti-Francis backlash (Gehring 2019). The pope's relentless critique of neoliberal economics posed clear challenges to a wealthy American church where Republican politicians and big donors enjoyed warm relations with conservative bishops (Cloutier 2015).

Timothy Busch for example, founder of the Napa Institute, formed a close alliance with Archbishop Charles Chaput, the former Archbishop of Philadelphia, within conservative Catholicism in the United States. Busch, who rejected minimum wages as 'anti-market regulation', hosted an annual $2,600-a-ticket gathering at his Napa vineyard every summer, an initiative which he co-founded with Chaput (Annett, 2015). The 'Napa Institute', served as a hub for conservative Catholic thought, hosting conferences that featured like-minded clergy and lay leaders. In 2019, a meeting of the institute featured the former Archbishop of St Louis, Cardinal Raymond Burke, a vehement opponent of Francis, who described the Church under the pope as a "ship without a rudder" (Gehring 2019).

The Napa Institute became a prominent platform for critiquing Pope Francis's approach to international diplomacy. Through its conferences and affiliated networks, the Institute expressed concerns over the Vatican's engagement with authoritarian regimes and its perceived departure from traditional Western alliances.

The criticisms levelled at Francis had two dimensions: one theological, the other socio-political. His attempts at rapprochement with China, his relations with Russia, and his dialogue with Islam led to fierce reaction

(Wetzel 2020). His perceived left-wing inclination fared no better in the eyes of critics. He drew denunciation from right- wing religious conservatives for lauding Gustavo Gutiérrez, Leonardo Boff, Jon Sobrino, and José María Castillo for their theological contributions to liberation theology (Lølan, 2021). He was disparaged for the annulment of the suspensions *a divinis* of Miguel d'Escoto and Father Ernesto Cardenal (Wooden 2019a). D'Escoto and Cardenal were radical members of the Sandinista in Nicaragua. Both priests accepted roles in the Sandinista left-wing government as the United States funded the Contras rebellion. D'Escoto and Cardenal had been suspended by John Paul II in 1985 (Becker 2017). Francis also canonised Oscar Romero, the assassinated Salvadoran Archbishop, branded communist by political conservatives. During his tenure, Romero resisted the Washington-backed ultra-right government of El Salvador, penning a letter to President Carter asking for the cessation of the United States' military aid to the Salvadorian regime (Maza 2018). Before Francis, resistance to his canonisation had endured for years (Rubén 2017).

This convergence of theological and political criticism against Francis aligned with powerful domestic and international interests for the United States. Despite its minority status, the American Catholic Church is wealthy and significantly influential, with affluent Catholic donors among Francis' fiercest critics (Oakes 2018). Ultra right-wing Catholic conservatives aligned readily with Donald Trump in campaigns to promote a common socio-political agenda of liberal economics, dramatically curbing the number of refugees received by the United States (especially Muslims), and rejecting climate accords. While Trump boasted the support of several high-profile right-wing Christian evangelical leaders, he also surrounded himself with conservative Catholics associated with organisations that many considered extremist (Young 2022). These groups candidly rejected numerous foreign policy initiatives implemented by Francis (Gayte, 2022).

In response, the pope's ambiguous relationship with the United States was epitomised by comments in September 2019 made on a papal flight en route to Mozambique, during a three-nation papal journey to Africa: "For me, it's an honour that Americans are attacking me," Francis said. He was speaking to Nicolas Seneze, author of *How America Wanted to Change the Pope*. John Allen contextualised the comment well. "In all honesty, Francis's beef has really never been with your average American Catholic, but elites who, in his own view, want to use the church for political ends... of which he doesn't approve" (Allen 2019). Seneze's book argued that influential conservative Catholics in the United States actively wanted to undermine the Francis (Collins 2019b). In the final analysis, Francis' impromptu comment, made informally but overheard by a group of journalists on the same flight, revealed a Latin American pope who could not but perceive arrogance in American privilege and power (Allen 2019).

Cardinal Raymond Burke and former Trump chief strategist Steve Bannon were also briefly united by a shared opposition to Francis's international diplomacy, especially his outreach to China and Russia. Their alignment was most visibly expressed through their involvement with the *Dignitatis Humanae Institute* (DHI), a conservative Catholic think tank, of which Burke was president from 2013 to 2019 (Altieri 2019). In attacking the pope's international diplomacy, Cardinal Burke and Bannon planned to construct a compound near Rome for hosting meetings and seminars with Church leaders and politicians interested in 'protecting Christendom' (Duncan 2019). Bannon used his media influence, and Burke, his religious authority. The academy, earmarked to be at the Trisulti monastery in Italy, intended to train future conservative leaders. The initiative failed to materialise and the alliance between Burke and Bannon eventually fractured over differing views on the intersection between religion and politics. Burke argued that Bannon's own political agenda subsumed the broader focus of their initiative (McCormick 2019).

Conclusion: The Pontiff and the Republic—Between Resonance and Resistance

John Paul II grew up in Soviet-era Poland, and became a fierce opponent of communism. He and Reagan made for natural allies on that front. The pope's opposition to liberation theology in Latin America also played well to the political objectives of the Reagan administration. (Hebblethwaite 1983, 1990). Pope Francis on the hand, grew up in Perónist Argentina and held alternate views of Western hegemony. He didn't feel compelled or indeed the need to privilege the United States.

In comparison with President Trump, Francis appeared more accommodating of Presidents Putin and Xi despite their abysmal human rights record. Although relations were markedly improved under the Biden administration, Francis continued to face substantial opposition from powerful religious and political conservatives in America and, for his part, in response, the pope maintained a distance.

Francis' immediate predecessors were in good measure a part of the transatlantic geopolitical alliance with the United States. In contrast, Francis' statements on the Ukrainian conflict were not kind to the West nor in unquestioned alliance with it. Francis was a multilateralist from Argentina with an inherent distrust of United States hegemony. In remaining committed to a Jesuit tradition deeply connecting theology and politics, the United States led economic order was in Francis' line of fire. The United States economic order was one that Pope Francis passionately critiqued. He felt this to be more important than the culture wars of conservative Catholic bishops in the United States.

His predecessors, in comparison, were connected more with Catholic conservatives on that front (Faggioli 2018). The religious right in the United States laboured to define the terms of political debate at the intersection of religion and politics, by placing emphasis upon issues like abortion and same-sex marriage. Francis maintained a relentless focus on the poor, the dispossessed, upon unhinged capitalism, climate change, and inequitable globalisation, choosing not to side unequivocally with a West led by the United States.

The Perónist tradition of non-alignment with the great power of the United States resonated with the pope's tendency to pursue alignments that he saw as better serving the future of his Church's long-term place and mission in the world. On the spectrum of American politics, Francis was readily perceived far to the left not only by Republicans but by some Democrats as well. Through that lens, it was easy for them to perceive in Francis, a left-wing Jesuit pope from a Perónist Argentina who refused to place Washington at the epicentre of his international relations (Neumayr 2017).

Francis did not assess global order from the perspective of those at the defined centre but from a polycentric space. For him this, by its very nature, necessitated even the inclusion of challenging emergent and revisionist non-Western powers. The pontiff acted in a fashion suggesting, at least in his view, that Euro-centrism and the hegemony of the United States was diminishing.

In the pope's view the United States itself faced a crisis with the advent of a new emergent multipolar world. He thus began positioning the Holy See in a polycentric fashion. China and Russia consequently received concerted diplomatic effort. In many ways, he was the first true post-Cold War pope, as his centre of gravity firmly located him beyond an American orbit. An unquestioned hegemony of the United States simply did not sit well with the Jesuit Argentinian pope.

The Holy See, and by extension, Francis, envisioned a diplomacy embedded within a theology of global witness. In this sense, Vatican diplomacy is by nature *teleological*. In Catholic thought, teleological refers to action that connects to purpose, goal, and an ultimate end (*telos* in Greek). A teleological view in religious terms interprets events, existence, and behaviour as directed toward a divinely ordained purpose or final goal.

The United States has traditionally also perceived itself in similar, yet secular, *teleological* terms with its self-understanding of a state with a 'manifest destiny' (Urio 2018, 108–195). For much of United States history, the nation constructed its own narrative of the unique nature of its international destiny. Historic discourses were anchored to belief in a 'manifest destiny' bestowed by 'the Divine' upon America, to lead globally while defending principles of freedom and enterprise (de Zoysa 2005). All this is not to say the Holy See under Francis had no common interests with Washington. There were of course common interests (Harris 2017a). The difference perhaps, rested in the greater paradox that both Catholicism and the United States share a common belief in their own versions of a 'manifest destiny'.

In the Holy See and the United States, we thus have two global actors who, in their foundational narratives, conceptualise a divinely inspired role in the international arena. The Holy See's 'manifest destiny' is *eschatological* and *teleological*, driven by the broad parameters of Catholic Social Teaching and a religious mission. American 'manifest destiny' is grounded in a politics seeking to enshrine a model that reflects how America comprehends liberal socio-political ideals. The Holy See and the United States, will at some level be forced to co-operate and simultaneously compete, both in their respective identities, and in their perceived 'destinies'. Their grand narratives overlap and at the same time diverge. Presidents and popes can choose whether to magnify areas of overlap, or highlight discrepancies. Pope Francis, for the large part, chose the latter.

If Pope Francis chose to highlight divergence with the United States, particularly for its global hegemony, it in part informed his cautious and strategically ambivalent approach to Russia. While his engagement with Washington was at least to some extent, shaped by shared values and mutual concerns over human rights, his relations with Moscow involved a more delicate balancing act. Russia, with its own 'messianic' self-understanding as defender of Orthodox Christendom and its subsequent historical tensions with the West, presented a whole set of different problems for a pope seeking to assert moral authority while promoting inclusion. The next chapter explores how Francis navigated the complexities of Vatican-Russia relations, especially in the context of Orthodox-Catholic tensions, geopolitical rivalry, and the moral crisis unleashed upon him by the war in Ukraine.

Chapter Seven: Pope Francis and the Geopolitics of Russia

This chapter explores the Vatican's engagement with Russia during the pontificate of Pope Francis, beginning with a contextual overview of the long and complex relationship forged through centuries of theological divergence, imperial rivalry, and geopolitical entanglement between the Holy See, the Russian state, and Eastern Orthodoxy. It then turns to the specific contours of this relationship under Francis, analysing his diplomatic overtures and ecumenical strategies against the backdrop of escalating Russian aggression in Ukraine. In so doing, the chapter seeks to evaluate both the symbolic and strategic dimensions of Vatican–Russia relations during a period of deepening global instability and moral ambiguity.

Bridging the Divide: Rome, Russia, and the Challenge of Orthodox Plurality

Though the Catholic Church in Russia remains small, Pope Francis devoted considerable diplomatic effort to fostering relations with both the Russian state and the Russian Orthodox Church. His engagement was not chiefly motivated by the needs of the Catholic minority in Russia, but by a more expansive vision: to advance a form of papal diplomacy unshackled from Western political alignments and crafted instead for the quest of inter-religious dialogue, particularly with the world's largest Orthodox Christian body. President Vladimir Putin, in turn, responded favourably to these overtures, discerning in them a strategic opportunity for alignment with a global moral authority.

Navigating the treacherous terrain of Vatican–Kremlin relations, Pope Francis was compelled to tread a diplomatic tightrope with careful, sometimes unsettling, precision. His engagement with Moscow, while couched in the language of inter-religious dialogue, often gave the impression that the strategic end might justify the ambiguous means. This dialogue was channelled primarily through the Russian Orthodox Church, yet the repeated visits of President Vladimir Putin to the Vatican signalled more than ecclesial courtesy. The audiences with the pope constituted tacit state endorsement of a relationship Moscow could leverage for geopolitical gain.

Francis, shaped in part by an Argentine Perónist ethos, and his Jesuit political inheritance, viewed the world through a lens resistant to binary geopolitical logic. He did not frame Russia as an adversary to be contained, but as a necessary participant within a multipolar order. Yet, his Jesuit sensibility, defined by an aptitude for embracing paradox and deferring final judgment, posed a profound moral tension. In privileging pragmatic engagement over prophetic denunciation, the papacy risked being seen as ethically ambivalent, if not complicit, in the face of aggression cloaked in ecclesial rapport.

Russia, home to the world's largest Orthodox Christian population, presents a paradox of religious identity: widespread affiliation yet low observance. As the Pew Research Centre reported in 2017, only 6% of Orthodox believers in Russia attend church services weekly, making it one of the least religiously observant among Orthodox-majority nations (Pew Research Centre 2017). The research highlights a disconnect between Orthodox religious identity and religious practice. Yet beneath this surface lies a potent civil religion, where Orthodoxy and nationalism are inseparably bound. The Russian Orthodox Church wields considerable influence, not necessarily through spiritual fervour, but through the strategic patronage of the state. In this fusion of altar and throne, religion serves less as a personal conviction than as a cornerstone of national identity lending metaphysical legitimacy to political power.

Unlike the Roman Catholic Church, with its centralised authority, Orthodox Christianity is decentralised, consisting of an ecclesial mosaic of autocephalous churches. Many Orthodox Churches are defined by the contours of ethnic identity, a characteristic that, by its very nature, introduces geopolitical fault through into inter-Orthodox relations. This ethno-national framing frequently impedes unity, fostering discord and diplomatic paralysis where a coherent ecclesial witness might otherwise emerge.

For Pope Francis, this ecclesial plurality within Orthodoxy posed formidable diplomatic and theological challenges. How might a pope engage meaningfully with a tradition that bears deep historical wounds and suspicions toward Rome? Whose voice, amid Orthodoxy's internal plurality, should be recognised as authoritative in dialogue? And with whom should the Holy See converse when the Orthodox world itself lacks a single, unified spokesperson? While Greek Orthodoxy retains a symbolic and sentimental resonance for the Vatican, rooted in a shared historical past, it is the Russian Orthodox Church that looms largest, both in demographic scale and geopolitical reach. In confronting this reality, Francis was drawn into a complex engagement not merely with faith, but with power cloaked in religion.

To understand the delicate contours of Pope Francis' engagement with Russia, one must first reckon with the long and often fraught history that precedes it. The Vatican's relationship with the Russian world has been shaped by centuries of theological estrangement, political rivalry, and mutual suspicion. Beneath the contemporary gestures of dialogue lies a legacy marked by schism, imperial ambition, and ideological confrontation, all of which have left enduring scars. Before examining Francis' efforts to navigate this terrain, it is essential to briefly trace the evolution of Vatican–Russia relations across time. It is within this historical tapestry that the meaning and limitations of Francis' diplomacy can be more fully discerned.

Past as Prologue: The Historical Arc of Vatican Diplomacy with Russia

Russia's international posture is that of a revisionist power seeking not merely to assert influence, but to define its regional geopolitical order. Its foreign policy toward Ukraine must be situated within a longue durée framework, in which the region has been cast as a liminal space between 'Russia' and 'the West,' a contested frontier of imperial, religious, and civilisational claims. This enduring narrative of antagonism has shaped the terrain upon which Vatican diplomacy has attempted to operate. For the Holy See, engaging with Russia has meant more than navigating contemporary political tensions; it has required confronting a legacy in which East–West polarities, historical grievances, and national mythologies continually resurface as barriers to sustained and meaningful dialogue.

The Christianisation of the Slavic world traces its roots to the ninth century, when Byzantine missionaries brought the Orthodox faith to Kievan Rus. Under their influence, Kyiv emerged as a spiritual and cultural centre of Slavic Orthodoxy, laying the foundations for a distinct ecclesial identity. Kyiv's prominence was violently disrupted in 1240, when the Mongol (Tartar) invasion led to its sacking, dramatically diminishing its religious and political influence. By the sixteenth century, significant portions of Ukrainian territory had come under the dominion of the Polish–Lithuanian Commonwealth. This shift in sovereignty brought with it an expanding Catholic presence, as Latin Christianity gained a foothold in the region, setting the stage for enduring tensions between Catholic and Orthodox traditions that would shape ecclesial allegiances and geopolitical contests for centuries to come

A significant minority of Ukrainians embraced Eastern Rite Catholicism, a development in which the Jesuit Order played an instrumental role. This process was formalised in the Union of Brest-Litovsk of 1596, with an ecclesial agreement allowing Orthodox clergy and faithful to enter into full communion with Rome while preserving their Byzantine liturgical heritage (la Rocca 2012, 4–5).

The union marked not only a theological convergence but also a geopolitical realignment, as Rome extended its influence along the western frontier of the Russian world. The establishment of what came to be known, often pejoratively within Orthodoxy, as the 'Uniate' Church sent tremors through the Orthodox East. For Russian Orthodoxy, this new ecclesial body represented a Latin incursion cloaked in Eastern vestments. The legacy of Brest-Litovsk endured as a source of enduring suspicion and periodic hostility, shaping Orthodox–Catholic relations and complicating papal diplomacy in the region well into the modern era (Avvakumov 2016).

Barbara Skinner, in her evaluation of Russian Orthodoxy's fraught relationship with Catholicism, captures the depth of ecclesial resentment provoked by the Union. She writes: "In the Russian Orthodox view, the creation of a 'Uniate' church was the most pernicious spawn of Roman heresy. The Uniate church, by absorbing formerly Orthodox Christians into the Roman fold, moved the boundaries of schism eastward, directly challenging the Russian Orthodox church" (Skinner 2005, 24–25). For Moscow, the emergence of an Eastern Rite Catholic presence on its western frontier was not merely a theological aberration, but a geopolitical provocation that undermined its spiritual jurisdiction and sowed the seeds of mistrust that would echo across subsequent centuries of Catholic–Orthodox interaction.

The Jesuit Order stood at the forefront of these developments, playing a fundamental role in advancing Catholic influence across the contested religious frontier. Through an ambitious network of educational institutions, the Jesuits promoted both intellectual formation and spiritual allegiance to Rome, deliberately focusing their efforts on the social and cultural elite. Under the tolerant patronage of Catherine the Great, they expanded their activities deep into Russian-controlled territories, embedding Catholic presence within traditionally Orthodox lands. These initiatives, while effective in cultivating a loyal Catholic intelligentsia, provoked ecclesiastical resentment. In the eyes of the Orthodox hierarchy, Jesuit efforts were not simply pedagogical but proselytising.

This history of contested presence and ecclesial rivalry created a cautious and strained diplomatic trajectory. While theological tensions and cultural suspicions persisted, the evolving political landscape of Europe necessitated new modes of engagement between the Holy See and the Russian state. From cautious gestures in the imperial era to clandestine contacts during Soviet repression, the Vatican's relationship with Russia gradually shifted from confrontation to dialogue, albeit under fragile and frequently shifting conditions. It is within this historical continuum that the evolution of formal relations took place.

The earliest formal contacts between the Holy See and the Russian state date back to the late fifteenth century (Dunn 2004), though full diplomatic relations were not established until the closing years of the eighteenth century. These fragile ties were abruptly severed following the Bolshevik Revolution, as the newly formed Soviet regime demonstrated no interest in renewing formal relations with the Vatican (Dunn 2016).

Despite the ideological hostilities and widespread religious persecution that defined the communist era, the Vatican began to seek a more pragmatic response to the existential threats facing Catholics behind the Iron Curtain (Dunn 1976; Dunn 1982a; 1982b). The Vatican's cautious approach was termed as a *modus vivendi*, a strategy of coexistence for survival in an otherwise hostile environment. Yet the policy achieved only limited success. Cardinal Agostino Casaroli, the principal architect of Vatican *Ostpolitik*, would later describe the approach more starkly as a *modus non moriendi*, a mode of not dying, more prominently underscoring its fundamentally defensive and survivalist orientation (Dunn 1976).

Popes John XXIII and Paul VI revised the Vatican's diplomatic framework by adopting Casaroli's strategy of *Ostpolitik* (a term borrowed from secular diplomacy to describe a policy of cautious rapprochement with Soviet bloc regimes). Cardinal Agostino Casaroli was the principal architect of the Vatican's Eastern policy. Between 1963 and the onset of Gorbachev's *perestroika* in the 1980s, he orchestrated a series of delicate negotiations and partial agreements with communist governments in Eastern Europe. While controversial for its perceived compromises, the strategy was adopted as an essential dimension aimed to alleviate the persecution endured by Catholic communities (Dunn 1982b).

The Soviet leadership, for its part, remained wary of the Catholic Church's international stature, transnational networks, and its potential to inspire ideological dissent. John XXIII's emphasis on papal neutrality, however, slowly began to soften the adversarial tone. His effectiveness as a moral intermediary was demonstrated during the Cuban Missile Crisis in 1962, when he issued a public appeal for peace in letters addressed to both President Kennedy and Premier Khrushchev. Through informal diplomatic channels, the Vatican helped facilitate the exchange of concerns. *Pravda* notably published the pope's message on its front page, providing Khrushchev with political cover to de-escalate the crisis in return for the withdrawal of the United States' missiles from Turkey (Hebblethwaite 1985). Later, in 1963, John XXIII received Alexei Adzhubei, Khrushchev's son-in-law and editor-in-chief of *Izvestia*, at the Vatican. Though no formal agreement followed, the meeting opened new lines of communication, and, significantly, Catholic clergy from Eastern Europe were permitted to attend the Second Vatican Council.

Vatican II notably avoided direct condemnation of communism, an omission reflecting John XXIII's desire to use diplomacy as a means of mitigating Catholic persecution and nurturing more open communication with Moscow (Fogarty 2017, 27–49). That same year, Soviet Foreign Minister Andrei Gromyko visited the Vatican following the publication of *Pacem in Terris* and went on to meet with Pope Paul VI on five further occasions. With the election of John Paul II in 1978 however, the Vatican's tone shifted decisively.

As the first pope from a Soviet bloc country, John Paul II presented an entirely new challenge to Moscow. A Polish national shaped by first-hand experience of communist oppression, he rejected the policy of accommodation and instead mounted a direct moral and theological attack against Marxist ideology. His landmark visit to Poland in 1979 drew millions and marked a turning point in Cold War history. There, he presented Christianity and communism as fundamentally incompatible worldviews.

John Paul II also reasserted the question of Ukrainian Catholicism, openly advocating for the full restoration of the Ukrainian Greek Catholic Church, an assertion that deeply unsettled Soviet authorities (Hvat' 1983). His unyielding stance and personal authority not only emboldened resistance movements across Eastern Europe but intensified Soviet anxieties about the Church's influence (Corley 1994).

A genuine thaw in relations came only under Mikhail Gorbachev, who, in 1989, became the first Soviet leader to visit the Vatican. Formal diplomatic relations were established a year later, in 1990, at the level of Representatives, and were elevated to full ambassadorial ties in 2010 under President Dmitry Medvedev (2008-2012) and Pope Benedict XVI (Catholic News Agency 2010). This détente fostered ongoing dialogue, and successive Russian leaders made official visits to the Vatican: Boris Yeltsin (1991-1999) met with John Paul II in 1998, while Vladimir Putin followed in 2000 and 2003. Pope Benedict XVI received Putin again in 2007.

Despite these diplomatic advancements, a fundamental obstacle persisted: widespread Orthodox hostility toward Catholicism (Uzzell 2002). In Russia, religious identity and nationalism were intertwined, fuelling entrenched anti-Latin sentiment that continued to shape ecclesial and public opinion. President Putin skilfully leveraged religion, embedding Orthodox symbolism into his national narrative and casting Russia as a bulwark of 'Christian values' in opposition to what he portrayed as a morally decadent West.

Into this charged atmosphere stepped Pope Francis. While he shared with Putin a rhetorical emphasis on traditional values, he confronted the formidable challenge of navigating a Russian nationalism where Church and state operated in ideological synchrony. His task in charting a terrain where historical memory, religious identity, and geopolitical ambition converged was a daunting one.

This complex historical legacy provides crucial context for understanding Russia's contemporary use of religious diplomacy. In the post-Soviet era, the Russian state has increasingly instrumentalised the Orthodox Church as a vehicle for projecting its power, both domestically and internationally. Far from relegating religion to the private sphere, the Kremlin has re-integrated Orthodoxy into its geopolitical strategy, framing Russia as a spiritual counterweight to the secular West. This fusion of political ambition with ecclesial authority has allowed Moscow to cast its foreign policy in terms that blur the boundaries between confession and statecraft.

Instrumentalising Faith: Russian Foreign Policy and Religious Diplomacy

A distinct form of religio-political *Messianism* characterises much of Russia's geopolitical imagination. Scholars Robert Blitt, Alicja Curanovic, Nozar Shafiee, Ehsan Fallahi, and Archana Upadhyay have examined this complex intersection of foreign policy and religious ideology (Blitt 2022; Curanovic 2012a; Shafiee and Fallahi 2018; Upadhyay 2021).

Maria Engström, analysing this fusion in depth, writes: "The 'conservative turn' in Russian politics is associated with the return to the cultural and political ideologeme of *Katechon*, which is proposed by several right-wing intellectuals as the basis for Russia's new state ideology and foreign and security policy. The theological concept of *Katechon* (from the Greek ὁ Κατέχων, 'the withholding') protects the world from the advent of the Antichrist and originates in the Byzantine Empire. In Russian tradition, this concept is presented in the well-known doctrine of Moscow as the Third Rome, dating back to the 16th century. The term *Katechon* in contemporary Russian political discourse is relatively new and can be traced to the post-Soviet reception of Carl Schmitt's political theology. The concept of Russia as *Katechon* is directly connected to national security and defence policy because it is used as the ideological ground for the new wave of militarization and anti-Western sentiment, as well as for Russia's actions during the Ukrainian crisis" (Engström 2014, 356–379).

This worldview classifies global affairs along civilisational lines, with religion functioning as a principal marker of identity. Within this framework, Russia imagines itself as a divinely appointed guardian of traditional Orthodox Christianity, casting Western liberalism as an existential and moral threat to a sacred order (Hill 2021). Religious diplomacy, therefore, becomes strategically useful, serving as an extension of statecraft through spiritual language.

Analysts of Russian strategic culture generally identify three broad schools of foreign policy thought: 'Westernisers,' who stress cooperation and shared values with the West; 'Statists,' who prioritise sovereignty, internal stability, and national security over liberal norms; and 'Civilisationists,' who affirm the uniqueness of Russian values and advocate their global projection. From a religious standpoint, civilisationists frequently invoke the doctrine of Moscow as the 'Third Rome', the heir to Rome and Constantinople, and the final bastion of authentic Orthodox Christian civilisation (Tsygankov 2019).

This 'civilisationists' narrative has become especially prominent under Vladimir Putin. It defines Russian identity in direct contrast to the West, and by extension, often to Catholicism (Tido 2018). Putin has increasingly deployed rhetoric rooted in spirituality, morality, and national exceptionalism to position Russia as a civilisational force with a providential mission (RT Television Network 2012). Utilising thinkers such as Alexander Dugin, who envisions Russia not merely as a nation-state but as a universal civilisation, Putin promotes a radically anti-Western and revisionist global posture (Barbashin and Thoburn 2014).

These ideological frameworks are not merely rhetorical. They serve strategic functions, particularly in reinforcing Russia's ambitions within its 'near abroad,' especially in Ukraine and Belarus (Tido 2018). Within this 'messianic' worldview, Russia's global role is cast in redemptive and salvific terms (Laurelle 2015). The Russian Orthodox Church plays a central role in legitimising this vision, promoting a tripartite Slavic identity—Great Russians (Moscow), Little Russians (Ukrainians), and White Russians (Belarusians)—that reflects the imperial narratives of tsarist Russia. Under Putin Russia potently deployed this narrative as a tool of regional integration and political control. However, Ukraine's national resistance and the reassertion of its own identity has seriously challenged, and in many ways undermined, Putin's civilisational claims (Petro 2018).

Putin's relationship with Pope Francis must be understood within this broader ideological and strategic context,. By portraying Russia as the last defender of traditional Christian values, Putin found it advantageous to seek alignment, or at least symbolic dialogue, with the Vatican. This afforded him greater opportunity to contrast Russia's moral conservatism with the perceived decadence of the liberal West, while simultaneously leveraging the Holy See's global moral authority to validate his civilisational narrative (Feifer 2018).

Between Two Altars: Russian Orthodoxy, Global Power, and Francis' Challenge

President Vladimir Putin strategically mobilised Russian cultural psychology by idealising the past, emphasising an East-West existential divide and casting Russia as the guardian of a 'sacred mission' to defend

Christian morality (Gessen 2017). The Russian Orthodox Church (ROC) plays a central role in sustaining his narrative. As Alicja Curanovic noted, the Church's international vision is deeply rooted in a form of nationalism that is imperial, autocratic, and messianic, positioning Orthodoxy as a civilisational alternative (Curanovic 2012b, 124).

Russian statecraft has long manipulated religious institutions to serve strategic ends. Even during the Soviet period the state occasionally utilised the ROC to improve its global image, particularly through involvement in peace movements (Helby 1993). The Church's transethnic identity, extending across Soviet republics, allowed it to wield a form of spiritual power that persisted into the post-Soviet era. The Moscow Patriarchate's continued assertion of ecclesial authority in Belarus, Estonia, and Ukraine reflects this. In the words of Curanovic, "The convergence of the Kremlin's and the ROC's visions concerning global order is a key component of the religious factor in Russian foreign policy. Both subjects perceive post-Soviet territory as Russia's sphere of influence, in which the activity of other subjects should be limited to the minimum" (Curanovic 2012b, 246).

In pursuit of strategic legitimacy, Putin sought a religious ally in the Vatican. Pope Francis, committed to inter-religious and inter-civilisational dialogue, created an opportunity. While the United States and the European Union imposed sanctions on Russia for its annexation of Crimea in 2014 and its full-scale invasion of Ukraine in 2022, Francis adopted a cautious stance. He refrained from overt condemnation, motivated by a constellation of factors: the Vatican's commitment to neutrality, the pursuit of reconciliation with the Orthodox world, the integration of Russia into a broader multipolar vision, and a cautious openness to Putin's civilisational rhetoric as a bulwark against the perceived erosion of global Christianity.

Among Francis' most deeply held aspirations was the healing of the schism with Eastern Orthodoxy. Yet, this project was complicated by the internal divisions within Orthodoxy itself, particularly between Moscow and Constantinople. When the Ecumenical Patriarchate granted autocephaly to the Ukrainian Orthodox Church in 2019, thereby removing it from the jurisdiction of the Moscow Patriarchate, Francis found himself navigating a delicate and polarising ecclesial landscape. From a Western perspective, the move enhanced Constantinople's authority. Paradoxically, however, it also aligned Eastern Rite Catholics in Ukraine more closely with anti-Russian Orthodox nationalists (Babynskyi 2020).

　　The Kremlin and the ROC responded forcefully. Their joint campaign to block the move included backchannel diplomacy, cyber espionage which included the hacking of Patriarch Bartholomew's emails, and public denunciations. Nonetheless, Bartholomew pressed forward, citing historical precedent and his Patriarchate's prerogative in bestowing autocephaly to emerging churches: the Ecumenical Patriarchate had historically granted autocephaly to the Orthodox Churches of Bulgaria, Serbia, Romania, and indeed Moscow itself (Coleman 2020).

　　Russian Orthodox leaders accused Bartholomew of acting as an instrument of United States foreign policy. The loss of the Ukrainian Church, which comprised more than 30 percent of the Moscow Patriarchate's faithful, was a significant blow to Russia's religious and geopolitical aspirations. The ROC suffered a dramatic loss of adherents, assets, and regional influence (Shestopalets 2020b). The episode revealed the high geopolitical stakes tied to ecclesiastical sovereignty in post-Soviet space.

　　Orthodox ecclesiology, lacking a centralised authority akin to Roman Catholicism, further complicated Vatican engagement. Although the Ecumenical Patriarch of Constantinople is formally recognised as *primus inter pares* (first among equals), the vast size, wealth, and political backing of the Moscow Patriarchate enables it to exert disproportionate influence. These internal rivalries within Orthodoxy hindered Francis' efforts to foster unified Catholic-Orthodox reconciliation.

Francis' broader geopolitical outlook also shaped his posture toward Russia. His consistent dedication to a multipolar order converged, to a degree, with Putin's own ambition to challenge Western hegemony (Chebankova 2017). As a result, Francis refrained from publicly denouncing Putin's authoritarianism. In a spirit of Jesuit pragmatism Francis' diplomatic style reflected ambiguity. He consistently resisted initiatives aimed at politically isolating Russia and, in several public interviews, expressed a striking degree of resonance with certain elements of Putin's worldview.

Early in his papacy, the pope called upon the West to engage in self-criticism and observed that "in part, there has been a convergence of analysis between the Holy See and Russia" (The Economist 2016a). This orientation was further affirmed by Vatican Secretary of State Cardinal Pietro Parolin during his 2017 visit to Moscow. Parolin stated: "Russia, for its geographical position, its history, its culture, and its past, present, and future, has an important role to play in the international community and in the world." Vatican analyst Gerard O'Connell observed, Parolin's remarks conveyed a subtle yet unmistakable message to Western powers: Russia should not be marginalised or excluded from global affairs (O'Connell 2017).

Francis and Kirill in Havana: Religion, Diplomacy, and Strategic Symbolism

Historically, the Vatican's ecumenical overtures to Orthodoxy were channelled through Constantinople. In 2016 however, Pope Francis secured a meeting with Patriarch Kirill in Havana. The historic encounter between Patriarch Kirill and Pope Francis at Havana Airport on 12 February 2016 marked the first meeting between a Roman Pontiff and the head of the Russian Orthodox Church. The meeting produced a Joint Declaration (Pope Francis and Patriarch Kirill 2016b), but its deeper significance lay in what it revealed: the close alignment between the Russian Church and state. The meeting unfolded in a coordinated manner, advancing the Kremlin's broader foreign policy objectives. While both Kirill and Putin derived considerable strategic benefit, Francis risked the appearance of complicity.

For Patriarch Kirill, the timing of the meeting was tactically astute. It allowed him opportunity to assert his leadership within global Orthodoxy just prior to the long-anticipated 2016 Pan-Orthodox Council in Crete. The 2016 Council in Crete was to be the first significant pan-Orthodox council since 787. For numerous reasons the Orthodox Church had not convened for a global Council in over a millennia.

The Russian Orthodox Church boycotted the Crete council at the last minute, persuading three other autocephalous churches to follow suit, Bulgaria, Georgia, and Antioch (Heller 2017). This severely limited the breadth of participation. The absence of key Churches, particularly the Russian Orthodox Church, meant that the 2016 Council in Crete did not represent a majority of the global Orthodox faithful.

By engaging with the pope in Havana, independently of the Ecumenical Patriarch of Constantinople, Kirill aimed to undercut the latter's authority, particularly given Patriarch Bartholomew's stronger alignment with Western geopolitical interests. In effect, Kirill used the Havana meeting to advance Moscow's 'Third Rome' narrative, seeking to assert primacy within the Orthodox world. By doing so, he strategically positioned Pope Francis within the context of intra-Orthodox rivalry, drawing the Vatican into a struggle for influence that primarily served Russian ecclesial and geopolitical interests. Beyond a symbolic prayer for unity, the encounter functioned more as diplomatic choreography than as a moment of substantive ecumenical dialogue.

The Joint Declaration addressed a range of global issues, including the plight of Christians in the Middle East, the conflict in Ukraine, and socio-cultural concerns such as secularism, abortion, euthanasia, and same-sex marriage. While the language of faith was present, the declaration leaned more toward geopolitical alignment than theological rapprochement, reinforcing Russia's effort to sacralise its foreign policy ambitions. Notably, the document offered no concrete progress on the conflict in Ukraine or the protection of the Catholic minority within Russia.

The neutral tone on Ukraine drew criticism, particularly from Ukrainian Greek Catholics, who felt betrayed by the Vatican's lack of support. Archbishop Sviatoslav Shevchuk, head of the Ukrainian Greek Catholic Church, described the text as filled with "half-truths". He expressed deep disillusionment with Rome's perceived neutrality. He stated: "Vatican officials are still calling this conflict a civil war, when it's really a Russian war of aggression... it's equally clear this declaration was mostly written in Moscow" (Luxmoore 2016, 5; Brauer 2017; Gallaher 2019; Zonova et al. 2023). For many, the Vatican appeared detached from the lived realities of Russian aggression in Ukraine, resulting in moral ambiguity instead of ethical advocacy.

The meeting echoed the Vatican's tradition of *Ostpolitik*, and the encounter lacked any hallmarks of authentic interfaith exchange. At Moscow's insistence, theological and ecclesiological issues were kept off the agenda, resulting in a declaration that reflected only platitudes. The Vatican's muted references to Ukraine were noted by critics as a capitulation to accommodate Kirill's conditions for the meeting.

Kirill clearly held the upper hand. The encounter enhanced Moscow's international stature reinforced its conservative ideological posture, and steered clear of any theological or political compromises that might have undermined its authority. Although Pope Francis achieved a symbolic breakthrough in Catholic–Orthodox relations, it came at a diplomatic and moral cost, especially for Ukrainian Catholics and others who had hoped for a more decisive stance on justice and human rights (Clarke 2016).

Francis' conciliatory tone thus alienated many Ukrainians, particularly in sharp contrast to the assertive stance of John Paul II during the Cold War who unequivocally aligned himself with Eastern European Catholics in their resistance to communist oppression. Pope Francis adopted a more cautious tone. Where John Paul II confronted Soviet influence head-on, Francis described Russia's 2014 invasion of Ukraine as a "fratricidal" war, framing it as a mutual tragedy rather than a clear act of aggression (Harris 2015). His response to the 2022 full-scale invasion was widely criticised for its ambivalence, perceived ineffectiveness, and lack of moral clarity at a moment many regarded as a defining test of international and ecclesial leadership.

Ukraine and the Vatican: The Limits of Jesuit Diplomacy

Ukraine presented a persistent and multifaceted challenge for Pope Francis. Geopolitically situated at the crossroads of Russian, European Union, and American spheres of influence, Ukraine has historically oscillated between alignment with Moscow and aspirations for European integration.

The 2014 election of President Petro Poroshenko signalled a decisive turn westward, triggering Russia's annexation of Crimea and its support for pro-Russian militias in Eastern Ukraine. This aggression catalysed a surge in pro-European sentiment and amplified calls within Ukraine for an independent Orthodox Church, free from the jurisdiction of the Moscow Patriarchate (Brüning 2016).

Complicating this religious landscape was the significant presence of Eastern Rite Catholics, or 'Uniates', the largest Eastern-Rite Catholic community in the world. Representing roughly 10% of the national population and up to 30% in western regions, they have long been viewed by Orthodox leaders as a provocative reminder of Catholic encroachment (Wawrzonek 2014).

From the perspective of both the Kremlin and the Moscow Patriarchate, Ukraine was expected to remain within Moscow's religious and political orbit. Yet the Ukrainian people increasingly asserted their national and ecclesial independence. Russia's military intervention further exacerbated tensions. Ukraine became a diplomatic grey zone for the Vatican, where ecclesiastical allegiance, national identity, and geopolitical strategy collided. Francis was tasked with a delicate balancing act: supporting the Ukrainian Catholic faithful, sustaining dialogue with the Moscow Patriarchate, and preserving diplomatic relations with the Russian state.

President Poroshenko's strategy to weaken Moscow's influence rested partly on securing religious independence for Ukraine. Frustrated by the silence of Moscow-loyal bishops during the Crimean crisis, Poroshenko obtained a unanimous parliamentary vote requesting ecclesial autocephaly. Patriarch Bartholomew responded affirmatively. Despite intra-Orthodox debates over jurisdiction, canon law upheld Constantinople's historical right to grant autocephaly. In January 2019, he issued the Tome of Autocephaly, formally recognising an independent Ukrainian Orthodox Church.

This decision triggered deep turmoil within global Orthodoxy. Patriarchates were forced to choose between Constantinople and Moscow. In response, the Russian Church appealed to Pope Francis for support while simultaneously mobilising Orthodox churches financially aligned with Moscow. The episode exposed how geopolitical strategy, and ecclesial rivalry had become deeply intertwined within the Orthodox Church (Griva and Yaksa 2020).

Constantinople's alignment with Western interests, particularly the United States, reinforced Russia's resentment. Historically backed by Washington during the Cold War, the Ecumenical Patriarchate retained strong Western ties. Bartholomew's action not only diminished Moscow's ecclesiastical influence in Ukraine but elevated his own standing in the West (Paris 2019). Pope Francis, by contrast, adopted a hesitant posture, waiting to see how the realignment might unfold. Yet the emergence of a newly independent Ukrainian Orthodox Church forced him to recalibrate his diplomatic approach: how could the Vatican maintain engagement with Moscow without alienating Kyiv?

Francis faced a further dilemma: failure to support Ukrainian ecclesial autonomy risked aligning the Vatican, however unintentionally, with the revisionist ambitions of Putin and Kirill. Yet, given Russia's regional dominance, Vatican access to Moscow was strategically valuable. Francis had to calibrate his response carefully, balancing moral authority with diplomatic pragmatism.

The situation dramatically escalated with Russia's full-scale invasion of Ukraine in 2022. The pope was placed in an excruciating bind. Defending the Vatican's diplomatic ties with Moscow risked undermining his moral credibility. Conversely, condemning Russia outright threatened to unravel years of delicate Vatican-Russian dialogue. Francis' public messaging appeared deliberately ambiguous. Despite an unprecedented visit to the Russian Embassy to the Holy See, he avoided naming Russia or Putin directly, and consistently refrained from using the term 'invasion.'

More provocatively, in a May 2022 interview with *Corriere della Sera*, Francis referenced NATO's "barking at Russia's door" as a factor in provoking Russia (Fontana 2022). In *La Civiltà Cattolica*, Francis cited a conversation with a 'wise' head of state who predicted the war, warning that NATO expansion ignored Russia's protective instincts (Spadaro 2022).

While insisting he was not pro-Putin, (He disclosed a private video call with Patriarch Kirill, warning him not to become "Putin's altar boy"), Francis yet resisted framing the war as an evil act of invasion. He acknowledged the brutality of Russian troops, but tried to underscore the broader context and deeper geopolitical causes. When asked whether arming Ukraine for self-defence was morally justifiable, he replied, "I don't know the answer" (Fontana 2022). His ambivalence clashed with traditional Catholic Just War theory. In *Fratelli Tutti*, Francis had questioned the continued applicability of Just War principles in the nuclear age, arguing that war's disproportionate risks nullified its legitimacy as a political solution (Pope Francis 2020, §258). He invoked this reasoning to challenge Kirill's religious justification for the war during their 16 March 2022 Zoom call (White 2022b). Yet this rejection of Just War left Francis vulnerable to criticism that he was insufficiently defending Ukraine's right to resist.

In an attempt at damage control, Archbishop Paul Gallagher, representing the Holy See in Ukraine (18–21 May 2022), reaffirmed Catholic teaching on legitimate self-defence and affirmed support for Ukraine's sovereignty (San Martin 2022). His stance exposed a tension within Vatican diplomacy: Gallagher offered moral clarity where Francis remained cautious. Though the pontiff repeatedly condemned the war in general terms, his reluctance to explicitly denounce Russia strained Vatican-Kyiv relations.

During the World Day of the Poor, he decried the war as a "direct intervention of a 'superpower' aimed at imposing its own will in violation of the principle of the self-determination of peoples" (Pope Francis 2022). The 'superpower' was not explicitly identified. Francis then also expressed a preference to visit Moscow before Kyiv, believing engagement with Putin was more essential to achieving peace. Despite Cardinal Parolin's efforts, no invitation from Moscow was forthcoming (White 2022c).

Francis' approaches ultimately failed to produce diplomatic breakthroughs. His calls for an Easter ceasefire were ignored. A planned June 2022 meeting with Kirill in Jerusalem was cancelled. Ukrainian backlash was swift when the Vatican featured both a Russian and a Ukrainian woman carrying the cross together at a Good Friday service, a gesture many interpreted as falsely equating aggressor and victim (Wooden 2022).

Moscow, for its part, carefully avoided dismissing Vatican efforts. Russian Foreign Ministry official Alexey Paramonov stated that all Vatican initiatives were viewed "with great respect" and might be activated "if appropriate conditions arise" (Agasso 2022). The statement was vague but preserved diplomatic space.

In June 2023, Francis sent Cardinal Matteo Zuppi as a peace envoy to Kyiv and Moscow. While Zuppi met President Zelenskyy in Ukraine, he did not meet Putin or Foreign Minister Lavrov in Russia. Instead, he spoke with Maria Lvova-Belova, a figure accused by the International Criminal Court of war crimes related to the unlawful deportation and transfer of Ukrainian children from occupied areas of Ukraine to the Russian Federation. Zuppi also gained an audience with Patriarch Kirill. Both sides issued general statements on peace. A month later, in July 2023, Zuppi visited Washington, where the Vatican positioned its diplomacy as humanitarian (Watkins 2023). Critics argued the pope's diplomatic approach risked legitimising Putin as a negotiating partner.

Francis' management of the crisis generated much internal Church debate. Some saw his reluctance to criticise Russia as evidence of an enduring bias shaped by his long-standing focus on relations with the Moscow Patriarchate. The Russian Church, in turn, selectively cited his statements to bolster its own narratives (Bremer et al. 2022). Others defended Francis' strategy as a continuation of Vatican neutrality, grounded in the hope of future mediation (Cahill 2022). Luke Cahill for example, argued that by maintaining ambiguity, Francis preserved access to all sides. The pope sought not to alienate Moscow, while also avoiding indifference to Ukrainian suffering. Tragically, Francis' ambiguity generated an image of chaos from the Vatican.

Crossing the Threshold of Moscow: The Limits of Dialogue

The collapse of the Soviet Union opened new avenues for the Holy See's engagement with Russia, allowing papal diplomacy to re-enter a region long sealed off by ideological barriers. Under Pope Francis, this renewed engagement found a distinctive shape, marked by his preference for a *diplomacy of encounter* and informed by the anti-alignment instincts of Perónism and the adaptable pragmatism of the Jesuit tradition.

His carefully balanced diplomacy with Moscow, particularly in the wake of the 2022 invasion of Ukraine, demonstrated both the possibilities and the constraints of a non-confrontational, morally-grounded *realpolitik*. Francis' silence on Putin's authoritarianism, his refusal to adopt the concerns of the West over Ukraine's invasion, and his efforts to maintain dialogue with the Russian Orthodox Church all pointed to a long-game strategy: positioning the papacy in a space of neutrality.

This strategy came at a price. His ambiguous stance on Ukraine, a country with strong Catholic roots in its west and a painful legacy of Soviet repression, raised questions about the limits of papal diplomacy when confronted with clear moral transgressions. The Holy See's muted response to Russian aggression was couched in broad and highly avoidant language. While it attempted to preserve diplomatic space with Moscow, it placed Francis' moral credibility under immense strain.

For Putin, his relationship with Francis provided a veneer of spiritual legitimacy; for Francis, it represented an opportunity to question the Western monopoly on moral discourse and global leadership. Although Francis' approach to Russia revealed a diplomatic style characterised by patience and a reluctance to reduce complex geopolitical conflicts to binary narratives, the results for Ukraine were nonetheless disastrous.

His engagement with the Russian Orthodox Church, especially through the historic meeting with Patriarch Kirill, underscored a commitment to ecumenical dialogue but achieved little. His cautious response to the war in Ukraine, balancing condemnation of violence with efforts to preserve channels of communication, drew criticism and highlighted the limitations of his approach when truth fails in speaking to power in a direct manner.

These tensions were just as apparent in Francis' evolving relationship with China. The next chapter turns to this delicate diplomatic arena, where questions of religious freedom, ecclesial authority, and geopolitical pragmatism converged, offering a revealing test case of the pope's long-game diplomacy and his willingness to pursue goals through strategic ambiguity.

Chapter Eight: The Dragon and the Cross Pope Francis and China

This chapter explores the complex and often fraught attempts at re-engagement between the Holy See and China. It considers how these interactions intersect with China's broader domestic and foreign policy ambitions while evaluating the extent to which papal diplomacy, particularly under Pope Francis, has had any impact. Despite the limited presence of Catholicism within China, Francis' status as the head of a sovereign state provoked suspicion within the Chinese Communist Party (CCP). This distrust stemmed not only from the CCP's ideological opposition to religion but also from historical precedent, namely, Pope John Paul II's instrumental role in the collapse of European communism (Ibrahim 2021).

Bridging Civilisations: Pope Francis and the Chinese Enigma

Pope Francis approached the question of China not as a marginal concern but as a necessary and inevitable frontier in a post-Cold War international order. In his vision of rapprochement, opportunity and contradiction were intimately intertwined. He was reaching toward a government known for its suppression of religious freedom, yet one whose vast population and cultural legacy offered an immense horizon for the Church's presence and mission. His diplomatic initiative sought to reconcile not only geopolitical estrangement but also a deep ecclesial divide within Chinese Catholicism.

Though formal diplomatic ties remained absent, a historic shift began in 2018 with the negotiation of a *Provisional Agreement* between the Holy See and Beijing concerning episcopal appointments. The agreement represented a calculated step toward ecclesial unity under conditions palatable to both Rome and the Chinese Communist Party (CCP). In the short term, Francis aimed to heal the longstanding schism between the state-sanctioned Catholic Patriotic Association (CCAP) and an underground Church loyal to the pope. But his longer gaze likely reached further, toward the dreams first imagined by the early Jesuits who ventured eastward, fired by the hope of a Christian China.

At the heart of Francis' diplomatic overtures lay a fundamental tension between two irreconcilable understandings of religious freedom. On one side stood *Dignitatis Humanae* (1965), the Vatican II declaration affirming the inviolable dignity of human conscience in matters of faith; on the other, the CCP's interpretation enshrined in its 1982 Constitution, which grants religious activity only within the boundaries of state control (Lynch 2014). The contradiction was stark, yet Francis chose not to confront it head-on. Instead, he moved with the patient subtlety characteristic of Jesuit strategy, prioritising encounter over denunciation, and seeking cracks in the wall through which dialogue might emerge.

Francis' fascination with China was not merely political, it was deeply personal and, in a sense, spiritual. Though the missionary efforts of the 16th and 17th centuries ultimately faltered, their legacy endured. As the first Jesuit pope, Francis seemed to inherit not only their dreams but also their methodology. He spoke often and warmly of China's "ancient and noble people," evoking admiration rather than criticism. Cardinal Pietro Parolin, Vatican Secretary of State, captured this tone in an interview with the *Global Times*. He said of Francis: "He sees China not only as a great country but also as a great culture, rich in history and wisdom" (Global Times 2019).

At the symbolic centre of this admiration stood Matteo Ricci (1552–1610), the Jesuit scholar-missionary who had once stood at the threshold of the imperial court. Francis identified with Ricci's method of cultural immersion, intellectual respect, and gentle evangelisation. In a 2016 interview with *Asia Times*, the pope reflected: "For me, China has always been a reference point of greatness... Later I looked into Matteo Ricci's life, and I saw how this man felt the same thing in the exact way I did—admiration—and how he was able to enter into dialogue with this great culture, with this age-old wisdom. He was able to 'encounter' it" (Zenit 2016).

Francis, then, did not engage China as a mere geopolitical actor but as a bearer of civilisational depth. Yet this civilisational outreach came at a price. Sensitive issues, like Taiwan, the erosion of democracy in Hong Kong, the tightening grip on religious minorities, were all conspicuously downplayed. Such omissions were not accidental but emblematic of a broader diplomacy rooted in calculated compromise. Francis' priority was not to challenge Beijing's authority but to foster a space in which the Church might survive, adapt, and eventually grow.

The echoes of the Jesuits' missionary approach were unmistakable. Like his spiritual predecessors, Francis and his envoys emphasised cultural respect and gradual integration. The early missionaries had immersed themselves in Chinese philosophy, adopted local customs, and adapted Catholic practices to accommodate Chinese identity. Yet their project had been curtailed by the Vatican's refusal to tolerate what was regarded as syncretism.

Francis, flexible in temperament, seemed willing to revisit that path diplomatically. Unlike his papal predecessors, he expressed not only ecclesial interest in China but a kind of spiritual kinship. Previous popes had spoken of China in grand terms, but from a distance. Francis, by contrast, engaged with an emotional immediacy, almost as if returning to a long-lost inheritance.

Admiration, nevertheless, could not obscure the moral dilemmas. To many observers, especially in Washington, Francis' diplomacy appeared dangerously deferential. Under the Trump administration, Secretary of State Michael Pompeo publicly criticised the Vatican's approach, accusing the pope of compromising moral clarity for political engagement (Sherwood 2020). Amid such criticism, Francis remained characteristically elusive. He avoided rhetorical confrontation and instead concentrated on ecclesial pragmatism. His priority was not formal recognition by Beijing but ecclesiastical cohesion. Unity among China's Catholics was, for him, both an end in itself and a means of gradually re-establishing the Church's presence in one of the world's most populous nation. Yet this careful balancing act raised larger questions: What was Francis ultimately seeking? And how much was he prepared to yield?

Taiwan loomed as a particularly fraught concern. The Holy See remains the last European sovereign entity to maintain full diplomatic relations with Taipei. Would Francis sacrifice this relationship to gain formal recognition from Beijing if the opportunity arose? Many in Taiwan feared precisely that outcome, suspecting that the Vatican's long-game plan extended well beyond pastoral care and into the terrain of political realignment (Josèph 2021).

Nor could Francis escape the weight of historical memory. In 2000, on China's National Day, Pope John Paul II canonised 120 Chinese martyrs, some of whom had died during the Boxer Rebellion. In China, the event was remembered not as a spiritual affirmation but as a provocation and a reminder of colonial humiliation amid

Western religious intrusion (Cohen 1992). The CCP weaponised such narratives in its anti-Western discourse, painting Catholicism as a foreign agent rather than a native faith.

Indeed, since the severing of ties in 1951, the Vatican has typically been viewed with suspicion by Beijing. Catholicism, in the eyes of the CCP, remains entangled with memories of imperialism, missionary overreach, and cultural subversion. It is not simply a religion; it is a symbol of the 'century of humiliation' and a potential challenge to CCP power. Francis' diplomacy, therefore, confronted not only the contemporary policies of the Chinese state but also the sedimented layers of historical grievance and ideological distrust.

In this context, Francis' engagement with China may be seen as one of the most delicate and daring aspects of his diplomacy. It fused a Jesuit longing for mission with a geopolitical sense of timing. It carried both hope and peril. And in the shadows of Matteo Ricci, the Boxer martyrs, and Vatican II, it asked whether the Church could once again plant seeds in Chinese soil, through patient encounter.

The Wounds of Encounter: A Historical Prelude to Francis
Catholicism's first arrival on Chinese soil came in 1294, carried by the Franciscan missionary Giovanni de Montecorvino (1246–1328). This initial incursion proved ephemeral. The Ming Dynasty's rise in 1368 ushered in an era of isolation, expelling foreign influence and extinguishing the Church's early flame. It was not until the 17th century, under radically different auspices, that Catholic missionaries would again attempt to plant their faith in Chinese soil, this time with the Jesuits at the helm and a more sophisticated, culturally attuned strategy.

The most luminous figure of this renewed effort was Matteo Ricci (1552–1610), a Jesuit scholar and missionary whose name would become synonymous with Catholic engagement in China. Ricci's method rested on the principle of *accommodation*. He employed a deliberate openness to Chinese customs, language, and philosophy. Along with his fellow Jesuits Ricci immersed himself in Confucian thought, translated classical texts, and adopted the robes and mannerisms of Chinese literati. Jesuit admiration for China extended beyond religion and on to governance. They framed the Qing empire as a Confucian polity ruled by philosopher-kings.

Far from imposing Western dogma, Matteo Ricci sought to present Christianity as consonant with the moral order of the Middle Kingdom. Soon after Ricci's efforts, this cultural sensitivity yielded tangible results: in 1674, the appointment of Gregory Lou Wenzao (1616–1691) as the first ethnically Chinese bishop marked a symbolic triumph (Laven 2011).

But the very flexibility that allowed early Jesuits to thrive soon became a source of controversy. The so-called *Chinese Rites Controversy*, which unfolded between 1645 and 1742, reflected growing tensions between Rome's theological orthodoxy and the Jesuits' contextual pragmatism. Practices such as ancestor veneration and the use of Confucian terminology, acceptable to the Jesuits, were increasingly viewed by curial theologians as syncretistic and doctrinally impure. In 1704, Pope Clement XI, under pressure from these critics, issued a decree forbidding the use of Chinese in liturgy and condemning ritual practices that had been tolerated or encouraged by Jesuit missionaries.

This papal intervention ruptured the tenuous equilibrium Jesuits had forged. The Qing court, which had accepted the missionaries on the condition of cultural respect, interpreted the papal decree as disrespectful. In 1724, the Yongzheng Emperor banned Christianity altogether, casting it as a subversive element within the empire (Entenmann 1996). These decisions, one Roman, the other Chinese, etched a legacy of mistrust that would haunt Vatican–China relations for centuries (Xiang 2018).

The underlying conflict was not purely theological. It was entangled in the cultural anxieties of early modern Europe and the socio-political structures of Confucian China. In demanding the renunciation of Confucianism, conservative voices in Rome effectively insisted on the erasure of Chinese identity for Christian converts. Such a posture reinforced Chinese perceptions of Christianity as a foreign and potentially destabilising influence.

The *Rites Controversy* became a proxy for wider philosophical and geopolitical reflection. It drew into its orbit three popes, two Qing emperors, hundreds of missionaries, and the full weight of the Sorbonne's theological faculty. Figures such as Leibniz, Rousseau, Kant, Montesquieu, and Voltaire weighed in, variously commenting on the Jesuit method (Xiang 2018, 91).

The the nineteenth century brought calamitous adversities. China's socio-political system bore the brunt of Europe's imperial ambition. Western powers advanced upon China not through full colonisation, but through a subtler erosion of sovereignty that was driven by economic ambition, strategic calculation, and the allure of imperial prestige. Exploiting the internal fragilities of a waning Qing dynasty, they imposed unequal treaties, carved out foreign enclaves, and exerted economic dominion. Though China retained the veneer of formal independence, the substance of its autonomy was steadily dismantled, its sovereignty hollowed out by the encroaching forces of semi-colonial subjugation.

Treaties often demanded the protection of Christian missionaries and Catholicism now came tethered to the vessels of empire and borne aloft by the winds of Western ambition. Far from a neutral spiritual presence, the Catholic mission was enmeshed in the architecture of imperial power. It was shielded by foreign treaties, upheld by diplomatic privilege, and inscribed into the geopolitical fabric of a fractured Qing state.

As China's sovereignty waned beneath the weight of foreign encroachment, Catholicism was increasingly seen as a foreign creed cloaked in cultural disruption and political intrusion. On one hand, it served as a conduit for Western education, medical care, and modernisation. On the other, it was perceived as undermining Chinese traditions and aligning local converts with foreign interests (Clark 2021).

Anti-Christian violence flared across numerous provinces, most notably in the Tianjin Massacre of 1870 and during the Boxer Rebellion of 1899–1901, where foreign missionaries and thousands of Chinese Catholics lost their lives. These eruptions of brutality were not merely spasms of xenophobic rage; they revealed the simmering tensions beneath China's encounter with the West, a potent blend of nationalist resentment and a profound cultural collision between Confucian traditions and the intrusive presence of Western religious influence (Hsia 2018). The bloodshed bore witness to a deeper crisis: the struggle to preserve indigenous identity amid the encroaching tide of imperial faith.

Resentment especially exploded in the Boxer Rebellion of 1900. What began as a populist uprising against Qing misrule morphed into a violent purge of foreign missionaries and Chinese Christians. Empress Dowager Cixi, seeking to reclaim authority, covertly backed the Boxers. The

Taiyuan massacre and other atrocities claimed thousands of lives, with converts labelled as traitors and missionaries cast as agents of foreign domination (Galli 1996). Catholicism in China was left decimated.

The Opium Wars (1839–1842 and 1856–1860) epitomised this collision of commerce, coercion, and religion. The Treaty of Nanjing, which ended the first war, opened China's ports to foreign trade and legalised Christianity. The second war culminated in the destruction of the Old Summer Palace; a symbol of Chinese cultural grandeur ironically designed in part by Jesuits. As Wang and Tong noted, missionary activity became entangled with the economic interests of Western powers, particularly the opium trade from British India (Wang and Tong 2000). The spiritual became inseparable from the imperial.

The trauma of this period; military defeat, addiction, and cultural desecration, was not forgotten. It formed the emotional bedrock of modern Chinese nationalism and is central to the Chinese Communist Party's narrative of resistance to Western interference. Within this narrative, Christianity was cast as a foreign vector of humiliation (Clarke 2013).

These layered traumas all converged to form a Chinese suspicion of Catholicism. Scholars such as Esherick (1987) and Powell (1955) have shown how these memories calcified into a political consciousness viewing Christianity not as a benign faith but as a colonial intrusion. Beatrice Leung summarises this enduring struggle in terms of sovereignty and spiritual authority: "The clash of authority has been a traditional theme of Catholic and China state relations for the last four centuries. The Chinese Rites Controversy (1715) resulted in a negative reaction from the Kangxi Emperor. It pitted the 'Vicar of Christ' against the 'Son of Heaven.' Later, the clash… at a local or provincial level between the local gentries and foreign missionaries in the late Qing Period resulted in the Boxer Rebellion… and various unequal treaties" (Leung 2005, 355).

These historical fissures shadow the present. The papacy's missteps, its rejection of cultural integration, its entanglement with colonial expansion, and its insensitivity to Chinese culture left scars that no diplomatic agreement can quickly erase. As Carbonneau (2015) and Farrelly (2019) argued, the failure to reconcile these histories has preserved an atmosphere of suspicion between Rome and Beijing.

For Pope Francis, this history posed a formidable backdrop. His gestures toward reconciliation, however sincere or strategic had to contend not only with contemporary political constraints but also with the ghosts of a past characterised by misunderstanding, mutual injury, and shattered trust.

Diplomatic Relations: Between Recognition and Rupture
The fall of the Qing Empire in 1912, catalysed by the Xinhai Revolution, marked the end of over two millennia of imperial rule and inaugurated the Republic of China. This seismic transition created new diplomatic openings for the Holy See. Keen to re-establish a foothold in the newly formed republic, Pope Pius XI appointed Celso Costantini in 1922 as the first Apostolic Delegate to China.

At the Council of Shanghai in 1924, the Holy See formally began preparations for a native Chinese hierarchy. These efforts witnessed the consecration of six Chinese bishops in Rome in 1926, a historic gesture toward indigenisation. In 1946, Pope Pius XII advanced this project further by naming the first Chinese Cardinal and establishing a fully-fledged ecclesiastical structure across the country, including archdioceses, dioceses, and apostolic prefectures.

By the early 20th century, the Vatican had been revising its long-standing theological posture toward Chinese culture. In 1939 for example, Pope Pius XII formally revoked the earlier papal bans imposed because of the Chinese rites controversy, recognising numerous Confucian customs as compatible with Catholicism. This significantly reversed the Rites Controversy and reflected a more dialogical approach to inculturation. As a result, the Chinese Church enjoyed a modest revival and emerged, for a brief moment, as the first Western religious institution to successfully transition leadership to indigenous hands (Mariani 2014).

However, this period of growth was short-lived. Two historic forces soon came together in undermining it: the rise of nationalist anti-foreign sentiment and the Communist revolution. In 1949, the establishment of the People's Republic of China (PRC) under Mao Zedong initiated a radical break from the past. Foreign missionaries were swiftly expelled, and Church operations came under state scrutiny. By 1951, diplomatic relations between the Holy See and the PRC were formally severed.

The Chinese Catholic Church was compelled to disavow allegiance to Rome. In its place, the government created the Chinese Catholic Patriotic Association (CCPA) in 1957 to regulate Catholic life independently of Vatican authority (Tong 2013). Clergy loyal to Rome were persecuted, driven underground, or imprisoned. Accusations of espionage were levelled against Vatican representatives, most notably the Apostolic Prefect Tarcisio Martina, who was accused of conspiring to assassinate Mao (Dikotter 2013, 117).

In parallel, the Holy See redirected its diplomatic efforts toward the exiled Republic of China, in Taiwan. After early attempts to reach out to Beijing were rebuffed in 1951, the Vatican re-established formal ties through Taipei, recognising the Nationalist government. However, following the United Nations' recognition of the PRC in 1971, the Holy See proceeded in downgrading its diplomatic presence in Taiwan to the level of chargé d'affaires. Still, it maintained official recognition of Taiwan, framing the relationship as a necessary channel for engagement with the broader Chinese cultural and political sphere.

To this day, Taiwan maintains a functioning embassy to the Holy See in Rome, which remains its only diplomatic mission in Europe and one of its most symbolically significant worldwide. The arrangement, nonetheless, hangs in delicate balance. A number of analysts agree that, should the Holy See succeed in establishing formal diplomatic relations with Beijing, it would almost certainly entail severing official ties with Taipei (Moody 2020). Such a move would be a political recalibration, reflecting the Church's evolving priorities in the face of China's rising global influence.

The Chinese Communist Party and the Holy See: Ideology, Sovereignty, and the Struggle for Religious Authority
Pope Pius XII presided over the Catholic Church during a period of immense disruption in China, as the Communist Party rose from revolutionary force to governing power. His response to the CCP's victory was unequivocal: the 1956 encyclical *Ad Sinarum Gentem* condemned communism outright and reaffirmed the Church's theological and political independence from the new regime. Two enduring sources of tension were thus enshrined, conflicting political ideologies and the Vatican's unwavering insistence on papal sovereignty in religious matters.

The CCP swiftly brought administration of the Church under state control, and Catholic institutions were subjected to ideological scrutiny and tight regulation. Bishops began to be ordained without papal approval, an act that constituted, in the eyes of the Vatican, a rupture with apostolic succession and ecclesial unity (Charbonnier 2013). The situation worsened during the Cultural Revolution (1966–1976), when religious life was driven underground and Catholic clergy endured widespread persecution until Mao Zedong's death.

A shift in tone followed the rise of Deng Xiaoping in 1978. With the introduction of economic liberalisation came a more tolerant approach to religion. While Deng did not see Catholicism as an existential threat, residual suspicions and Marxist ideological constraints persisted. Hopes for a tentative rapprochement with the Vatican surfaced in 1981 when Cardinal Agostino Casaroli, then Vatican Secretary of State, made discreet approaches to Beijing. Yet the Holy See's recognition of Taiwan remained a formidable barrier to progress (Criveller 2020).

Throughout this period, CCP propaganda continued to frame Catholicism as a tool of Western imperialism. Although Article 36 of the 1982 Constitution guaranteed religious freedom, it did so under strict qualification, allowing the state to prevent what it termed "foreign infiltration." Papal sovereignty, and in particular the Holy See's exclusive right to appoint bishops, remained a point of irreconcilable difference. For the Vatican, this was a matter of spiritual integrity; for Beijing, it represented an unacceptable surrender of national sovereignty (Lynch 2014).

The collapse of the Soviet Union in 1989 further hardened Chinese attitudes toward the papacy. The CCP was acutely aware of the role played by the Catholic Church, especially in Poland, in the unravelling of communist regimes across Eastern Europe. Analysts within the Party concluded that religion, rather than economic inefficiency or authoritarianism, had catalysed the fall of the Eastern Bloc. From this perspective, institutional faith was not merely tolerated dissent but a systemic threat to political stability (Leung 2005a). This insight, drawn from the collapse of Marxist governments abroad, continues to shape Chinese religious policy today (Powers 2019).

The anxieties of Beijing were only amplified by Pope John Paul II's 1991 encyclical *Centesimus Annus*, which celebrated the moral triumph of the Church over communism in Europe. To the CCP, this document was not merely theological, but a geopolitical statement that intensified their fears of Catholic subversion (Leung 1992; Madsen 1998; Chu 2012). In response, Beijing redoubled its efforts to insulate Chinese Catholics from foreign influence, and to sever perceived ties between the Church and what the Party labelled "Western imperial powers" (Goossaert and Palmer 2011, 158).

Despite this hostile backdrop, John Paul II did allow for an albeit measured diplomatic track to continue. Cardinals Casaroli and, later, Angelo Sodano were tasked with maintaining unofficial contact with Chinese authorities. In 1999, Sodano publicly declared the Holy See's willingness to sever ties with Taiwan if Beijing were open to formal relations (Union of Catholic Asian News 1999). The same year, the CCP's Central Committee and State Council released a joint statement affirming conditional openness to normalised relations with the Vatican on the non-negotiable condition that the Catholic Church in China operate independently of papal authority. This position was codified in *Document No. 26*, which reaffirmed the role of the CCPA as the state's instrument for regulating Catholic affairs (Leung 2005a, 353).

Hopes of reconciliation flickered anew in 2002, when Pope John Paul II appointed Pietro Parolin as Undersecretary of State and entrusted him with normalising ties with both Vietnam and China. Progress with Hanoi was promising following a 2007 meeting between Pope Benedict XVI and Vietnamese Prime Minister Nguyen Tan Dung, formal talks began, and the Vatican eventually appointed its first envoy to Vietnam in 2011 (*New York Times* 2007). China, however, remained resistant. In 2007, Benedict XVI issued a pastoral letter to Chinese Catholics expressing hope for dialogue, but also criticising the CCPA, calling its existence "incompatible with Catholic doctrine" (Pope Benedict XVI 2007a). The letter was met with disapproval in Beijing, and diplomatic efforts once again stalled.

The tension between ecclesiastical universality and national sovereignty came into stark relief on 6 January 2000, when the CCP unilaterally ordained five bishops without Vatican approval. The Vatican responded symbolically but forcefully: that same year, Pope John Paul II canonised 120 Chinese martyrs, many of whom had died during the Boxer Rebellion. This act was read in Beijing not as a gesture of religious commemoration, but as a provocation (Criveller 2020).

A central dilemma endured across papacies: can the Catholic Church maintain spiritual sovereignty while engaging a regime that insists on political control over religious expression? Beneath the technical debates over episcopal appointments and diplomatic recognition lies a deeper clash, that between a universal Church and a communist state that views religious authority as a threat to ideological control. This unresolved contest of legitimacy remained the defining struggle in a long and often difficult relationship between the Chinese Communist Party and the Holy See.

Chinese Foreign Policy under President Xi Jinping: Power, Legitimacy, and the Vatican's Long View

Since assuming power in late 2012, President Xi Jinping articulated a vision of China anchored in three interwoven objectives: the accumulation of national wealth, the expansion of global influence, and the preservation of the Chinese Communist Party's one-party rule. His leadership was a decisive shift away from the ethos of Deng Xiaoping, who famously urged China to "hide its strength and bide its time." In its place, Xi advanced a bold doctrine, one that seeks not only to secure China's rise but to redefine the rules of global engagement.

Central to Xi's foreign policy strategy is an ambiguous but mutually beneficial relationship with Russia. While the Kremlin under Vladimir Putin presents a convenient partner in opposing American dominance, Beijing remains clear-eyed in maintaining a pragmatic approach. Russia is viewed less as a strategic equal than as a useful counterbalance in the broader struggle to limit the reach of the United States. Xi's overarching goal is not an outright rejection of the current international order but its gradual transformation to enshrine China as a dominant participant. Beijing participates in the structures of global governance, while working methodically to reshape them according to Chinese interests and values (Zhu 2021).

Under Xi's leadership, this ambition has found expression in what is now widely known as '*Major Country Diplomacy*' (*daguo waijiao*). This policy signals China's departure from low-profile diplomacy and proclaims its intent to be a central actor on the global stage. This assertiveness has often been embodied in the combative tone of '*Wolf Warrior Diplomacy*', a style of international diplomacy characterised by forceful rhetoric, swift rebuke of criticism, and a refusal to accept Western moral judgments without retaliation (Wang 2019; Smith 2021).

Beneath this veneer lies a deeper strategic aspiration: to become a 'norm shaper' in the international system (Zeng 2017). This entails positioning China not simply as a geopolitical power but as a civilisational model that offers a compelling alternative to Western liberal democracy. In Xi's speeches, one hears frequent invocations of shared destiny, global peace, and moral rejuvenation, a rhetoric that blends Confucian heritage with socialist ambition, aiming to craft a new moral legitimacy for China's global leadership (Wang 2019).

Such a posture brings Xi's China into a subtle but profound tension, and perhaps at some future point, dialogue with the Holy See. For the Vatican, whose diplomatic identity has long been grounded in moral prestige, China's civilisational claims cannot be ignored. Both the Vatican and Beijing seek to project influence, each invoking its own vision of an international order. Xi's insistence on civilisational leadership intersects, sometimes awkwardly, with the Vatican's universal mission. In this diplomatic theatre, the question emerges: *What does China seek from a pope? And what can a pope afford to seek from China?*

At the heart of China's motivation lies the pursuit of international legitimacy. Despite its economic and military rise, China remains acutely aware that its political system is met with scepticism across much of the democratic world. A relationship with the Holy See possibly offers some symbolic capital: an alliance, however tenuous, with the world's oldest religious diplomatic actor and one of its most enduring moral voices. For Beijing, engaging the Vatican would not merely be about religious management; it would be about enhancing its stature in the international order (Koesel 2014).

For the Vatican, the strategic calculation is no less delicate. The Holy See cannot afford to ignore China not simply because of its sheer demographic and geopolitical weight, but also because of its divided Catholic population, split between underground communities and state-sanctioned institutions. Under Francis' diplomacy, the Vatican was taking a long-term approach: prioritising engagement over confrontation, and presence over immediate results.

In an age of shifting power and moral contestation, the encounter between Xi Jinping's China and the Holy See represents a dialogue not merely of states, but of worldviews. It is a meeting of two ancient institutions, each claiming authority, each pursuing legitimacy, each navigating the demands of the global stage with strategies shaped by very different histories.

CCP Control of Religious Groups: Sinicisation, Surveillance, and the Erosion of Religious Autonomy
Prior to Xi Jinping's ascent to power, religious practice in China was governed by a relatively pragmatic and loosely enforced framework. As Thomas DuBois observed, the Chinese Communist Party (CCP) pursued a largely utilitarian policy toward religion that sought not to eradicate belief but to absorb and appropriate it in the service of nation-building (DuBois 2010). Confucianism, as an indigenous and non-confrontational tradition, received implicit state endorsement and was often deployed as a cultural resource to reinforce social harmony and loyalty to the Party. Other religious traditions, particularly those seen as foreign or socially mobilising, were treated with suspicion but often tolerated, so long as they remained politically quiescent.

This uneasy accommodation changed under President Xi Jinping. Religious freedom has been significantly curtailed. What was once tolerated is now increasingly criminalised. China maintains one of the largest prison populations in the world for religious activity, and despite official claims of openness, only state-sponsored religious institutions are legally permitted. In 2017, the *State Council's Regulations on Religious Affairs* imposed sweeping restrictions on religious education, publication, property ownership, financial contributions, and the training and appointment of clergy (The State Council 2017).

Catholicism, viewed as a 'foreign' religion with global allegiances, has come under especially intense scrutiny. The CCP's objective is not only to contain Christianity but to domesticate it, reinterpreting its teachings through a nationalist lens. Under the banner of *Sinicisation*, new campaigns have sought to revise Christian scripture to align with socialist values and Chinese cultural narratives. Possession or distribution of unapproved Bibles is punishable by fines or imprisonment (del Turco 2020). While the growth of Christianity remains modest in proportion to China's population, the CCP perceives it as a latent threat due to its transnational connections and moral independence.

For Catholics in China, this presents a profound dilemma. Fidelity to the pope, and the universal character of the Church, stand in stark contrast to the CCP's demand for political and ideological subordination. The sovereign status of the papacy complicates the Party's efforts to assert total control over Chinese Catholics. As Yang notes, the global reach of Catholicism continues to trouble the CCP elite, who remain wary of any institution capable of commanding loyalty beyond state borders (Yang 2017). Beatrice Leung captures this longstanding concern succinctly, writing that the Chinese state views the Catholic Church as historically aligned with "the imperialist enemy" and marked by "cultural exploitation" (Leung 1992, 95).

The intensification of religious repression under Xi raised the stakes for Pope Francis. Churches have been demolished, crosses removed, and surveillance cameras installed inside places of worship. Children under the age of eighteen are legally forbidden from attending religious services. Regulations enacted in February 2018 further prohibited unauthorised religious teaching and foreign travel for religious purposes. Foreign donations were capped at USD $15,000, and in some provinces, public servants, including teachers and medical professionals, have been required to renounce their religious beliefs (Albert and Maizland 2020).

These policies are justified by the CCP as necessary measures to protect national security and social cohesion. Xi Jinping has consistently framed *Sinicisation* as an ideological imperative demanding that all religious expression conform to the Party's understanding of socialism with Chinese characteristics. The campaign is not simply about alignment with state goals but about the redefinition of religious identity itself.

In 2015, the Party took a decisive step by dissolving the State Administration for Religious Affairs and transferring its responsibilities directly to the United Front Work Department, an agency tasked with enforcing ideological conformity and managing relations with non-Party actors. This structural shift was formalised by the Politburo in 2017 and signalled the end of even the appearance of religious autonomy.

By 2018, all 'officially' recognised religious organisations in China were required to submit comprehensive five-year plans for their own *Sinicisation*.

These plans had to articulate how their doctrines, practices, and institutional structures would be brought into conformity with CCP ideology. One of the most extreme consequences of this policy has been the mass internment of Uighur Muslims in the Xinjiang Uyghur Autonomous Region, under the guise of 're-education' and counter-extremism measures (Wang 2018).

The Catholic Church was not exempt. In June 2018, the state-endorsed Chinese Catholic Patriotic Association, alongside the government-approved Bishop's Conference of the Catholic Church in China, issued its own five-year *Sinicisation* plan. Every diocese in the country was ordered to produce a corresponding plan within two months, each incorporating explicit statements on political loyalty, cultural identity, and social values aligned with CCP directives.

These developments illuminate the profound challenges that confronted Pope Francis. The Holy See's commitment to spiritual sovereignty stands in stark and irreconcilable tension with the CCP's unyielding demand for political control. Under Xi Jinping, religious policy is not merely repressive in function, but transformational in intent, aiming to remould any remnant of religion into the fabric of a nation whose identity remains acutely controlled and shaped by regime propaganda. It seeks not coexistence but convergence, leaving scant space for authentic pluralism and rendering the Church's mission in China an act of both witness and resistance.

Francis and China: Playing with the Dragon
With the retirement of Cardinal Agostino Casaroli in 1990, Vatican engagement with China entered a hiatus. Casaroli's departure saw the close of a defining chapter in Vatican diplomacy that was shaped by his leadership of the Holy See's *Ostpolitik*, a carefully calibrated policy of dialogue with Eastern Bloc regimes during the Cold War. His

successor, Cardinal Angelo Sodano, brought a different set of priorities to the role of Secretary of State and placed far less emphasis on China (Leung 2003).

Relations between the Holy See and China remained stagnant, particularly after the Vatican continued to recognize Taiwan rather than the People's Republic of China. The delicate and incremental strategy forged under Casaroli found little continuity under Sodano, due in large part to Beijing's persistent resistance to dialogue and ongoing concerns within the Vatican over the repression of religious freedom in China.

Diplomatic responsibility for China shifted from the Secretariat of State to the more conservative Congregation for the Evangelisation of Peoples (*Propaganda Fide*), whose approach lacked both the political nuance and the institutional prowess of Casaroli's legacy. Cardinal Jozef Tomko, then prefect, made overtures to Beijing, but these were hampered by his lack of diplomatic training. His successor, Cardinal Crescenzio Sepe, convened a 2002 consultative meeting on the Chinese mission, yet acknowledged a persistent vacuum of knowledge within the Roman Curia (Chu 2013).

Francis brought a strong re-focus upon China in his diplomatic agenda. China was elevated from diplomatic periphery to ecclesial priority. This pivot was driven by both geopolitical calculation and spiritual conviction. China's demographic scale and global influence offered opportunities for Catholic expansion, while its political climate presented immense pastoral challenges (Mok 2021; O'Connell 2015). The Jesuit pope appeared determined to resume the Society of Jesus' long-interrupted mission, not merely as an act of historical homage but as a strategic commitment to patient dialogue.

When Francis became pope in 2013, he revitalised this diplomatic path. As Sino-Vatican scholar Xiang observed: "The Society of Jesus once displayed an admirable open-mindedness toward Chinese culture that seems to have all but disappeared among Western governments. Now that a Jesuit has ascended to the papacy for the first time, it seems like the ideal moment for the Vatican and China to resume the healthy cultural dialogue that was so brutally broken off in 1742" (Xiang 2018, 94). Francis' strategy echoed a language of cultural respect and slow engagement with the CCP. His was a diplomacy of paradox: rhetorical continuity cloaked in *realpolitik*, and an openness constrained by surveillance and repression.

Francis had inherited a Vatican ill-equipped for the complexities of Chinese diplomacy. He dissolved the largely ineffective China Committee and returned Sino-Vatican policy to the Secretariat of State. Secretary of State Cardinal Parolin, was tasked by Francis with resuming leadership of the initiative, drawing from his earlier experience negotiating with Hanoi. In a 2021 interview with the Spanish broadcaster COPE, Francis explicitly invoked Casaroli's legacy: "Slowly, slowly, slowly, he [Casaroli] was achieving reserves of diplomatic relations which in the end meant appointing new bishops and taking care of God's faithful people" (Pullela 2021).

The groundwork for a strategy had been laid years earlier. In 2005, then-Archbishop Pietro Parolin negotiated a landmark agreement with Vietnam over episcopal appointments. By 2009, he had reportedly reached a similar understanding with Beijing, an accord that Pope Benedict XVI declined to ratify, leading to renewed tensions (Wiest 2014).

Francis proved more open. In a symbolic gesture as a result, he became the first pope permitted to fly through

Chinese airspace. On 14 August 2014, en-route to South Korea, he sent a message to President Xi Jinping, invoking "divine blessings of peace and well-being upon the nation" (Wan 2014). Similar actions followed in 2015 and beyond, each time expressing goodwill and cultural respect.

These gestures stirred controversy. Critics feared the Vatican was legitimising authoritarianism. Citing historical precedent, from concordats with fascist and communist regimes, figures like the elderly Cardinal Joseph Zen of Hong Kong denounced Francis dangerously accommodating Beijing (Mok 2021). His policy, they argued, risked the pope's moral credibility, especially at a time of increasing religious repression in China.

An appeal for gradualism failed to satisfy those who expected prophetic resistance. Francis' silence during Xi Jinping's 2019 visit to Rome, where the Chinese leader conspicuously avoided meeting with the pontiff, was seen by some as a symbolic submission. Xi's omission of Matteo Ricci in speeches celebrating Sino-European ties were also met with reticence (Cervellera 2019). To many observers, Francis' posture was ambiguous and came at the cost of moral clarity.

Still, his strategy bore some fruit. In 2018, the Holy See, and the Chinese government did sign a *Provisional Agreement* concerning the appointment of bishops. Though the details remained confidential, it was widely understood that the agreement granted Beijing substantial input over episcopal nominations. Critics warned of capitulation. Supporters stressed its provisional and narrow scope, limited to episcopal appointments and intended as a first step toward deeper future progress.

The Vatican made notable concessions to secure the agreement. Bishops previously ordained without papal mandate were pardoned and legitimised. In some cases, bishops loyal to Rome were asked to step down. Bishop Huang Bingzhang, once excommunicated and a member of the National People's Congress, was reinstated. Bishop Guo Xijin, a 59-year-old underground bishop from Mindong, was asked to cede his position to state-recognised Bishop Zhan Silu. Bishop Peter Zhuang Jianjian, too, was reportedly requested to vacate his post for a government-approved successor (Catholic News Agency 2018).

These actions wounded many in the underground Church, who had endured decades of persecution in fidelity to Rome. For some, the agreement seemed to erase their sacrifice. Nevertheless, Jesuit commentator Thomas Reese offered a different interpretation: "The Vatican's job is to make martyrdom unnecessary wherever possible... This is why negotiations are conducted by diplomats, not saints or martyrs" (Reese 2018). Even so, repression continued. Clergy were pressured to register with the CCPA. Churches remained under surveillance. Children were banned from religious services. Critics warned that the 2018 agreement had not loosened the grip of state control, but rather institutionalised it.

Francis' engagement with China, then, remains a study in diplomatic paradox. It draws upon the memory of Matteo Ricci and the legacy of Casaroli, yet it unfolds in an era shaped by authoritarian nationalism and digital surveillance. It is at once pastoral and political, spiritual and strategic, hopeful and deeply compromised. Whether this careful diplomacy yields long-term positive outcomes, or further marginalises the Church remains an open question. But for Francis, it represented a wager: that presence, however limited, is better than absence, and that quiet engagement, even when misunderstood, could yet sow seeds of encounter even in the soil of repression.

Francis, China, and the Fragility of Taiwan

The Holy See's relationship with Taiwan occupies a precarious and deeply symbolic space at the intersection of moral principle and geopolitical pragmatism. While the details of the *Provisional Agreement* signed between the Holy See and the People's Republic of China in 2018, and quietly extended in 2024, remain officially undisclosed, its implications are unmistakable.

Taiwan, often described as a 'virtual international orphan,' finds itself diplomatically adrift amid the shifting tides of global power. For the island, formal recognition by the Holy See is not merely symbolic but existential. The Vatican remains one of the few sovereign entities to maintain official ties with Taipei. To lose this recognition would be not just a diplomatic loss, but a deep wound. Yet for the Holy See, this relationship may represent a singular bargaining chip and a precious token to be exchanged in pursuit of a larger strategic goal: full diplomatic relations with Beijing.

The shadow of this possibility has loomed over Vatican diplomacy for decades. Pope Francis inherited this tension and followed an arc of diplomatic logic, that looked to the legacy of Cardinal Agostino Casaroli, as a model of strategic engagement with authoritarian regimes. For Francis, Casaroli's approach offered a template for patient bridge-building, in which long-term spiritual goals justified short-term compromise (UCA News 2021). Francis' strategy was not without peril. Severing ties with Taiwan, one of Asia's most robust democracies and a haven of religious liberty, in favour of formal engagement with a state known for its repression of religious groups would raise serious questions about the papacy's moral coherence.

The stakes are high on all sides. For Beijing, prying the Vatican away from Taipei would represent a symbolic and strategic triumph, another piece removed from Taiwan's shrinking circle of allies. For Taiwan, its embassy to the Holy See is more than a diplomatic mission; it is a visible, living sign of sovereign dignity, and its only permanent diplomatic foothold in Europe. The CCP's long-term strategy of isolating Taiwan relies on precisely such moments of attrition, subtle realignments that quietly erode international recognition.

Francis, too, recognised Taiwan's value, not only as a loyal partner but as a diplomatic lever. Taiwan offers Rome negotiating strength as Beijing seeks to neutralise it. Any future shift in the Holy See's position would almost certainly require firm guarantees from the CCP, a delicate and perhaps illusory promise given the Party's track record in keeping to agreements.

Pope Francis thus adopted a strategy of deliberate ambiguity. While maintaining official diplomatic ties with Taipei, he consistently refrained from visiting the island. He neither endorsed the CCP's 'One China' policy nor issued statements that would imply recognition of Taiwanese statehood. In doing so, Francis walked a narrow diplomatic tightrope, attempting to preserve a fragile equilibrium between prophetic witness and political realism.

In the unfolding drama of Vatican–China relations, Taiwan remains both a symbol and a scapegoat: a nation whose fate may be shaped not only by its own resilience but by the outcome of negotiations in which it has no seat at the table. Francis' balancing act may yet preserve this fragile status quo. But in the long sweep of Vatican diplomacy, Taiwan's position remains vulnerable, a fragile ember caught between competing fires.

Stabilising the Church in China: Francis' Urgent Diplomatic Goal

Five interwoven concerns shaped Pope Francis' short- and long-term diplomatic strategy with regard to China:

1. The division of authority in the appointment of Catholic bishops within the PRC.
2. The future role and status of a papal nuncio in Beijing, should formal diplomatic relations be established.
3. The reconciliation of China's underground Church with its state-recognised counterpart.
4. The Vatican's delicate posture toward Taiwan, particularly the challenge of transferring diplomatic recognition to Beijing without publicly humiliating Taipei.
5. The CCP's uncompromising insistence on ideological loyalty, and the fundamental tensions this presents with Catholic teaching.

Among these, the issue of episcopal appointments emerged as the keystone of negotiations. Unlike the Holy See's arrangement with Vietnam, where shared consultation on bishops allowed for a workable *modus vivendi*, China's case remained uniquely fraught.

The signing of Provisional Agreements, and done so in secrecy, signalled a departure from the Vatican's prior position, which had consistently defended the autonomy of ecclesial authority from state control. Francis, in contrast, was willing to take what many perceived as a 'leap of faith.' On Francis' strategy Chit Wai John Mok noted, "The realpolitik of Pope Francis... led the Vatican to take a 'leap of faith' and embrace the PRC. Francis' personal attachment to the Jesuit tradition... allowed him to politick boldly and make concessions that his predecessors were unwilling to agree to" (Mok 2021, 399).

Francis' actions became deeply polarising. Critics decried them as moral capitulation, a diplomatic accommodation that undermined the suffering and loyalty of China's underground Catholics. Supporters, by contrast, hailed them as a historic breakthrough, an effort to ensure the Church's survival and future growth in one of the world's most challenging religious environments. Yet the CCP's longstanding pattern of disregarding international agreements cast a shadow over the Vatican's trust. Whether the Holy See's willingness to compromise would be met with reciprocal good faith from Beijing remained an open and consequential question.

That question indeed, did not take long to be tested. In October 2022, Chinese authorities unilaterally appointed Peng Weizhao as auxiliary bishop of the Diocese of Jiangxi, a diocese not recognised by the Holy See. Bishop Peng had been clandestinely appointed by Pope Francis in 2014 as the bishop of Yujiang, a diocese recognized by the Vatican but not by the Chinese government. For this, the bishop was detained by Chinese authorities for six months.

Peng's 2022 re-appointment (to the Diocese of Jiangxi) was made without Vatican approval and was not in accordance with the 2018 Provisional Agreement between Rome and Beijing. The Vatican expressed "surprise and regret" over the event, noting that it did not align with the spirit of dialogue established by the agreement and that Bishop Peng's civil recognition was reportedly preceded by prolonged and intense pressure from local authorities (Vatican News 2022).

The appointment was conducted under the auspices of the Chinese Catholic Patriotic Association and the Council of Chinese Bishops, both state-sanctioned organisations. During his installation, Bishop Peng reportedly pledged to "guide Catholicism to adapt to socialist society" and contribute to the "dream of the great rejuvenation of the Chinese nation," aligning with the Chinese government's policy of Sinicising religion (Catholic World Report 2022).

Despite the Vatican's public protest, Beijing offered no formal response. In April 2023, Chinese authorities again, unilaterally appointed Bishop Joseph Shen Bin as the Bishop of Shanghai without consulting the Vatican—a move that contravened the spirit of the 2018 Provisional Agreement. Shen Bin had previously served as Bishop of Haimen since 2010, an appointment made with Vatican approval. His installation in Shanghai was organised by the state-sanctioned Council of Chinese Bishops, a body not recognised by the Holy See. Functioning as a government-aligned episcopal conference, the Council operates under the oversight of the CCP and maintains close ties to the Chinese Catholic Patriotic Association (CCPA), whose mission is to align Catholic life and doctrine in China with state policy and ideological directives (Catholic News Agency 2023). Despite this, on 15 July 2023, Pope Francis formally recognised Shen Bin's appointment, which shocked observers and reinforced concerns over the Vatican's muted response to CCP transgressions.

Francis' silence on acts of repression and episcopal irregularity stood in contrast to his predecessor, Pope Benedict XVI, who had set clear boundaries in his 2007 *Letter to Chinese Catholics*: "The solution to existing problems cannot be pursued via an ongoing conflict with the legitimate civil authorities; at the same time, though, compliance with those authorities is not acceptable when they interfere unduly in matters regarding the faith and discipline of the Church" (Pope Benedict XVI 2007a).

The fragility of Francis' Sino-Vatican relationship reflected the complexity of a diplomatic experiment. Francis moved with caution, sensitivity, and, some would say, necessary compromise. But whether the *Provisional Agreement* ultimately strengthens the Church's position in China, or entangles it in a web of state control, remains unresolved. The papacy's perennial challenge is how to defend the faith without abandoning the faithful.

Both China and the Holy See are custodians of institutional memory measured not in centuries but in millennia. Yet history, with its shifting empires and fallen powers, has more often favoured the Church in its endurance through the tempests of authoritarianism. The papacy has withstood the rise and ruin of all types of regime; authoritarian, totalitarian, and colonial. Each was consigned, in time, to the margins of memory. Perhaps this was Francis' quiet confidence: that the Chinese Communist Party, like so many before it, would one day fade into the annals of history, while the papacy, rooted in deeper soil, would remain.

In Francis, the world witnessed a pontiff who embodied a transnational spiritual institution unmatched in its reach, symbolic depth, and historical resilience. His détente with the CCP, at once strategic and pastoral, must be read against this broader horizon: not merely as present policy, but as an expression of a papacy seasoned by centuries, and confident in its capacity to outlast the impermanence of secular power.

Chapter Nine: Legacies in Light and Shadow The Horizons of Pope Francis

This book has explored the distinctive diplomatic style and enduring legacy of Jorge Mario Bergoglio, Pope Francis, the first Jesuit pontiff. It traced the diverse threads of his formation, from Jesuit spirituality and Latin American theology to the Perónist political ethos of Argentina, the *aggiornamento* spirit of the Second Vatican Council, and key theological and philosophical voices from across globe. These influences coalesced into a papal identity that both challenged and expanded conventional expectations of Vatican diplomacy. Francis emerged as a maverick pope, whose diplomatic approach was unorthodox but never without deliberation.

At the heart of his diplomatic project lay an enduring paradox for the papacy: the need to reconcile the Church's spiritual mission with its temporal engagement in global affairs. Under Francis, this tension was not avoided but embraced.

Francis' diplomacy was above all pragmatic, deeply rooted in the Jesuit tradition. This allowed him a space of comfort with ambiguity, the capacity to accommodate tension, and a scope in remaining open to unexpected outcomes. In all this, his diplomacy was process-orientated rather than a chessboard of fixed strategies. He privileged relationship over dissociative formality.

Throughout his pontificate, Francis navigated precarious lines between spiritual witness and geopolitical necessity. In places like China and Russia, he practiced a renewed Vatican *Ostpolitik*, an ecclesiastical *realpolitik* that drew a strategic and sadly often needed, demarcation between what the Church proclaims and how it acts. This was not duplicity, but the acceptance that diplomacy frequently unfolds in silence, subtlety, and longitudinally. The Jesuit capacity to live with unresolved tension, and a Perónist instinct for ideological non-alignment, equipped the pope with tools to survive in the morally compromised theatre of international politics.

This grounded gaze, though noble, exacted a cost. Francis' path of dialogue, though paved with goodwill, sometimes blurred the sharp lines of moral witness. When he held his tongue amid Putin's assault on Ukraine, or offered cautious overtures to Beijing, critics saw not discernment but disquieting silence. To many in the liberal West, his diplomacy, measured and deliberate, seemed to falter where they felt clarity was most needed, trading thunder for whisper in the face of storm.

Francis did not seek the echo of applause nor the comfort of ideological consistency. His measure of diplomacy was not purity, but an endurance cultivated through patience, cultural listening, and the courage to dwell with uncertainty. For him, diplomacy was not transaction but relationship, a slow art of presence across divides. To reach all without prejudice was no mark of naivety, but of something deeper. Beneath the papacy's open face, welcoming, disarming, and inclusive, lay a quiet mastery of signal and symbol, of unexpected gestures and unorthodox moves. And though this often gave the impression of disorder, it was, in truth, the choreography of a different kind of power.

Though rich in symbol and tempered by strategic restraint, Pope Francis' diplomacy could not always bend the arc of geopolitics. His persistent overtures to Vladimir Putin, tendered with care and conscience, ran aground on the hard shores of *realpolitik*. The invasion of Ukraine proceeded undeterred, exposing the frailty of moral persuasion against imperial ambition. Likewise, his bold accommodation with the Chinese Communist Party, sealed in Provisional Agreements, did little to still the machinery of repression. The persecution of believers continued, unmoved by dialogue. In these moments, the limits of papal soft power stood starkly revealed, and the cost of appeasement, when unreciprocated, was paid.

Yet to judge Francis' choices solely through the lens of diplomatic shortfall is to miss the deeper current beneath his course. His gaze turned deliberately eastward and southward, loosening the Vatican from the gravitational pull of Western primacy. In redrawing the map of papal engagement, Francis envisioned not failure, but a quiet revolution that embraced a multipolar world over the certainties of dominance. His tempered stance toward American hegemony was no mere rebuke, but a sign of the Holy See's emerging posture: post-Western, dialogical, and globally attuned. Through subtle realignment, Francis gestured toward a new centre of gravity in the Church's international imagination.

Francis entered the global stage at a time of shifting geopolitical fault lines. World order was fragmenting, and new poles of power were emerging. He attended to a multipolar world. Manlio Graziano observed poignantly, the West was no longer the centre of the world it once commanded. In his words: "Europe, which had 'commandeered the world', and which had shaped it, has been destined, 'since the mid-twentieth century', to be but 'a simple part' of a universe that once 'was its own'; it is condemned to 'again become a mere fraction of humanity, its erstwhile project'" (Graziano 2017, 195). Francis did not lament this; he embraced it with a polyhedron view of the world.

Within this shifting landscape, the pontiff sought new paths and unexpected companions, reaching across divides even to those whose values did not mirror his own, in the hope of planting seeds where none had grown. Francis beheld the rise of a multipolar world not as a threat to global order, but as an invitation to reimagine it. Where others saw fragmentation and the decline of Euro-American hegemony, he discerned the possibility of a more inclusive international communion. Drawing upon his polyhedron metaphor, Francis envisioned unity not through uniformity, but through the dignified coexistence of difference. This vision animated his efforts to move the Church beyond its conventional alliances, toward a posture of listening, encounter, and shared responsibility.

In confronting the dominant currents of globalisation, Francis sought to voice an alternative vision of world order (Ferrara, 2015). In this task, he cast both himself and the papacy as counter-hegemonic actors, untethered from empire, yet deeply engaged with the shifting tectonics of global power. His dual vocation as sovereign and shepherd allowed him to traverse the fault lines between the sacred and the secular, between the transient affairs of state and the enduring claims of the spirit. In a world increasingly fractured, he moved with a singular grace across realms, offering not control, but connection as the currency of a different kind of leadership.

This dual role endowed Francis with a rare diplomatic versatility. At times, he engaged global powers like Russia, China, and the United States as a head of state; at others, he addressed their populations, especially Catholics, as a pastoral figure. Such manoeuvrability afforded him a space within which to bypass conventional diplomatic constraints, leveraging the Church's transnational nature to project influence across national borders. His multivalent identity, straddling both religious and political spheres, underpinned a distinctly Catholic form of diplomacy that could operate simultaneously within and beyond the state system.

At its heart, the animating narrative of Pope Francis' diplomacy was one of encounter; of a Church stepping beyond its walls not with clenched fists but with open hands. His was a vision not of confrontation, but of dialogue across divides, of presence rather than proclamation. Yet this very openness unveiled the fault lines within a diplomacy of encounter: the peril of drawing near to power without losing the clarity of prophetic distance. Francis' approach, at once aspirational and uneven, exposed the delicate balance between principle and pragmatism. But rather than retreat from this tension, he accepted it. His aim was never to assert authority from afar, but to plant the Church within the messy centre of the world's stage even when the path was dimmed by ambiguity.

He did not shy away from a readiness to engage a fractured world through calibrated compromise, equating the pursuit of peace not with the elimination of difference but with sustained negotiation of coexisting tensions. Compromise, in this light, was not a betrayal of principle but a necessary instrument within a broader, spiritually informed calculus. He was at once a pastor and a politician, a bridge-builder and a disruptor, a saint and a strategist.

Francis' 'encounter process-orientated diplomacy' was 'messy' at times. It didn't necessarily come with preconceived goals, but rather, in Jesuit fashion, opened pathways that required frequent reworking and substantial fluidity. In this regard, Pope Francis was less concerned with closure than with gradual and relational progress. His theological anthropology and idiosyncratic political imagination evaded categorisation within conventional binaries. His strategic ambiguity, far from incoherence, enabled Francis to operate within complexity.

Francis' reflected the example of Peter Faber, an early Jesuit forebearer known for his ability to dialogue even with ideological adversaries. It is telling that in *Evangelii Gaudium*, Francis highlighted Faber's patience for dialogue by quoting his statement… "time is God's messenger" (Pope Francis 2013f, §171). This maxim encapsulated Francis' willingness to forgo immediate outcomes for the sake of prospective transformation.

Assessing the effectiveness of Francis' diplomacy is challenging, particularly given its longitudinal and sometimes intangible nature. Was he primarily motivated by religious witness, strategic calculation, or a deliberate fusion of both? This book concludes that Francis operated as a religious witness *through* calculated diplomacy.

At the heart of this paradox lies a deeper ecclesiological tension: how the Church is to be "in the world but not of the world" (John 17:14–15). This perennial Christian challenge was addressed by Francis in a manner distinctively his own. As a Latin American Jesuit, he brought to this ancient question an approach that embraced contextual awareness, pastoral pragmatism, and political flexibility. His pontificate exemplified the ongoing paradox of the Church itself: situated within history yet oriented toward transcendence, shaped by contingency yet tasked with proclaiming the eternal.

The full measure of Francis' diplomacy will only emerge across decades. Marked by ambiguity, touched by contradiction, and uneven in its immediate outcomes, it defied the neat metrics of success. Yet beneath its shifting forms lay a coherence anchored in spiritual depth, shaped by pastoral realism, and animated by a profound empathy.

Whatever its flaws, his diplomacy bore the unmistakable imprint of a conscience formed not in strategy alone, but in spirituality, discernment, and the frequently painful process of encounter. His was a diplomacy of relationship, not dominance; of tension, not resolution; of faith navigating power.

In a time of disillusionment with institutions and diplomacy alike, Pope Francis offered a humble but radical model of engagement. He did not claim to resolve the world's conflicts, but insisted on the Church's responsibility to walk alongside humanity. His legacy should be judged not by his geopolitical results, but by the example he set: a papacy willing to take risk, to dwell in ambiguity, and to reimagine diplomacy as an act of accompaniment in an age of fracture. Like his Jesuit ancestors, he focused on 'seed planting,' accepting that in reality he wouldn't see the fruits harvested in his lifetime. Perhaps eternity was the timeframe.

Pope Francis' diplomatic legacy will not be etched in treaties signed or empires swayed, but in the quiet resonance of a deeper alignment between the man he became through Jesuit formation, the world he engaged as shepherd, and the imagination that guided his choices. He did not strive to please all, nor did he chase the winds of favour. His mission was steadier: to carry the voice of his Church into the fractured geometry of global power.

Through gestures that disarmed, silences that provoked, and words that unsettled, he practiced a diplomacy of presence to the complexities of the age. In a world shaped by spectacle and strategy, he remained attentive to the long patience of transformation.

If history judges him with delay, it will do so rightly, for his project was never the short aim of success, but the long arc of fidelity. And in that arc, Francis stands not only as pope or diplomat, but as a rare witness: one who bore the weight of the world without surrendering the light within.

And so, in the long reckoning of time, Francis may not be remembered as a pope who changed the world, but as one who walked within it—between altars and alliances—with a heart open to the other, and a diplomacy quietly guided by the currents of a transcendental call. He did not seek dominion, but relationship, not triumph, but transformation. And in that sacred tension between the spiritual and the political, he carved a path that may long outlast those forces that questioned it.

Epilogue: From Francis' Legacy to Leo's Dawn

The close of any papacy invites reflection, but the end of Pope Francis' tenure arrived with particular weight. His was a pontificate shaped not only by his charismatic personality but by the global upheavals through which he shepherded the Church. The world had come to recognise his voice, gentle yet provocative, sometimes ambiguous, at other times sharp. When the bells tolled once more for the Conclave, it marked not only the cessation of a pontifical reign, but the final epoch of a diplomatic chapter indelibly stamped with the character of Francis himself.

The College of Cardinals assembled bore the imprint of Francis himself. Over a decade, he had reshaped its geographic composition, elevating voices from Africa, Asia, and Latin America. The electors who gathered in the Sistine Chapel were thus not only voting for a new pope, but they were also voting amid the ecclesial map Francis had drawn.

Pope Francis enacted a deliberate departure from the patterns of his predecessors, who had largely drawn their cardinalate appointments from Europe and North America. Cardinals were named from countries like Myanmar, Mongolia, Brunei, Iraq, and Bangladesh, many of which had never had a cardinal before. African countries like South Sudan, Congo, and Mozambique gained greater prominence. Francis often bypassed major archdioceses traditionally expected to receive red hats. Instead, he elevated bishops from remote dioceses or places marked by conflict, poverty, or Catholic minority status (Lavenburg 2025). Francis sought to reflect the universal character of the Church, bringing voices from peripheral and often underrepresented regions into the heart of Vatican decision-making.

From the 2025 Conclave emerged Pope Leo XIV. Cardinal Robert Francis Prevost was relatively unknown outside ecclesial and theological circles prior to his election. Unlike high-profile figures in the Roman Curia or prominent cardinals, he did not hold a globally visible position. He was not frequently featured in international Catholic media or mainstream global press. His name was not widely circulated among leading 'papabili' (potential popes) in pre-Conclave speculation (Meichtry et al. 2025). His election was seen by many analysts as a consensus choice, a pope capable of balancing continuity with renewal after the highly distinctive papacy of Francis.

Pope Leo XIV is from the Augustinian Order. While it's too early to assess the full impact, analysts and theologians are likely to interpret Leo XIV's Augustinian background as a symbolic pivot from Francis' Jesuit improvisational approach to a possibly greater unifying model of papal governance. Pope Francis' Jesuit formation shaped a diplomacy of adaptability and strategic ambiguity.

Unlike the Jesuit model of engagement that informed the diplomacy of Pope Francis. Augustinian diplomacy is likely to place considerable emphasis upon the inner coherence of the Church as a moral and metaphysical actor in global affairs. In the Augustinian imagination, diplomacy is likely to be grounded in realism about human nature and political structures, eschewing utopian visions in favour of cautious moral engagement (Niebuhr 1953; Loriaux 1992). This worldview, embedded in St Augustine's seminal work *The City of God* (Augustine 1950), lends itself to a diplomacy that is less about accommodation and more about witness and bearing the weight of divine truth in a fractured world.

Before his election, Prevost served in various roles, a missionary in Peru (1985-1986 and 1988-1999), Prior General of the Augustinian Order (2001-2013), Bishop of Chiclayo

(2015-2023), and for a short period, in the Roma Curia as Prefect of the Dicastery for Bishops (2023-2025). Francis had created him a Cardinal on 30 September 2023 (Vatican News 2025).

The newly elected pope's choice of the name *Leo* was a deliberate evocation of Leo XIII (1878–1903), signalling continuity with his intellectual and pastoral legacy. That pope had penned **Rerum Novarum,** a foundational papal encyclical issued on May 15, 1891. Its full title, *Rerum Novarum: On the Condition of Labor*, is widely considered the beginning of modern Catholic Social Teaching (Boyle 2019). The encyclical was published during a time of intense social upheaval caused by the Industrial Revolution and addressed the plight of the working class, the rise of socialism, and the effects of capitalism. Pope Leo XIV articulated a continuity between the socio-economic upheavals addressed by Leo XIII in the late nineteenth century and the transformative forces shaping the present age, most notably, the emergence of artificial intelligence and the onset of a new industrial paradigm.

Pope Leo XIV's adoption of the name *Leo* serves as an indicative cue that his international diplomacy will likely echo the moral and intellectual posture of Leo XIII. Rather than conveying a geopolitical realignment, the choice suggests a principled engagement with international affairs. His diplomacy is expected to emphasise human dignity, justice, and the common good, offering a continuity of moral witness amid the complexities of the emerging global order.

While Pope Francis brought to the papacy a distinctive blend of Latin American populism and Jesuit adaptability, Pope Leo XIV enters the role with a different formation and temperament. His Augustinian background suggests a more cohesive approach, emphasising ecclesial unity, and moral clarity. Where Francis often prioritised symbolic gestures, Leo XIV appears poised to reassert the Church's role as a stabilising moral presence. His election signals not a rupture but a shift, from an era of relational diplomacy to one more deeply anchored in institutional continuity. Early commentary describes him as a 'bridge pope' whose mandate is to consolidate, rather than revolutionise, the trajectory set by Francis. He may turn out to be for Francis what Paul VI was for John XXIII (Heatherington 2025). As such, Leo XIV's first steps have been cautious but not unremarkable.

In one of his first public remarks on China, Pope Leo XIV expressed pastoral concern for Chinese Catholics, urging prayers for their strength, joy, and unity with the Holy See during the World Day of Prayer for the Church in China (Winfield 2025). His tone was measured and conciliatory, emphasising peace and harmony amid trials. One notable absence, however, at Pope Leo XIV's inaugural Mass was President Lai Ching-te of Taiwan. Despite earlier hopes expressed by Taiwan's foreign ministry that the president would be present, the delegation was led instead by former vice-president Chen Chien-jen. The decision for a former, rather than the sitting, head of state to attend has been interpreted as a diplomatic compromise by the Holy See, an effort to maintain its unique relationship with Taiwan without further antagonizing Beijing Rogers 2025). This stood in contrast to precedent: sitting Taiwanese presidents attended both the funeral of Pope St. John Paul II and the inauguration of Pope Francis.

This shift in diplomatic protocol raises serious concerns. As one of the few remaining states to maintain formal diplomatic ties with Taiwan, the Vatican's apparent sensitivity to Chinese pressure—evidenced by the absence of President Lai—suggests a continuation of a broader trend toward accommodation. This gesture appears not merely incidental but reflective of the strategic caution that has come to define the Holy See's engagement with Beijing, particularly since the 2018 Sino-Vatican agreement. Viewed in this light, the decision to forgo a full invitation to Taiwan's sitting head of state may be interpreted as yet another compromise in a pattern of concessions. It prompts renewed scrutiny of the Vatican's evolving diplomatic orientation in East Asia and its capacity to maintain both moral consistency and geopolitical relevance. It remains to be seen whether Leo will continue Francis' policy framework or seek a recalibration in the Vatican's engagement with China.

On Russia, Leo XIV may take a notably firmer stance. In 2022, as Bishop Prevost, Leo characterised Russia's invasion of Ukraine as "a true invasion, imperialist in nature, where Russia seeks to conquer territory for reasons of power" (Pakhnyuk 2025). These candid statements, made at a time when Francis was restrained in his messaging, are now amplified by his Leo's papal authority. Pope Leo XIV is charting a path that maintains the Vatican's commitment to dialogue while adopting a more morally clear approach to Russia. Without directly repudiating Francis' much-criticised ambiguity during the war in Ukraine, the new pope has made it clear the Church will utilise its soft diplomacy for resolution of the conflict in Ukraine (Di Giorgio 2025).

Despite Leo's unequivocable comments in 2022, he has nevertheless offered the Vatican as a venue for peace talks. Russia has not accepted the pope's offer to host peace talks between Russia and Ukraine at the Vatican. Russian officials have expressed scepticism about the Vatican as a neutral venue. Factors contributing to this scepticism include the Vatican's location within Italy (a NATO and EU member) and the predominantly Eastern Orthodox affiliations of both Russia and Ukraine, contrasting with the Vatican's Catholic identity (Reuters 2025).

In other areas, the echoes of Francis seem unmistakable. Leo has retained the language of synodality, affirming the unfinished work of the Synod on Synodality initiated under his predecessor. He upholds the global orientation of Vatican diplomacy, continuing engagements with the Islamic world, the African continent, and the peripheries of Latin America.

What, then, does this transition tell us? First, that the grand narrative of Francis' legacy is too embedded to be erased. His pontificate was not simply a papacy of gestures, it was one of institutional realignment, spiritual repositioning, and geopolitical reframing. The College of Cardinals that elected Leo XIV was itself a reflection of Francis' vision, just as global expectations for Vatican leadership continue to echo the tone and rhythm of his diplomatic legacy.

Second, the election of Leo XIV confirms the Church's capacity for both continuity and contrast. If Francis stirred the world with gestures rich in ambiguity and provocation, Leo may steady it with a voice tempered by clarity and anchored in a different type of statesmanship. These differences are not oppositional but complementary. Where Francis expanded the diplomatic imagination of the Church, Leo may now seek to consolidate its institutional coherence.

There is a theological rhythm to this as well. The Church does not move only by innovation but by reception, correction, and deepening. Just as Vatican II required decades of reception by subsequent popes, so too will the diplomatic grammar of Francis be tested, interpreted, and either absorbed or adjusted by Leo XIV. And in this resides the enduring question: How will the Church carry forward the diplomacy of a Latin American Jesuit, if the global order demands clarity, resolve, and institutional authority?

In many ways, Francis' legacy will be determined not only by what he did, but by how his successor carries his memory. Successors, history shows, may either sanctify the legacy they inherit or carefully delimit its reach. John Paul II redefined the legacy of John XXIII and Paul VI through his own charismatic rearticulation of conciliar ideals. Benedict XVI, in turn, interpreted Vatican II through the lens of 'reform in continuity.' Now Leo XIV, while unlikely to disown Francis, appears poised to render his legacy intelligible through perhaps a more structured register.

But it is too early to judge. Papacies unfold not only in words but in decades. Leo XIV inherits a Church that is globalised, decentralised, and in many ways more plural than ever before. Francis made it so, not through doctrinal rupture, but through symbolic leadership and diplomatic innovation. Whether that legacy flourishes or fades will depend on whether Leo XIV chooses to inhabit the space Francis opened or retreat into safer ecclesial ground.

Yet even in transition, the image of Francis will endure. A pope who knelt more than he ruled. A pastor who preferred the margins to the throne. A diplomat who embraced tension as the crucible of discernment. If Leo XIV becomes the pope of synthesis, then Francis will remain, like John XXII, a pope of the threshold, the one who opened the window and let the winds of the world rush in.

And so, the story continues. Between altars and alliances, between charism and institution, between memory and mission. The papacy endures not because it clings to power, but because it adapts, at times boldly, at times cautiously, to the changing tides of history. With Francis, the Church learned to speak a new diplomatic language. With Leo XIV, it now learns whether that language can become a durable grammar.

BIBLIOGRAPHY

Albert, Eleanor, and Lindsay Maizland. 2020. "The State of Religion in China." Council on Foreign Relations. 2020. https://www.cfr.org/backgrounder/religion-china.

Alfeyev, Hilarion. 2018. "Meeting in Havana: Outcomes and Prospects." *Horizons: Journal of International Relations and Sustainable Development* (10): 152–167.

Agasso, Domenico. 2022. "Mosca Elogia La Mediazione Di Francesco. 'Dialogo Aperto e Riservato Col Vaticano'." *La Stampa*. June 14, 2022. https://www.lastampa.it/vatican-insider/it/2022/06/14/news/mosca_elogia_la_mediazione_di_francesco_dialogo_aperto_e_riservato_col_vaticano_-5403406/.

Allen, Elise Ann. 2022. "In New Interview, Pope Defends Himself on China and Russia." *Crux*. November 28, 2022. https://cruxnow.com/vatican/2022/11/in-new-interview-pope-defends-himself-on-china-and-russia.

Allen, John L. 2006. "Who Is Joséph Ratzinger?" In *The Political Papacy: John Paul II, Benedict XVI, and Their Influence*, edited by Chester Gillis, 7–22. New York: Routledge.

———. 2015a. *The Francis Miracle: Inside the Transformation of the Pope and the Church*. New York: Time Books.

———. 2015b. "Pope Francis Anniversary Vatican Political Accomplishments." *Time*. March 5, 2015. https://time.com/3729869/francis-politics/.

———. 2019. "Fallout from the Latest Chapter in Pope Francis's Love/Hate Bond with the US." *Crux*. September 5, 2019. https://cruxnow.com/news-analysis/2019/09/05/fallout-from-the-latest-chapter-in-pope-franciss-love-hate-bond-with-the-us.

———. 2022. "Why Did Francis Really Pull the Plug on Summit with Russian Orthodox Leader?" *Crux*. April 24, 2022.

https://cruxnow.com/news-analysis/2022/04/why-did-francis-really-pull-the-plug-on-summit-with-russian-orthodox-leader.

Altieri, Christopher R. 2019. "Cardinal Burke cuts ties with Dignitatis Humanae Institute amid Steve Bannon rows." *Catholic Herald.* June 26, 2019. https://thecatholicherald.com/cardinal-burke-cuts-ties-with-dignitatis-humanae-institute-amid-steve-bannon-row/?utm_source=chatgpt.com

Amiri, Sohasia. 2015. "The Public Diplomacy of Pope Francis." USC Center on Public Diplomacy. September 25, 2015. https://uscpublicdiplomacy.org/blog/public-diplomacy-pope-francis.

Andrews-Lee, Caitlin. 2021. *The Emergence and Revival of Charismatic Movements: Argentine Perónism and Venezuelan Chavismo.* Cambridge: Cambridge University Press.

Annett, Anthony. 2015. "Papal Economics." *Commonweal* 142 (5): 10.

Augustine. 1950. *The City of God.* Translated by Dods, Marcus. New York: Modern Library.

Auza, Archbishop Bernardito. 2016. "An Overview from the Point of View of Pope Francis." *Journal of Corporate Citizenship* (64): 16–22. http://doi.org/10.9774/GLEAF.4700.2016.de.00004

Avvakumov, Yury P. 2016. "Ukrainian Greek Catholics, Past and Present." In *Churches in the Ukrainian Crisis,* edited by Andrii Krawchuk and Thomas Bremer, 21–44. Cham: Palgrave Macmillan. https://doi.org/10.1007/978-3-319-34144-6_2.

Babynskyi, Anatolii. 2020. "The Orthodox Church of Ukraine (OCU) and the Ukrainian Greek-Catholic Church (UGCC): A Meeting After the Tomos." *Canadian Slavonic Papers* 62 (3–4): 488–96. https://doi.org/10.1080/00085006.2020.1834710.

Baker-Smith, Dominic. 2010. "Erasmus and More: A Friendship Revisited." *Recusant History* 30 (1): 7–25. https://doi.org/10.1017/S0034193200012607.

Banchoff, Thomas, and José Casanova. 2016. "Introduction: The Jesuits and Globalization." In *The Jesuits and Globalization: Historical Legacies and Contemporary Challenges*, edited by Thomas Banchoff and José Casanova, 1–24. Washington, District of Columbia: Georgetown University Press.

Bangert, William V. 1986. *A History of the Society of Jesus*. United States: Institute of Jesuit Sources.

Barbato, Mariano. 2013a. "A State, a Diplomat, and a Transnational Church: The Multi-Layered Actorness of the Holy See." *Perspectives* 21 (2): 27–48.

———. 2013b. *Pilgrimage, Politics, and International Relations: Religious Semantics for World Politics*. 1st ed. New York: Palgrave Macmillan.

BBC. 2014. "Pope's Peace Doves Attacked by Crow and Seagull." *BBC News*. January 26, 2014. https://www.bbc.com/news/world-europe-25905108.

Beaumont, Peter. 2014. "Pope Francis Offers Prayers at Israeli Separation Wall in Bethlehem | Pope Francis." *The Guardian*. May 25, 2014. https://www.theguardian.com/world/2014/may/25/pope-francis-israeli-separation-wall-bethlehem.

Becker, Marc. 2017. *Twentieth-Century Latin American Revolutions*. New York: Rowman and Littlefield.

Bella, Timothy, and Sammy Westfall. 2022. "Don't Be 'Putin's Altar Boy,' Pope Francis Warns Russian Orthodox Church Leader Patriarch Kirill." *The Washington Post*. May 4, 2022. https://www.washingtonpost.com/world/2022/05/04/patriarch-kirill-pope-francis-russian-orthodox-church-ukraine/.

Bergoglio, Jorge. 2013. "Cardinal Jorge Mario Bergoglio's 'Letter on the Year of Faith'." *The Catholic World Report*. March 15, 2013. https://www.catholicworldreport.com/2013/03/15/cardinal-jorge-mario-bergoglios-letter-on-the-year-of-faith/.

Bergoglio, Jorge M., and Phillip Endean (trans.). 2013. "Writings on Jesuit Spirituality II." *Studies in the Spirituality of Jesuits* 45 (3): 1–38.

Bergoglio, Jorge M., and Abraham Skorka. 2014. *On Heaven and Earth*. United Kingdom: Bloomsbury.

Bin, Yu. 2018. "Absorbing Shock and Awe: Trump Style." *Comparative Connections* 20 (1): 121–43.

Bingemer, Maria, and Clara Lucchetti. 2016. *Latin American Theology: Roots and Branches*. Orbis Books.

Borelli, John. 2013. "In the Footsteps of John XXIII: Pope Francis and the Embodiment of Vatican II." *E-International Relations.* May 16, 2013. https://www.e-ir.info/2013/05/16/in-the-footsteps-of-john-xxiii-pope-francis-and-the-embodiment-of-vatican-ii/.

Borghese, Massimo. 2019. "The Polarity Model: The Influences of Gaston Fessard and Romano Guardini on Jorge Bergoglio." In *Discovering Pope Francis: The Roots of Jorge Mario Bergoglio's Thinking*, edited by Brian. Y. Lee and Thomas. L. Knoebel. Collegeville, MN: Liturgical Press.

Borghese, Massimo, and Barry Hudock. 2018a. *The Mind of Pope Francis: Jorge Mario Bergoglio's Intellectual Journey*. Collegeville, MN: Liturgical Press.

———. 2018b. "The Theory of Polar Opposition: Bergoglio and Romano Guardini." In *The Mind of Pope Francis: Jorge Mario Bergoglio's Intellectual Journey*, 99–139. Collegeville, MN: Liturgical Press.

Bourg, Julian. 2015. "The Enduring Tensions Between Catholicism and Modernity." *Integritas* 6 (1): 1–22.

Boyle. Joseph. 2019. "Rerum Novarum (1891)." In *Catholic Social Teaching*, edited by Gerard V. Bradley and E. Christian Brugger, 69-89. Cambridge: Cambridge University Press

Blitt, Robert C. 2022. "Russia's 2020 Constitutional Amendments and the Entrenchment of the Moscow Patriarchate as a Lever of Foreign Policy

Soft Power." In *The Geopolitics of Religious Soft Power: How States Use Religion in Foreign Policy*, edited by Peter Mandaville. New York: Oxford University Press. https://papers.ssrn.com/sol3/papers.cfm?abstract_id=3930235.

Brackley, Dean. 2004. *The Call to Discernment in Troubled Times: New Perspectives on the Transformative Wisdom of Ignatius of Loyola*. New York: Crossroad.

Brauer, Martin. 2017a. "Pope Francis and Ecumenism." *Ecumenical Review* 69 (1): 4–14.

Brennan, Sean. 2019. "Henry Cabot Lodge Jr. and the Catholic Church." *U.S. Catholic Historian* 37 (1): 97–122. https://doi.org/10.1353/cht.2019.0004.

Burns, James. 2018. "Fullness of Power? Popes, Bishops and the Polity of the Church 1215–1517." In *The Medieval World*, edited by Peter Linehan, Janet Nelson, and Marios Costambeys. Florence: Taylor & Francis Group

Cahill, Luke. 2020. "Special and Not Special: The Holy See, the 1991 Iraq War, and the United Nations Conferences of 1994 and 1995." *Diplomacy & Statecraft* 31 (3): 509–33. https://doi.org/10.1080/09592296.2020.1782676.

———. 2022. "Neutrality as an Aid to Holy See Diplomacy." In *The Vatican and Permanent Neutrality*, edited by Marshall. J. Breger and Herbert. R. Reginbogin. Lanham: Rowman & Littlefield.

Carbonneau, Robert. E. 2015. "Ecclesiastical Colony: China's Catholic Church and the French Protectorate." *The China Journal* 73: 269–71.

Casanova, José. 1997. "Globalizing Catholicism and the Return to a 'Universal' Church." In *Transnational Religion and Fading States*, edited by Susanne. H. Rudolph and James Piscatori, 1st ed., 121–43. New York: Routledge. https://doi.org/10.4324/9780429503467-6.

Casanova, José. 2016. "The Jesuits Through the Prism of Globalization, Globalization through a Jesuit Prism." In *The Jesuits and Globalization*, edited by Thomas Banchoff and José Casanova. Washington, District of Columbia: Georgetown University Press.

Catholic News Agency. 2010. "Holy See and Russia Establish Full Diplomatic Ties." *Catholic News Agency.* July 28, 2010. https://www.catholicnewsagency.com/news/20397/holy-see-and-russia-establish-full-diplomatic-ties.

———. 2018. "After China Deal, Two Underground Bishops Step down at Vatican's Request." *Catholic News Agency.* December 14, 2018. https://www.catholicnewsagency.com/news/40151/after-china-deal-two-underground-bishops-step-down-at-vaticans-request.

———. 2023. "Pope Francis Confirms Shanghai Bishop Appointed in Violation of Vatican-China Deal." *National Catholic Register*, July 15, 2023. https://www.ncregister.com/cna/pope-francis-confirms-shanghai-bishop-appointed-in-violation-of-vatican-china-deal.

Catholic World Report. 2022. "Vatican Says China Violated Terms of Agreement with Bishop Installation." *Catholic World Report*, November 26, 2022. https://www.catholicworldreport.com/2022/11/26/vatican-says-china-violated-terms-of-agreement-with-bishop-installation/.

Cervellera, Bernardo. 2019. "China-Vatican Matteo Ricci and the Cultural Revolution Absent in Ode to Friendship between China and Italy Sung by Xi Jinping." *Asia News.* March 20, 2019. https://www.asianews.it/news-en/Matteo-Ricci-and-the-Cultural-Revolution-absent-in-ode-to-friendship-between-China-and-Italy-sung-by-Xi-Jinping-46554.html.

Charbonnier, Jean. 2013. "The 'Underground' Church." In *The Catholic Church in Modern China: Perspectives*, edited by Edmond Tang and Jean-Paul Wiest, 52–70. Eugene, OR: Wipf and Stock Publishing.

Chebankova, Elena. 2017. "Russia's Idea of the Multipolar World Order: Origins and Main Dimensions." *Post-Soviet Affairs* 33 (3): 217–34. https://doi.org/10.1080/1060586X.2017.1293394.

Chia, Edmund Kee-Fook. 2020. "The Church and Other Religions." In *The Cambridge Companion to Vatican II*, edited by Richard R. Gaillardetz, 303–17. Cambridge: Cambridge University Press. https://doi.org/10.1017/9781108698610.017.

Childs, James M., and George W. Forell. 2012. "Pope John XXIII and Vatican II." In *Christian Social Teachings: A Reader in Christian Social Ethics from the Bible to the Present*, edited by James. M. Childs and George. W. Forell, 2nd ed., 224–32. Minneapolis: Augsburg Fortress Publishers. https://doi.org/10.2307/j.ctt22nm868.32.

Chitadze, Nika. 2021. "Modern System of International Relations and Role of the USA." *Journal in Humanities* 10 (1): 15–20.

Christiansen, Drew. 2006. "Catholic Peacemaking, 1991–2005: The Legacy of Pope John Paul II." *The Review of Faith & International Affairs* 4 (2): 21–28. https://doi.org/10.1080/15570274.2006.9523246.

Christiansen, Drew. 2017. "The Global Vision of Evangelii Gaudium: Cultural Diversity as a Road to Peace." In *Pope Francis and the Future of Catholicism: Evangelii Gaudium and the papal Agenda*, edited by Gerard. Mannion, 203–20. Cambridge: Cambridge University Press. https://doi.org/10.1017/9781316529621.012.

Chu, Cindy Yik-Yi. 2012. *The Catholic Church in China: 1978 to the Present*. New York: Palgrave Macmillan.

Chu, Lan T. 2013. "Vatican Diplomacy in China and Vietnam." In *Religion and Public Diplomacy*, edited by Philip Seib, 57–73. Cham: Palgrave Macmillan.

Chu, Yun-han, and Yongniang Zheng. 2020. "Introduction to the Decline of the Western-Centric World and the Emerging New Global Order." In *The Decline of the Western-Centric World and the Emerging New Global order: Contending Views*, edited by Yun-han Chu and Yongniang Zheng, 1–14. New York: Routledge.

Clark, Anthony E. 2021. "Roman Catholic Foreign Missionaries, Nineteenth-Century China." In *The Palgrave Handbook of the Catholic*

Church in East Asia, edited by Cindy Yik-yi Chu and Beatrice Leung, 1–33. Singapore: Palgrave Macmillan, 2021. https://doi.org/10.1007/978-981-15-9365-9_4-1.

Clarke, Jeremy. 2013. *The Virgin Mary and Catholic Identities in Chinese History*. Hong Kong: Hong Kong University Press.

Clarke, Kevin. 2016. "Pope and Patriarch Meet in Cuba." *America: The Jesuit Review* 214 (6): 10–11.

Clossey, Luke. 2008. *Salvation and Globalization in the Early Jesuit Missions*. Cambridge: Cambridge University Press.

Cloutier, David. 2015. "Pope Francis and American Economics." *Horizons* 42 (1): 122–28. https://doi.org/10.1017/hor.2015.47.

Cohen, Paul A. 1992. "The Contested Past: The Boxers as History and Myth." *The Journal of Asian Studies* 51 (1): 82–113. https://doi.org/10.2307/2058348.

Coleman, Heather. J. 2020. "Orthodoxy and Autocephaly in Ukraine: Editor's Introduction." *Canadian Slavonic Papers* 62 (3–4): 421–25. https://doi.org/10.1080/00085006.2020.1841415.

Collins, Charles. 2019a. "Vatican Issues Guidelines on Clergy Registration in Communist China." Crux. June 28, 2019. https://cruxnow.com/church-in-asia/2019/06/28/vatican-issues-guidelines-on-clergy-registration-in-communist-china.

———. 2019b. "Pope Endorsement of Journal's Controversial Articles Shines Light on His View of U.S." *Crux*. September 27, 2019. https://cruxnow.com/news-analysis/2019/09/pope-endorsement-of-journals-controversial-articles-shines-light-on-his-view-of-u-s.

Corkery, James, and Thomas Worcester. 2010. *The Papacy Since 1500: From Italian Prince to Universal Pastor*. Cambridge; New York: Cambridge University Press.

Corley, Felix. 1994. "Soviet Reaction to the Election of Pope John Paul II." *Religion, State and Society: The Keston Journal* 22 (1): 37–64 Criveller, Gianni. 2020. "An Overview of the Catholic Church in Post-Mao China." In *People, Communities, and the Catholic Church in China*, edited by Cindy Yik-yi Chu and Paul P. Mariani, 9–27. Singapore: Palgrave Pivot. https://doi.org/10.1007/978-981-15-1679-5_2.

Curanovic, Alicja. 2012a. "The Religious Diplomacy of the Russian Federation." *Russia/NIS Center*. www.ifri.org.
— — —. 2012b. *The Religious Factor in Russia's Foreign Policy*. London: Routledge.

D'Costa, Gavin. 2017. "Nostra Aetate." In *The Reception of Vatican II*, edited by Matthew Lamb and Matthew Levering. Oxford: Oxford University Press.

Demacopoulos, George E. 2013. *The Invention of Peter: Apostolic Discourse and Papal Authority in Late Antiquity*. Philadelphia: University of Pennsylvania Press. Wessel, Susan. 2008. *Leo the Great and the Spiritual Rebuilding of a Universal Rome*. Leiden: Brill. https://doi.org/10.1163/ej.9789004170520.i-422.

Deye, Joséph M., and Gail T. Fairhurst. 2019. "Dialectical Tensions in the Narrative Discourse of Donald J. Trump and Pope Francis." *Leadership* 15 (2): 152–78. https://doi.org/10.1177/1742715018806404.

Díaz, Bárbara, and Ramiro Podetti. 2017. "Catholicism and the Building of Latin American Culture: The Reflections of Alberto Methol Ferré." *Religion Compass* 11 (9–10): e12239. https://doi.org/10.1111/rec3.12239.

Di Giorgio, Valentina. 2025. "Zelensky Calls Leo XIV: Ukrainian President Invited Pope to Visit the Country." *ZENIT News*. May 12, 2025. https://zenit.org/2025/05/12/zelensky-calls-leo-xiv-ukrainian-president-invited-pope-to-visit-the-country/?utm

Dikotter, Frank. 2013. *The Tragedy of Liberation: A History of the Chinese Revolution 1945–1957*. London: Bloomsbury.

DuBois, Thomas David. 2010. "Religion and the Chinese State: Three Crises and a Solution." *Australian Journal of International Affairs* 64 (3): 344–58. https://doi.org/10.1080/10357711003736501.

Duffy, Eamon. 2011. *Ten Popes Who Shook the World*. New Haven: Yale University Press.

Duncan, Robert. 2019. "Cardinal Burke: Limiting Muslim Immigration Is Patriotic." *Catholic Herald*, May 20.

Dunn, Dennis. 1976. "The Kremlin and the Vatican: Ostpolitik." *Religion in Communist Lands* 4 (4): 16–19.

Dunn, Dennis. J. 1982a. "The Vatican's 'Ostpolitik'." *Journal of International Affairs* 36 (2): 247–55.

— — —. 1982b. "The Vatican's Ostpolitik: Past and Present." *Journal of International Affairs* 36 (2): 247–55.

— — —. 2004. *The Catholic Church and Russia: Popes, Patriarchs, Tsars and Commisars*. London: Routledge. https://doi.org/https://doi.org/10.4324/9781315240879.

Dunn, Dennis. 2016. *The Catholic Church and Soviet Russia, 1917-39*. London: Routledge.

Dwight, Emma. 2015. "Dissecting a Miracle: Pope Francis the Peacemaker." *Harvard International Review* 36 (3): 7–9.

Enenkel, Karl. 2013. "Introduction – Manifold Reader Responses: The Reception of Erasmus in the Early Modern Europe." In *The Reception of Erasmus in the Early Modern Period*, edited by Karl. Enenkel, 1–21. Leiden: Brill. https://doi.org/10.1163/9789004255630_002.

Engström, Maria. 2014. "Contemporary Russian Messianism and New Russian Foreign Policy." *Civilization, Security, and Its Discontents* 35 (3): 356–79.

Entenmann, Robert E. 1996. "Catholics and Society in Eighteenth Century Sishuan." In *Christianity in China: From the Eighteenth Century to the Present*, edited by Daniel. H, Bays, 180–93. Stanford: Stanford University Press.

Esherick, Joséph. 1987. *The Origins of the Boxer Uprising*. Berkeley: University of California Press.
Essig, Andrew M. and Jennifer L. Moore. 2009. "U.S.–Holy See Diplomacy: The Establishment of Formal Relations, 1984." *The Catholic Historical Review* 95 (4): 741–64. https://doi.org/10.1353/cat.0.0555.

Evennett, Henry O., and John Bossy. 1970. "The Spirit of the Counter-Reformation: The Birkbeck Lectures in Ecclesiastical History Given in the University of Cambridge in May 1951." Notre Dame: University of Notre Dame.

Fabre, Pierre Antoine. 2019. "The 'First Fathers' of the Society of Jesus." In *The Oxford Handbook of the Jesuits*, edited by Ines. G. Zupanov. New York: Oxford University Press.

Faggioli, Massimo. 2012. *Vatican II: The Battle for Meaning*. Mahwah, NJ: Paulist Press.

———. 2013. "Vatican II and the Church of the Margins: In Commemoration of Vatican Council II." *Theological Studies* 74 (4): 808–18.

———. 2014. *John XXIII: The Medicine of Mercy*. Collegeville: Liturgical Press.

———. 2015a. *A Council for the Global Church: Receiving Vatican II in History*. Minneapolis, Minnesota: Fortress Press.

———. 2015b. *Pope Francis: Tradition in Transition*. Mahwah, NJ: Paulist Press.

———. 2016. "Reading the Signs of the Times through a Hermeneutics of Recognition: 'Gaudium et Spes' and Its Meaning for a Learning Church." *Horizons* 43 (2): 332–50. https://doi.org/10.1017/hor.2016.109.

———. 2017a. *Catholicism and Citizenship: Political Cultures of the Church in the Twenty-First Century*. Collegeville: Liturgical Press.

———. 2017b. "Evangelii Gaudium as an Act of Reception of Vatican II." In *Pope Francis and the Future of Catholicism:, Pope Francis and the Future of Catholicism: Evangelii Gaudium and the papal Agenda*, edited by Gerard. Mannion, 38–54. Cambridge: Cambridge University Press. https://doi.org/10.1017/9781316529621.004.

———. 2018a. "Francis & the 'Religious Left'." *Commonweal Magazine*. July 30, 2018. https://www.commonwealmagazine.org/francis-religious-left.

———. 2018b. "Pope Francis and the Catholic Crisis: Why His Opponents in the U.S. Are Changing Their Narrative." *Foreign Affairs*, November.

———. 2019a. *The Church in a Change of Era: How the Franciscan Reforms Are Changing the Catholic Church*. La Croix International. https://international.la-croix.com/uploads/the-church-in-a-change-of-era/the-church-in-a-change-of-era.pdf.

———. 2019b. "The Geopolitics of Pope Francis and the USA." In *The Geopolitics of Pope Francis*, edited by Jan de Volder, 47–60. Leuven: Peeters.

———. 2020a. *The Liminal Papacy of Pope Francis*. New York: Orbis.

———. 2020b. "No Easy Solutions: A Response to Weigel's Critique of the Vatican-China Deal." *National Catholic Reporter*. September 17, 2020. https://www.ncronline.org/news/opinion/no-easy-solutions-response-weigels-critique-vatican-china-deal.

———. 2021. *Joe Biden and Catholicism in the United States*. New London: Bayard.

Farrelly, Paul J. 2019. "Rapprochement with the Vatican." In *Power (China Story Yearbook Series)*, edited by Jane Golley, Linda Jaivin, Paul J. Farrelly, and Sharon Strange, 123–27. Canberra: ANU Press. https://doi.org/10.22459/CSY.2019.04B.

Federico, Christopher M. 2021. "The Ideological and Religious Bases of Attitudes Toward Pope Francis in the United States." *Journal for the Scientific Study of Religion* 60 (4): 830–51. https://doi.org/10.1111/jssr.12741.

Feifer, Gregory. 2018. "What Vladimir Putin's Past Tells Us About Russia's Post-Election Future." *Foreign Affairs*. March 16, 2018. https://www.foreignaffairs.com/articles/russian-federation/2018-03-16/putins-past-explains-russias-future.

Ferrari, Lisa L. 2006. "The Vatican as a Transnational Actor." In *The Catholic Church and the Nation State: Comparative Perspectives*, edited by Paul Christopher Manuel, Lawrence. C. Reardon, and Clyde Wilcox, 33–50. Washington, DC: Georgetown University Press.

Ferrarotti, Franco. 1990. "Toward the End of Constantinian Christendom." *International Journal of Politics, Culture and Society* 3 (4): 433–61. https://doi.org/10.1007/BF01384971.

Flynn, George. 1972. "'Franklin Roosevelt and the Vatican: The Myron Taylor Appointment.'" *The Catholic Historical Review* 58 (2): 171–94.

Flynn, James. 1970. "The Role of the Jesuits in the Politics of Russian Education." *The Catholic Historical Review* 56 (2): 249–65.

Fogarty, Gerald. P. 2017. "Vatican II and the Cold War." In *Vatican II Behind the Iron Curtain*, edited by Piotr. H. Kosicki, 27–49. Washington: Catholic University of America Press.

Fontana, Luciano. 2022. "Intervista a Papa Francesco: «Putin Non-Si Ferma, Voglio Incontrarlo a Mosca. Ora Non-Vado a Kiev." *Corriere Della Sera*. May 3, 2022. https://www.corriere.it/cronache/22_maggio_03/intervista-papa-francesco-putin-694c35f0-ca57-11ec-829f-386f144a5eff.shtml.

Formicola, Jo R. 1996. "U.S.-Vatican Relations: Toward a Post-Cold War Convergence?" *Journal of Church and State* 38 (4): 799–815. https://doi.org/10.1093/jcs/38.4.799.

———. 2006. "The Political Papacy: John Paul II, Benedict XVI, and Their Influence." In *The Political Papacy: John Paul II, Benedict XVI, and Their Influence,* edited by Chester. Gillis, 1–6. New York: Routledge.

Foreign Relations of the United States, 1952-1954, Volume IV, The American Republics. Kane, Stephen N., Sanford, Jr. William F. (Eds). Washington: Government Printing Office. Document 125. 1983. https://history.state.gov/historicaldocuments/frus1952-54v04/d125

Franco, Massimo. 2004. "Papal Rebuke: The Vatican vs. Pre-Emptive War." *Survival* 46 (1): 38–39. https://doi.org/10.1080/00396330412331343643.

Franco, Massimo, and Roland Flamini (trans.). 2008. *Parallel Empires: The Vatican and the United States —Two Centuries of Alliance and Conflict.* 1st ed. New York: Doubleday.

Friedrich, Markus. 2019. "Jesuit Organization and Legislation: Development and Implementation of a Normative Framework." In *The Oxford Handbook of the Jesuits,* edited by Ines. G. Zupanov. New York: Oxford University Press.

Friedrich, Markus, and John Noel Dillon. 2022. *The Jesuits: A History.* Princeton: Princeton University Press.

Gaetan, Victor. 2019. "Pope Francis' Holy Diplomacy in Ukraine: Why Washington and the Vatican Don't See Eye to Eye." *Foreign Affairs,* September 2019. https://www.foreignaffairs.com/ukraine/pope-francis-holy-diplomacy-ukraine
———. 2021. *God's Diplomats: Pope Francis, Vatican Diplomacy, and America's Armageddon.* Lanham: Rowman and Littlefield.

Galli, Mark. 1996. "Fury Unleashed: The Boxer Rebellion Revealed the Courage of Missionaries – and the Resentment They Sparked." *Christian History* 15 (4).

Gessen, Masha. 2017. *The Future Is History: How Totalitarianism Reclaimed Russia.* New York: Riverhead Books.

Gagliarducci, Andrea. 2016. "What Archbishop Shevchuk Saw in the Meeting of the Pope and Patriarch Kirill." *Catholic News Agency*. February 24, 2016. https://www.catholicnewsagency.com/news/33470/what-archbishop-shevchuk-saw-in-the-meeting-of-the-pope-and-patriarch-kirill.

———. 2018. "Will Pope Francis Have an Impact on Orthodoxy's Ukraine Dispute?" *Catholic News Agency*. November 6, 2018. https://www.catholicnewsagency.com/news/39828/will-pope-francis-have-an-impact-on-orthodoxys-ukraine-dispute.

———. 2022. "What Message Is Pope Francis Sending with His Choice of New Cardinals?" *Catholic News Agency*. May 30, 2022. https://www.catholicnewsagency.com/news/251408/what-message-is-pope-francis-sending-with-his-choice-of-new-cardinals.

Gaillardetz, Richard. R. 2015. *An Unfinished Council: Vatican II, Pope Francis, and the Renewal of Catholicism*. Collegeville: Liturgical Press

——— (ed). 2020. *The Cambridge Companion to Vatican II*. Cambridge: Cambridge University Press

Gallaher, Brandon. 2019. "The Pure Signifier of Power: Remembering, Repeating and Working Through the Significance of the Papacy and Pope Francis for Eastern Orthodoxy." In *The Geopolitics of Pope Francis*, edited by Jan de Volder, 169–98. Leuven: Peeters.

Ganns, G.E. 1991. *Ignatius of Loyola: The Spiritual Exercises and Selected Works*. Edited by G.E. Ganns. New York: Paulist Press.

Gayte, Marie. 2011. "The Vatican and the Reagan Administration: A Cold War Alliance?" *The Catholic Historical Review* 97 (4): 713–36. https://doi.org/10.1353/cat.2011.0170.

———. 2012. "'I Told the White House If They Give One to the Pope, I May Ask for One': The American Reception to the Establishment of Diplomatic Relations between the United States and the Vatican in 1984." *Journal of Church and State* 54 (1): 33–56. https://doi.org/10.1093/jcs/csr008.

———. 2022. "A Climax in the Culture Wars? The US Bishops and the 2020 Election." In *Catholics and US Politics After the 2020 Elections: Biden Chases the 'Swing Vote'*, edited by Marie Gayte, Blandine Chelini-Pont, and Mark J. Rozell, 103–32. Cham: Palgrave Macmillan.

Gehring, John. 2019. "Pope Francis Will Have the Last Word: The Pontiff Is Responding to His U.S. Critics." *New York Daily News*. September 14, 2019. https://www.nydailynews.com/opinion/ny-oped-pope-francis-will-have-the-last-word-20190913-b35hse2qnnflrp5gsysmu2m7te-story.html.

Gibson, David. 2016. "While Francis Frustrates Foes with Silence, Fr. Antonio Spadaro Nails Them with Tweets." *National Catholic Reporter*. December 27, 2016. https://www.ncronline.org/news/people/while-francis-frustrates-foes-silence-fr-antonio-spadaro-nails-them-tweets.

———. 2018. "Five Years of Francis: The Keys to His Papacy." *America: The Jesuit Review*. February 21, 2018. https://www.americamagazine.org/faith/2018/02/21/five-years-francis-keys-his-papacy.

Gill, George J. 1987. "The Truman Administration and Vatican Relations." *The Catholic Historical Review* 73 (3): 408–23.

Giovagnoli, Agostino. 2019. "Pope Francis: A New Way of Looking at the World." *Journal of Modern Italian Studies* 24 (3): 456–67. https://doi.org/10.1080/1354571X.2019.1605728.

Gonçalves da Câmara, Luis, Alexander Eaglestone, and Joséph. A. Munitiz (trans.). 2004. *Remembering Iñigo: Glimpses of the Life of Saint Ignatius of Loyola, The Memoriale of Luís Gançalves Da Câmara*. Saint Louis: The Institute of Jesuit Sources

Goossaert, Vincent, and David A. Palmer. 2011. *The Religious Question in Modern China*. Chicago: University of Chicago Press.

Global Times. 2019. "Pope Francis Sees China as Great Country, Says Cardinal." *Global Times*. May 12, 2019. https://www.globaltimes.cn/page/201905/1149623.shtml.

Gray, Hanna H. 1963. "Renaissance Humanism: The Pursuit of Eloquence." *Journal of the History of Ideas* 24 (4): 497–514. https://doi.org/10.2307/2707980.

Graziano, Manlio. 2017. *Holy Wars and Holy Alliance: The Return of Religion to the Global Stage*. New York: Columbia University Press.

Gregg, Samuel. 2017. "Understanding Pope Francis: Argentina, Economic Failure, and the Teología Del Pueblo." *The Independent Review* 21 (3): 361–74.

Griva, O.A., and N.V. Yaksa. 2020. "The Fight of Ukraine for the Autocephal Church in the Context of Politicization of Religion." *Post-Soviet Issues* 7 (2): 250–58. https://doi.org/10.24975/2313-8920-2020-7-2-250-258.

Guardini, Romano. 2001. *The End of the Modern World*. 2nd ed. United States: ISI Books.

Hadro, Matt. 2021. "Congressional Report: Biden Administration Should Push Vatican to 'Revaluate' China Deal." *Catholic News Agency*. January 14, 2021. https://www.catholicnewsagency.com/news/246104/congressional-report-biden-administration-should-push-vatican-to-reevaluate-china-deal.

Hanvey, James. 2013. "Vatican II: For the Life of the World." In *The Second Vatican Council: Celebrating Its Achievements and the Future*, edited by Gavin D'Costa and Emma J. Harris. London; New York: Bloomsbury.

Harris, Elise. 2015. "Pope Francis Urges End to Scandal of 'Fratricidal' Violence in Ukraine." *Catholic News Agency*. February 4, 2015. https://www.catholicnewsagency.com/news/31444/pope-francis-urges-end-to-scandal-of-fratricidal-violence-in-ukraine.

— — —. 2017a. "What Common Ground Could Trump and Pope Francis Find?." *Catholic News Agency*. May 22, 2017. https://www.catholicnewsagency.com/news/36086/what-common-ground-could-trump-and-pope-francis-find.

———. 2017b. "China, Vatican Use 'Diplomacy of Art' to Foster Relations." *Catholic News Agency.* November 21, 2017. https://www.catholicnewsagency.com/news/37239/china-vatican-use-diplomacy-of-art-to-foster-relations.

———. 2018. "The Theological Formation of Pope Francis." *Catholic News Agency.* March 17, 2018. https://www.catholicnewsagency.com/news/37989/the-theological-formation-of-pope-francis.

———. 2019. "Love It or Hate It, Francis's China Deal Has a Deep Vatican Pedigree." *Crux.* April 6, 2019. https://cruxnow.com/vatican/2019/04/love-it-or-hate-it-franciss-china-deal-has-a-deep-vatican-pedigree.

Hastings, Martin. 1958. "United States-Vatican Relations." *Records of the American Catholic Historical Society of Philadelphia* 69 (1): 20–55.

Healy, Patrick. 2016. "Donald Trump Fires Back at Sharp Rebuke by Pope Francis." *New York Times*, February 18, 2016.

Heatherington, Kimberley. 2025. "As new pontificate begins, papal historians share first impressions of Francis' successor." *OSV News*, May 9, 2025. https://www.osvnews.com/as-new-pontificate-begins-papal-historians-share-first-impressions-of-francis-successor/

Hebblethwaite, Peter. 1983. "Liberation and John Paul II: The Vatican's Perception of Latin America." *Index on Censorship* 12 (5): 10–14.

———. 1984. *John XXIII: Pope of the Council*. London: Chapman.

———. 1985. *Pope John XXIII: Shepherd of the Modern World*. New York: Doubleday.

———. 1990. "The Vatican's Latin American Policy." In *Church and Politics in Latin America*, edited by Dermot Keogh, 49–64. London: Palgrave Macmillan UK. https://doi.org/10.1007/978-1-349-09661-9.

Hebblethwaite, Peter, and Margaret Hebblewaite. 2000. *John XXIII: Pope of the Century*. New York: Continuum.

Hehir, J. Bryan. 1990. "Papal Foreign Policy." *Foreign Policy*, 78: 26–48. https://doi.org/10.2307/1148627.

Helby, Hans. 1993. "The State, the Church, and the Oikumene: The Russian Orthodox Church and the World Council of Churches, 1948–1985." In *Religious Policy in the Soviet Union*, edited by Sabrina. P. Ramet. New York: Cambridge University Press.

Heller, Dagmar. 2017. "The (Holy and Great) Council of the Orthodox Churches: An Ecumenical Perspective." *The Ecumenical Review* 69 (2): 288–300. https://doi.org/10.1111/erev.12289.

Hill, Ian. 2021. "Russia's National Security Strategy: Same Book, New Cover." *The Interpreter*. Lowy Institute. July 19, 2021. https://www.lowyinstitute.org/the-interpreter/russia-s-national-security-strategy-same-book-new-cover.

Hobbes, Thomas, Nancy A. Stanlick (ed.), and Daniel. P Collete (eds). 2016. *The Essential Leviathan: A Modernized Edition*. Indianapolis: Hackett Publishing Company, Inc.

Hoffmann, Peter. 1989. "Roncalli in the Second World War: Peace Initiatives, the Greek Famine and the Persecution of the Jews." *The Journal of Ecclesiastical History* 40 (1): 74–99. https://doi.org/10.1017/S0022046900035430.

Höpfl, Harro. 2004. *Jesuit Political Thought: The Society of Jesus and the State, c.1540–1630*. Cambridge, UK; New York: Cambridge University Press.

Horowitz, Jason, and Lara Jakes. 2021. "Rebuffed by Vatican, Pompeo Assails China and Aligns with Pope's Critics." *New York Times*, November 21, 2021.

Hsia, R. Po-chia. 2018. "Christianity and Empire: The Catholic Mission in Late Imperial China." *Studies in Church History* 54: 288-308.

Hvat', Ivan. 1983. "The Ukrainian Catholic Church, the Vatican and the Soviet Union During the Pontificate of Pope John Paul II." *Religion in Communist Lands* 11 (3): 264–94.

———. 1985. "The Moscow Patriarchate and the Liquidation of the Eastern-Rite Catholic Church in Ukraine." *Religion in Communist Lands* 13 (2): 182–88. https://doi.org/10.1080/09637498508431189.

Ibrahim, Azeem. 2021. "Why the Chinese Communist Party Fears Religion." *Foreign Policy*. July 1, 2021. https://foreignpolicy.com/2021/07/01/chinese-communist-party-scared-of-christianity-religion/.

Ignatius, David. 2015. "The Paradox of Pope Francis's Power." *The Washington Post*. September 25, 2015. https://www.washingtonpost.com/opinions/the-paradox-of-the-popes-power/2015/09/24/9533401a-62ca-11e5-b38e-06883aacba64_story.html?utm_term=.40b9821ba57a.

Ikenberry, John G. 2017. "The Plot Against American Foreign Policy: Can the Liberal Order Survive?" *Foreign Affairs* 96: 2–9.

Ivereigh, Austen. 1995. *Catholicism and Politics in Argentina, 1810–1960*. London: Palgrave Macmillan UK. https://doi.org/10.1007/978-1-349-13618-6.

———. 2014. *The Great Reformer: Francis and the Making of a Radical Pope*. 1st ed. New York: Henry Holt and Company.

———. 2019. *Wounded Shepherd: Pope Francis and His Struggle to Convert the Catholic Church*. New York: Henry Holt.

Jaffe, Alexander. 2021. "Presidents and Popes Over the Years: Gifts, Gaffes, Grief." *Crux*. October 28, 2021. https://cruxnow.com/church-in-the-usa/2021/10/presidents-and-popes-over-the-years-gifts-gaffes-grief.

Jensen, Jack. 2020. "Joe Biden's Catholic Politics Are Complicated – But Deeply American." *America: The Jesuit Review*, August.

Jesuit Conference of Canada and the United States. 2020. "Contemplation and Political Action: An Ignatian Guide to Civic Engagement." *Jesuit Conference of Canada and the United States*. Jesuit Conference of Canada and the United States. https://www.jesuits.org/wp-content/uploads/2020/08/CivicEngagement-v10.pdf.

Karush, Matthew B. 2010. "Populism, Melodrama, and the Market." In *The New Cultural History of Perónism: Power and Identity in Mid-Twentieth Century Argentina*, edited by Matthew B. Karush, Oscar Chamosa, and Natalia Milanesio, 21–51. North Carolina: Duke University Press. https://doi.org/10.1215/9780822392866-002.

Keeley, Theresa. 2020. *Reagan's Gun-Toting Nuns: The Catholic Conflict Over Cold War Human Rights Policy in Central America*. Ithaca: Cornell University Press.

Kengor, Paul. 2017. *A Pope and a President: John Paul II, Ronald Reagan, and the Extraordinary Untold Story of the 20th Century*. Wilmington, Delaware: ISI Books.

Kent, Peter C. 1981. *The Pope and the Duce: The International Impact of the Lateran Agreements*. London: Macmillan.

Kinzelbach, Katrin. 2014. *The EU's Human Rights Dialogue with China*. London: Routledge.

Kirby, Dianne. 2018. "The Roots of the Religious Cold War: Pre-Cold War Factors." *Social Sciences* 7 (4): 56.

Koesel, Karrie. J. 2014. *Religion and Authoritarianism: Cooperation, Conflict, and the New Consequences*. New York: Cambridge University Press.

Komonchak, Joséph. A. 2011. "Popes Pius Xi and Pius Xii and the Idea of an Ecumenical Council." https://jakomonchak.files.wordpress.com/2012/01/pius-xi-pius-xii-on-a-council.pdf.

Kramer, John. M. 1980. "The Vatican's 'Ostpolitik.'" *The Review of Politics* 42 (3): 283–308.

Krames, Jeffrey. A. 2015. *Lead with Humility: 12 Leadership Lessons from Pope Francis*. New York: AMACON Books.

Kuivala, Petra. 2017. "Policy of Empowerment: Pope Francis in Cuba." *International Journal of Cuban Studies*, 9(1), 19–36. https://doi.org/10.13169/intejcubastud.9.1.0019

La Rocca, Francesco. 2012. "At the Crossroads: The History of the Greek-Catholic Church in Lithuania." *Occasional Papers on Religion in Eastern Europe* 31 (1).

Laurelle, Marlene. 2018. "Russian Soft Power in France: Assessing Moscow's Cultural and Business Para-Diplomacy." Carnegie Council for Ethics in International Affairs. https://www.carnegiecouncil.org/media/series/russian-soft-power-in-france/russian-soft-power-in-france-assessing-moscows-cultural-and-business-para-diplomacy.

———. 2015. *The 'Russian World': Russia's Soft Power and Geopolitical Imagination*. Centre on Global Interests. http://globalinterests.org/wp-content/uploads/2015/05/FINAL-CGI_Russian-World_Marlene-Laruelle.pdf.

Laven, Mary. 2011. *Mission to China: Matteo Ricci and the Jesuit Encounter with the East*. London: Faber and Faber.

Lavenburg, John. 2025. "A Vision for a Globalized College of Cardinals." *The Tablet*. April 21, 2025. https://thetablet.org/pope-francis-globalized-college-of-cardinals/?utm_source=chatgpt.com

Leung, Beatrice. 1992. *Sino-Vatican Relations: Problems in Conflicting Authority 1976–1986*. Cambridge: Cambridge University Press.

———. 2003. "The Sino-Vatican Negotiations: Old Problems in a New Context." *The China Quarterly*, no. 174: 386–403. https://doi.org/10.1017/S0009443903000246.

———. 2005a. "Sino–Vatican Relations at the Century's Turn." *Journal of Contemporary China* 14 (43): 353–70. https://doi.org/10.1080/10670560500065553.

———. 2005b. "China's Religious Freedom Policy: The Art of Managing Religious Activity." *The China Quarterly* 184 (December): 894–913. https://doi.org/10.1017/S030574100500055X.

———. 2020. "Joséph Cardinal Zen Ze-Kiun of Hong Kong." In *People, Communities, and the Catholic Church in China*, 61–77. Singapore: Springer Singapore. https://doi.org/10.1007/978-981-15-1679-5_5.

Leung, Beatrice, and Marcus Wang. 2016. "Sino–Vatican Negotiations: Problems in Sovereign Right and National Security." *Journal of Contemporary China* 25 (99): 467–82. https://doi.org/10.1080/10670564.2015.1104921.

Leung, Beatrice, and Tony Yun-chung Li. 2018. "Taiwan-Vatican Relations From 1949 to the Present." In *The Catholic Church in Taiwan: Birth, Growth, and Development*, edited by Francis. K.H. So, Beatrice K.F. Leung, and Ellen Mary Mylod, 103–28. Singapore: Palgrave Macmillan.

Lewis, Pericles. 2011. "Modernism and Religion." In *The Cambridge Companion to Modernism*, edited by Michael Levenson, 2nd ed., 178–96. Cambridge: Cambridge University Press.

Løland, Ole Jakob. 2021. "The Solved Conflict: Pope Francis and Liberation Theology." *International Journal of Latin American Religions* 5 (2): 287–314. https://doi.org/10.1007/s41603-021-00137-3.

Lonergan, Bernard. 2016. "The Transition from a Classicist Worldview to Historical Mindedness." In *A Second Collection*, edited by R. Doran and J. Dadosky, 13: 1–10. Toronto: University of Toronto Press. https://doi.org/10.3138/9781487511579-002.

Loriaux, Michael. 1992. "The Realists and Saint Augustine: Skepticism, Psychology, and Moral Action in International Relations Thought." *International Studies Quarterly* 36 (4): 401-420. https://doi.org/10.2307/2600732

Luciani, Rafael. 2017. *Pope Francis and the Theology of the People*. Maryknoll: Orbis Books.

———. 2020. "Francis and the Pastoral Geopolitics of Peoples and Their Cultures: A Structural Option for the Poor." *Theological Studies* 81 (1): 181–202. https://doi.org/10.1177/0040563920906135.

Luxmoore, Jonathon. 2016. "Pope's Russian Outreach Stirs Anxieties." *National Catholic Reporter*. March 8, 2016. https://www.ncronline.org/news/vatican/popes-russian-outreach-stirs-anxieties.

———. 2018a. "Russia's Catholics Weigh the Benefits of Vatican-Orthodox Exchanges." *National Catholic Reporter*. May 14, 2018. https://www.ncronline.org/news/vatican/russias-catholics-weigh-benefits-vatican-orthodox-exchanges.

———. 2018b. "Eastern Europe's Catholics Steer through Inter-Orthodox Feud." *National Catholic Reporter*. October 16, 2018. https://www.ncronline.org/news/world/eastern-europes-catholics-steer-through-inter-orthodox-feud.

———. 2023. "Moscow Visit Had Humanitarian, Not Political, Aims, Says Cardinal." *Church Times*. July 7, 2023. https://www.churchtimes.co.uk/articles/2023/7-july/news/world/moscow-visit-had-humanitarian-not-political-aims-says-cardinal

Lynch, Andrew P. 2014. "Beijing and the Vatican." *SAGE Open* 4 (4): 1–10. https://doi.org/10.1177/2158244014554196.

Lyon, Alynna J., Christin A. Gustafson, and Paul Christopher Manuel. 2018. "Eluding Established Categories: Toward an Understanding of Pope Francis." In *Pope Francis as a Global Actor Where Politics and Theology Meet*, edited by Alynna J. Lyon, Christine A. Gustafson, and Paul Christopher Manuel, 3–22. Cham: Springer International Publishing. https://doi.org/10.1007/978-3-319-71377-9_1.

Madsen, Richard. 1998. *China's Catholics: Tragedy and Hope in an Emerging Civil Society*. Berkeley: University of California Press.

Magister, Sandro. 2016. "The Four Hooks on Which Bergoglio Hangs His Thought." May 19, 2016. http://chiesa.espresso.repubblica.it/articolo/1351301bdc4.html?eng=y.

Mansini, Guy. 2017. "Lumen Gentium." In *The Reception of Vatican II*, edited by Matthew Lamb and Matthew Levering. Oxford: Oxford University Press.

Mariani, Paul P. 2014. "The First Six Chinese Bishops of Modern Times: A Study in Church Indigenization." *The Catholic Historical Review* 100 (3): 486–513. https://doi.org/10.1353/cat.2014.0143.

Martens, Kurt. 2006. "The Position of the Holy See and Vatican City State in International Relations." *University of Detroit Mercy Law Review* 83 (5): 729.

Massaro, Thomas. 2018. "The First Jesuit Pope: The Contribution of His Jesuit Charism to His Political Views." In *Pope Francis as a Global Actor Where Politics and Theology Meet*, edited by Alynna J. Lyon, Christine A. Gustafson, and Paul Christopher Manuel, 41–57. Cham: Springer International Publishing. https://doi.org/10.1007/978-3-319-71377-9_3.

Maza, Cristina. 2018. "Who Is Oscar Romero? Vatican to Canonize Murdered Salvadorian Bishop Associated with Communism." *Newsweek*, July 3, 2018. https://www.newsweek.com/who-oscar-romero-vatican-canonize-murdered-salvadoran-bishop-associated-835521.

McElwee, Joshua J. 2021. "Francis: 'No Concession' to Those Who Deny Vatican II Teachings." *National Catholic Reporter*. February 1, 2021. https://www.ncronline.org/news/quick-reads/francis-no-concession-those-who-deny-vatican-ii-teachings.

McCormick, Bill. 2019. "*Steve Bannon's dubious crusade.*" America: The Jesuit Review. September 4, 2019. https://www.americamagazine.org/faith/2019/09/04/steve-bannons-dubious-crusade?utm_source=chatgpt.com

McLarren, Katharina, and Bernhard Stahl. 2020. "The Holy See as Hybrid Actor: Religion in International, Transnational, and World Society." In *The Pope, the Public, and International Relations*, edited by Mariano Barbato, 189–201. Cham: Springer International Publishing. https://doi.org/10.1007/978-3-030-46107-2_11.

Meichtry, Stacy, Stancati, Margherita, Tucker-Smith, Owen, and Lovett, Ian. 2025. "American Is Elected Pope for First Time." *Wall Street Journal*. May 8, 2025. https://www.wsj.com/world/new-pope-elected-white-smoke-vatican-f9a52ef5?utm

Menkhaus, James. 2009. "Ignatian Spirituality and the Just Peacemaking Theory." *Peace Review* 21 (4): 448–56. https://doi.org/10.1080/10402650903323439.

Mettepenningen, Jurgen. 2010. *Nouvelle Theologie – New Theology: Inheritor of Modernism, Precursor of Vatican II*. London: T & T Clark.

Miller, Zeke, and Aamer Madhani. 2021. "Biden Says Pope Has Brought Him Comfort After Son's Death." *AP News*. November 1, 2021. https://apnews.com/article/pope-francis-joe-biden-g-20-summit-christianity-barack-obama-b2bede6af864017433c1b1e14db371a1.

Mladenov, Nicolai S. 2021. "New System of International Relations? Which Way Forward into the Rest of the Twenty-First Century?" In *China's Rise to Power in the Global Order: Grand Strategic Implications*, 259–355. Cham: Palgrave Macmillan

Modras, Ronald. 2004. *Ignatian Humanism*. Chicago: Loyola Press.

Mok, Chit Wai John. 2021. "Sino-Vatican Rapprochement: An Assessment of Pope Francis' Realpolitik and the Provisional Agreement on the Appointment of Bishops." *Journal of Contemporary China* 30 (129): 386–401. https://doi.org/10.1080/10670564.2020.1827352.

Molina, J. Michelle. 2013. *To Overcome Oneself: The Jesuit Ethic and Spirit of Global Expansion, 1520–1767*. Berkeley, California: University of California Press.

Moody, Peter. 2020. "The Vatican and Taiwan: An Anomalous Diplomatic Relationship." *Journal of Contemporary China* 29 (124): 553–67. https://doi.org/10.1080/10670564.2019.1677364.

Morello, Gustavo. 2015. *The Catholic Church and Argentina's Dirty War*. New York: Oxford University Press.

Moyn, Samuel. 2018. *Not Enough: Human Rights in an Unequal World*. Cambridge, MA: The Belknap Press of Harvard University Press.

Murphy, Francis X. 1974. "Vatican Politics: Structure and Function." *World Politics* 26 (4): 542–59. https://doi.org/10.2307/2010100.

Nauert, Charles G. 2006a. *Humanism and the Culture of Renaissance Europe*. 2nd ed. New York: Cambridge University Press.

New York Times. 2007. "Vatican Calls Pope's Meeting with Vietnam's Prime Minister 'Important Step'." New York Times. January 25, 2007.

Neumayr, George. 2017. *The Political Pope: How Francis Is Delighting the Liberal Left and Abandoning Conservatives*. New York: Hachette.

Nicholas, Peter. 2021. "Biden's Catholic Identity Politics." *The Atlantic*. October 29, 2021. https://www.theatlantic.com/politics/archive/2021/10/biden-pope-meeting/620513/.

Nicholson, Jim. 2004. *The United States and the Holy See: The Long Road*. Rome: Trenta Giorni Società Cooperativa.

Niebuhr, Reinhold. 1953. *Christian Realism and Political Problems*. New York: Charles Scribner's Sons.

Nisley, Thomas J. 2018. "You Can't Force a Friendship? An Analysis of US/Argentine Relations." *International Politics* 55 (5): 612–30. https://doi.org/10.1057/s41311-017-0092-2.

Norwich, John Julius. 2012. *The Popes*. London: Vintage Books.

Nullens, Patrick. 2019. "From Spirituality to Responsible Leadership: Ignatian Discernment and Theory-U." In *Leading in a VUCA World: Integrating Leadership, Discernment and Spirituality*, edited by Jacobus Kok and Steven C. van den Heuvel, 185–207. Cham: Springer International Publishing. https://doi.org/10.1007/978-3-319-98884-9.

Oakes, Kaya. 2018. "The Conservative Resistance Inside the Vatican." *The New Republic.* October 8, 2018. https://newrepublic.com/article/151589/conservative-resistance-inside-vatican.

O'Collins, Gerald. 2015. *The Second Vatican Council on Other Religions*. Oxford: Oxford University Press.

O'Connell, Gerard. 2015. "Francis Looks East. (Pope Francis I and the Bishops in China and Russia)." *America: The Jesuit Review* 213 (16): 26.

———. 2016. "Pope Francis: 'Globalization of Indifference' Contributes to Killing." *America: The Jesuit Review* 214 (10): 9.

———. 2017. "How the Vatican Is Encouraging Dialogue Between Russia and the West." *America: The Jesuit Review*, September.

———. 2019. "Pope Francis Wants the World to Know About His Jesuit Spiritual Director." *America: The Jesuit Review*, December.

———. 2021. "Pope Francis Sends Greeting to President Biden, Contrasting with Sharper Message from Head of U.S. Bishops." *America: The Jesuit Review*, January. https://www.americamagazine.org/faith/2021/01/20/pope-francis-message-joe-biden-prayer-239772.

———. 2023. "Analysis: Why Pope Francis recognized a bishop appointed in violation of Vatican-China deal." *America: The Jesuit Review*, July. https://www.americamagazine.org/faith/2023/07/17/vatican-china-bishop-shanghai-245694

Oftestad, Bernt T. 2018. *The Catholic Church and Liberal Democracy*. London: Routledge. https://doi.org/10.4324/9781315229102.

O'Malley, John W. 1971. "Reform, Historical Consciousness, and Vatican II's Aggiornamento." *Theological Studies* 32 (4): 573–601. https://doi.org/10.1177/004056397103200401.

———. 1974. "Erasmus and Luther, Continuity and Discontinuity as Key to Their Conflict." *The Sixteenth Century Journal* 5 (2): 47–65.

———. 1984. "To Travel to Any Part of the World: Jerónimo Nadal and the Jesuit Vocation." *Studies in the Spirituality of Jesuits* 16 (2). https://doi.org/10.1163/9789004257375_010.

———. 1990. "Renaissance Humanism and the Religious Culture of the First Jesuits." *The Heythrop Journal* 31 (4): 471–87. https://doi.org/10.1111/j.1468-2265.1990.tb00148.x.

———. 1993. *The First Jesuits*. Cambridge, Mass.: Harvard University Press.

———. 2000. "How Humanistic Is the Jesuit Tradition?: From the 1599 Ratio Studorium to Now." In *Jesuit Education: Conference Proceedings on the Future of Jesuit Education*, 189–201. Philadelphia: St. Joseph's University Press. https://www.bc.edu/content/dam/files/offices/mission/pdf1/ju7.pdf.

———. 2006a. "Vatican II: Did Anything Happen?" *Theological Studies* 67 (1): 3–33. https://doi.org/10.1177/004056390606700101.

———. 2006b. "Ignatius Special Way of Proceeding." *America: The Jesuit Review* 195 (3).

———. 2010. *What Happened at Vatican II*. Cambridge: Harvard University Press.

———. 2013. *Saints or Devils Incarnate? Studies in Jesuit History*. Lieden: Brill.

———. 2014. *The Jesuits: A History from Ignatius to the Present*. Lanham: Rowman and Littlefield.

———. 2016a. "Historical Perspectives on Jesuit Education and Globalization." In *The Jesuits and Globalization: Historical Legacies and Contemporary Challenges*, edited by Thomas Banchoff and José Casanova, 147–66. Washington: Georgetown University Press.

———. 2016b. "The Distinctiveness of the Society of Jesus." *Journal of Jesuit Studies* 3 (1): 1–16. https://doi.org/10.1163/22141332-00301001.

O'Sullivan, Michael. 1990. "Trust Your Feelings but Use Your Head: Discernment and the Psychology of Decision Making." *Studies in the Spirituality of Jesuits* 22 (4): 1-5.

Padberg, John. 2014. "A Genius for Friendship: The Gentle, Grace-Filled Life of Peter Faber." *America: The Jesuit Review* 210 (10): 24–27.

———. 1996. *The Constitutions of the Society of Jesus and Their Complementary Norms: A Complete English Translation of the Official Latin Texts*. St Louis, MO: The Institute of Jesuit Sources. https://jesuitas.lat/uploads/the-constitutions-of-the-society-of-jesus-and-their-complementary-norms/Constitutions%20and%20Norms%20SJ%20ingls.pdf.

———. 2006. "A Saint Too Little Known." *America: The Jesuit Review* 195 (2): 16–19.

Pakhnyuk, Lucy. 2025. "In 2022 Interview, Pope Condemns Russia's 'Imperialist' Invasion of Ukraine." *The Kyiv Independent*, May 10, 2025. https://kyivindependent.com/pope-condemns-russias-imperialist-invasion-of-ukraine-in-2022-interview/#:~:text=Russia's%20abuse%20of%20its%20own,10%3A25%20AM

Paris, Francesca. 2019. "Ukrainian Orthodox Church Officially Gains Independence from Russian Church: NPR." *NPR*. January 5, 2019. https://www.npr.org/2019/01/05/682504351/ukrainian-orthodox-church-officially-gains-independence-from-russian-church.

Pavone, Sabina. 2016. "The History of Anti-Jesuitism: National and Global Dimensions." In *The Jesuits and Globalization*, edited by Thomas Banchoff and José Casanova, 111–30. Washington, DC: Georgetown University Press.

Petro, Nicolai N. 2018. "The Russian Orthodox Church." In *Handbook of Russian Foreign Policy*, edited by Andrei P. Tsygankov, 217–32. London: Routledge.

Perón, Juan D. 1952. *Perónist Doctrine*. Buenos Aires.

Pew Research Centre. 2017. "Religious Belief and National Belonging in Central and Eastern Europe." Pew Research Centre. May 10, 2017. https://www.pewresearch.org/religion/2017/05/10/religious-belief-and-national-belonging-in-central-and-eastern-europe/.

Pique, Elisabetta. 2014. *Pope Francis: Life and Revolution: A Biography of Jorge Bergoglio*. Chicago: Loyola Press.

Poggioli, Sylvia. 2016. "How Pope Francis Became a Foreign Policy Player: Parallels." *NPR*. April 14, 2016. https://www.npr.org/sections/parallels/2016/04/14/474130428/how-pope-francis-became-a-foreign-policy-player.

Pope Francis. 2013a. "Lumen Fidei (29 June 2013)." Encyclical Letter Lumen Fidei of the Supreme Pontiff Francis to the Bishops Priests and Deacons Consecrated Persons and The Lay Faithful On Faith. June 29, 2013. https://www.vatican.va/content/francesco/en/encyclicals/documents/papa-francesco_20130629_enciclica-lumen-fidei.html.

— — —. 2013b. "Letter to H.E. Mr Vladimir Putin, President of the Russian Federation, on the Occasion of the G20 St. Petersburg Summit (4 September 2013)." September 4, 2013. https://www.vatican.va/content/francesco/en/letters/2013/documents/papa-francesco_20130904_putin-g20.html.

— — —. 2013c. "7 September 2013: Vigil of Prayer for Peace." September 7, 2013.

https://www.vatican.va/content/francesco/en/homilies/2013/documents/papa-francesco_20130907_veglia-pace.html.

———. 2013d. "To Participants in the Plenary of the Pontifical Council for Promoting New Evangelization (14 October 2013) | Francis." October 14, 2013 https://www.vatican.va/content/francesco/en/speeches/2013/october/documents/papa-francesco_20131014_plenaria-consiglio-nuova-evangelizzazione.html.

———. 2013e. "Evangelii Gaudium: Apostolic Exhortation on the Proclamation of the Gospel in Today's World (24 November 2013)." November 24, 2013. https://www.vatican.va/content/francesco/en/apost_exhortations/documents/papa-francesco_esortazione-ap_20131124_evangelii-gaudium.html.

———. 2013f. "Evangelii Gaudium: Apostolic Exhortation on the Proclamation of the Gospel in Today's World (24 November 2013)." November 24, 2013. https://www.vatican.va/content/francesco/en/apost_exhortations/documents/papa-francesco_esortazione-ap_20131124_evangelii-gaudium.html#No_to_a_sterile_pessimism.

———. 2015a. "Apostolic Journey - Cuba: Welcoming Ceremony at 'José Martí' International Airport (Havana, 19 September 2015) | Francis." 2015. https://www.vatican.va/content/francesco/en/speeches/2015/september/documents/papa-francesco_20150919_cuba-benvenuto.html.

———. 2015b. "Laudato Si' (24 May 2015)." May 24, 2015. https://www.vatican.va/content/francesco/en/encyclicals/documents/papa-francesco_20150524_enciclica-laudato-si.html.

———. 2015c. "Meeting with representatives of the civil society at León Condou stadium of San José School (Asunción, 11 July 2015)." *The Holy See*, Libreria Editrice Vaticana, 11 July 2015, https://www.vatican.va/content/francesco/en/speeches/2015/july/documents/papa-francesco_20150711_paraguay-societa-civile.html.

———. 2016a. "Amoris Laetitia of the Holy Father Francis to Bishops, Priests and Deacons Consecrated Persons Christian Married Couples and All the Lay Faithful on Love in the Family," March.

———. 2016b. "Address of the Holy Father during the 36th General Congregation of the Society of Jesus (24 October 2016)." October 24, 2016. https://www.vatican.va/content/francesco/en/speeches/2016/october/documents/papa-francesco_20161024_visita-compagnia-gesu.html.

———. 2017. "Message of the Holy Father to the President of the United Nations Conference to Negotiate a Legally Binding Instrument to Prohibit Nuclear Weapons, Leading Towards Their Total Elimination [New York, 27–31 March 2017] (23 March 2017)." March 2017. https://www.vatican.va/content/francesco/en/messages/pont-messages/2017/documents/papa-francesco_20170323_messaggio-onu.html.

———. 2018. "Message of the Holy Father to the Catholics of China and to the Universal Church (26 September 2018)." September 26, 2018. https://www.vatican.va/content/francesco/en/messages/pont-messages/2018/documents/papa-francesco_20180926_messaggio-cattolici-cinesi.html.

———. 2019. "To the Diplomatic Corps Accredited to the Holy See for the Traditional Exchange of New Year Greetings (7 January 2019)." January 7, 2019. https://www.vatican.va/content/francesco/en/speeches/2019/january/documents/papa-francesco_20190107_corpo-diplomatico.html.

———. 2020. "Fratelli Tutti (3 October 2020)." October 3, 2020. https://www.vatican.va/content/francesco/en/encyclicals/documents/papa-francesco_20201003_enciclica-fratelli-tutti.html.

———. 2022. "Sixth World Day of the Poor, 2022: For Your Sakes Christ Became Poor (Cf. 2 Cor 8:9) | Francis." November 13, 2022. https://www.vatican.va/content/francesco/en/messages/poveri/documents/20220613-messaggio-vi-giornatamondiale-poveri-2022.html.

———. 2023. "Legge fondamentale dello Stato della Città del Vaticano, 13.05.2023.
https://press.vatican.va/content/salastampa/it/bollettino/pubblico/2023/05/13/0365/00791.html

Pope Gregory XVI. 1832. "Encyclical Mirari Vos (August 15, 1832)." August 15, 1832. https://www.vatican.va/content/gregorius-xvi/it/documents/encyclica-mirari-vos-15-augusti-1832.html.

Pope John Paul II. 1982. "Message to the Second Special Session of the United Nations for Disarmament (June 7, 1982)." June 7, 1982. https://www.vatican.va/content/john-paul-ii/en/messages/pont_messages/1982/documents/hf_jp-ii_mes_19820607_disarmo-onu.html.

———. 1987. "Sollicitudo Rei Socialis (30 December 1987)." December 30, 1987. https://www.vatican.va/content/john-paul-ii/en/encyclicals/documents/hf_jp-ii_enc_30121987_sollicitudo-rei-socialis.html.

———. 1991. "Centesimus Annus (1 May 1991)." May 1, 1991. https://www.vatican.va/content/john-paul-ii/en/encyclicals/documents/hf_jp-ii_enc_01051991_centesimus-annus.html.

———. 1996. "Message on the 70th Anniversary of the Ordination in Rome of the First Group of Chinese Bishops and on the 50th Anniversary of the Establishment of the Ecclesiastical Hierarchy in China (December 3, 1996)." December 3, 1996. https://www.vatican.va/content/john-paul-ii/it/messages/pont_messages/1996/documents/hf_jp-ii_mes_19961203_china-church.html.

———. 2001. "Message to the International Conference Commemorating the Fourth Centenary of the Arrival in Beijing of Father Matteo Ricci (October 24, 2001)." October 24, 2001. https://www.vatican.va/content/john-paul-ii/en/speeches/2001/october/documents/hf_jp-ii_spe_20011024_matteo-ricci.html.

Pope John XXIII. 1962. "Address at the Feast of the SS. At the Inauguration of the Council, d. 11 m. October a. 1962, Pope John XXIII John XXIII." October 11, 1962. https://www.vatican.va/content/john-xxiii/la/speeches/1962/documents/hf_j-xxiii_spe_19621011_opening-council.html.

———. 1963. "Pacem in Terris (April 11, 1963)." https://www.vatican.va/content/john-xxiii/en/encyclicals/documents/hf_j-xxiii_enc_11041963_pacem.html.

Pope Leo XIII. 1891. "Rerum Novarum (May 15, 1891)." May 15, 1891. https://www.vatican.va/content/leo-xiii/en/encyclicals/documents/hf_l-xiii_enc_15051891_rerum-novarum.html.

Pope Paul VI. 1964. *Ecclesiam Suam* (Encyclical Letter), August 6, 1964, https://www.vatican.va/content/paul-vi/en/encyclicals/documents/hf_p-vi_enc_06081964_ecclesiam.html.

———. 1965. "Visit to the United Nations: Speech to the United Nations Organization (October 4, 1965)." October 4, 1965. https://www.vatican.va/content/paul-vi/en/speeches/1965/documents/hf_p-vi_spe_19651004_united-nations.html.

———. 1967. "Populorum Progressio (March 26, 1967)." https://www.vatican.va/content/paul-vi/en/encyclicals/documents/hf_p-vi_enc_26031967_populorum.html.

Pope Pius IX. 1864. "Encyclical Quanta Cura (Rome, 8 December 1864)." December 8, 1864. https://www.vatican.va/content/pius-ix/it/documents/encyclica-quanta-cura-8-decembris-1864.html.

Pope Pius X. 1907. "Pascendi Dominici Gregis (September 8, 1907)." September 8, 1907. https://www.vatican.va/content/pius-x/en/encyclicals/documents/hf_p-x_enc_19070908_pascendi-dominici-gregis.html.

Pope Pius XXII. 1944. "Christmas Radio Message to the Peoples of the Whole World (24 December 1944)." December 24, 1944.

https://www.vatican.va/content/pius-xii/it/speeches/1944/documents/hf_p-xii_spe_19441224_natale.html.

Pope Paul VI. 1964. "Lumen Gentium." November 21, 1964. https://www.vatican.va/archive/hist_councils/ii_vatican_council/documents/vat-ii_const_19641121_lumen-gentium_en.html.

Powell, Ralph L. 1955. "The Hundred Days and the Boxer Rebellion: 1898–1900." In *Rise of the Chinese Military Power: 1895–1912*, 90–128. Princeton, NJ: Princeton University Press.

Powers, John. 2019. "China's Religion Problem: Why the Chinese Communist Party Views Religious Belief as a Threat." University of Nottingham Asia Research Institute. https://theasiadialogue.com/2019/10/17/chinas-religion-problem-why-the-chinese-communist-party-views-religious-belief-as-a-threat/.

Prieto, Andrés I. 2017. "The Perils of Accommodation: Jesuit Missionary Strategies in the Early Modern World." *Journal of Jesuit Studies* 4 (3): 395–414. https://doi.org/10.1163/22141332-00403002.

Primus, Richard A. 1999. "Rights after World War II." In *The American Language of Rights*, 177–233. Cambridge: Cambridge University Press. https://doi.org/10.1017/CBO9780511490699.006.

Pullela, Philip. 2021. "Pope Defends Deal with China, Says Dialogue Necessary." *Reuters*. September 1, 2021. https://www.reuters.com/world/china/pope-defends-deal-with-china-says-dialogue-necessary-2021-09-01/.

Purcell, Mary. 2014. *The Quiet Companion: The Life of Peter Faber*. Chicago: Loyola Press.

Quade, Quentin L. 1982. "The Pope and Revolution: John Paul II Confronts Liberation Theology." Washington, DC.

Rahner, Karl. 1981. "Basic Theological Interpretation of the Second Vatican Council." In *Theological Investigations, [Vol. 20]: Concern for the Church*, edited by Karl Rahner. Vol. 20. New York: Crossroads.

Rapanyane, Makhura Benjamin. 2021. "The New World [Dis]order in the Complexity of Multi-Polarity: United States of America's Hegemonic Decline and the Configuration of New Power Patterns." *Journal of Public Affairs* 21 (1). https://doi.org/10.1002/pa.2114.

Reese, Thomas. 2013. "Francis, the Jesuits and the Dirty War." *National Catholic Reporter*. March 17, 2013. https://www.ncronline.org/blogs/ncr-today/francis-jesuits-and-dirty-war.

———. 2017. "Pope Francis, Like Trump, Is Reluctant to Condemn Russia on Syria and Ukraine." *National Catholic Reporter*. June 8, 2017. https://www.ncronline.org/blogs/faith-and-justice/pope-francis-trump-reluctant-condemn-russia-syria-and-ukraine.

———. 2018. "The Vatican and China: Making the Best of a Bad Situation." *The Gazette*, February 20, 2018. http://gazette.com/the-vatican-and-china-making-the-best-of-a-bad-situation/article/1621381.

Regan, Ethna. 2019. "The Bergoglian Principles: Pope Francis' Dialectical Approach to Political Theology." *Religions* 10 (12): 670. https://doi.org/10.3390/rel10120670.

Remeseira, Claudio Ivan. 2015. "Pope Francis, Perón, and God's People: The Political Religion of Jorge Mario Bergoglio." *Medium*. September 17, 2015. https://medium.com/@hispanicnewyork/pope-francis-per%C3%B3n-and-god-s-people-the-political-religion-of-jorge-mario-bergoglio-2a85787e7abe.

Reuters. 2025, "Russia Does Not See Vatican as Serious Arena for Peace Talks, Sources Say." *Reuters*. May 26, 2025. https://www.reuters.com/world/europe/russia-does-not-see-vatican-serious-arena-peace-talks-sources-say-2025-05-26/?utm_source=chatgpt.com

Rockefeller, Nelson A. 1969. *The Rockefeller Report on the Americas; The Official Report of a United States Presidential Mission for the Western Hemisphere*. Chicago, IL: Quadrangle Books.

Rogers, Benedict. 2025. "Will Pope Leo End Appeasement of Beijing Bullies?" *UCA News*, May 19, 2025. https://www.ucanews.com/news/will-pope-leo-end-appeasement-of-beijing-bullies/109040

Rourke, Thomas R. 2016. *The Roots of Pope Francis's Social and Political Thought: From Argentina to the Vatican*. Lanham, Maryland: Rowman & Littlefield.

RT Television Network. 2012. "Putin Trumpets Russia's 'Cultural Dominance'." January 23, 2012. https://www.rt.com/russia/putin-immigration-manifest-article-421/.

Rubén, Rosario Rodríguez. 2017. *Christian Martyrdom and Political Violence*. Cambridge and New York: Cambridge University Press. https://doi.org/10.1017/9781316941058.

Rummel, Erika. 1989. *Erasmus and His Catholic Critics, II: 1523–1536*. Vol. 2. Nieuwkoop, Netherlands: De Graaf.

Rychlak, Ronald J. 2011. "A War Prevented: Pope John XXIII and the Cuban Missile Crisis." *Crisis Magazine*. November 11, 2011. https://www.crisismagazine.com/2011/preventing-war-pope-john-xxiii-and-the-cuban-missile-crisis

Salai, Sean. 2021. "What Pope Francis Has Said About Covid-19 Since His Iconic Urbi Et Orbi Blessing One Year Ago." *America: The Jesuit Review*. https://www.americamagazine.org/faith/2021/03/26/pope-francis-covid-19-orbi-et-urbi-240310

San Martin, Ines. 2022. "Vatican Foreign Minister Emphasizes Respecting Ukraine's Territorial Integrity." *Crux*. June 15, 2022. https://cruxnow.com/church-in-europe/2022/06/vatican-foreign-minister-emphasizes-respecting-ukraines-territorial-integrity.

Scannone, Juan Carlos. 2016. "Pope Francis and the Theology of the People." *Theological Studies* 77 (1): 118–35. https://doi.org/10.1177/0040563915621141.

Second Vatican Council. 1964. *Lumen Gentium: Dogmatic Constitution on the Church*. 21 November 1964.
https://www.vatican.va/archive/hist_councils/ii_vatican_council/documents/vat-ii_const_19641121_lumen-gentium_en.html.

———. 1965a. *Gaudium et Spes: Pastoral Constitution on the Church in the Modern World*. 7 December 1965.
https://www.vatican.va/archive/hist_councils/ii_vatican_council/documents/vat-ii_const_19651207_gaudium-et-spes_en.html.

———. 1965b. *Nostra Aetate: Declaration on the Relation of the Church to Non-Christian Religions*. 28 October 1965.
https://www.vatican.va/archive/hist_councils/ii_vatican_council/documents/vat-ii_decl_19651028_nostra-aetate_en.html.

———. 1965c. *Dei Verbum: Dogmatic Constitution on Divine Revelation*. 18 November 1965.
https://www.vatican.va/archive/hist_councils/ii_vatican_council/documents/vat-ii_const_19651118_dei-verbum_en.html.

———. 1965d. *Dignitatis Humanae: Declaration on Religious Freedom*. 7 December 1965.
https://www.vatican.va/archive/hist_councils/ii_vatican_council/documents/vat-ii_decl_19651207_dignitatis-humanae_en.html.

Shafiee, Nozar, and Ehsan Fallahi. 2018. "The Church and Religious Diplomacy in Russia's Foreign Policy." *Journal of Iran and Central Eurasia Studies* 1 (1): 93–105.

Schaller, Michael. 1992. *Reckoning with Reagan: America and Its President in the 1980s*. New York: Oxford University Press.

Schelkens, Karim., Dick, John A., Mettepenningen, Jürgen. 2013. *"Aggiornamento? Catholicism from Gregory XVI to Benedict XVI."* Leiden and Boston. Brill.

Schelkens, Karim. 2020. "Papal Leadership in the First Half of the Twentieth Century." In *The Cambridge Companion to Vatican II*, edited by Richard R. Gaillardetz, 41–61.

Schilson, Arno. 1995. "The Major Theological Themes of Romano Guardini." In *Romano Guardini: Proclaiming the Sacred in a Modern World*, edited by Robert A. Krieg, 31–42. Chicago: Liturgy Training Publications.

Schloesser, Stephen. 2006. "Against Forgetting: Memory, History, Vatican II." *Theological Studies* 67 (2): 275–319. https://doi.org/10.1177/004056390606700203.

———. 2014. "Accommodation as a Rhetorical Principle." *Journal of Jesuit Studies* 1 (3): 347–72. https://doi.org/10.1163/22141332-00103001.

Schurhammer, Georg, and Joséph. M. Costelloe (trans.). 1973. *Francis Xavier: His Life, His Times*. Rome: Jesuit Historical Institute.

Sessa, Kristina. 2012. *The Formation of Papal Authority in Late Antique Italy*. New York: Cambridge University Press.

Shapiro, Judith. 1987. "From Tupã to the Land Without Evil: The Christianization of Tupi-Guarani Cosmology." *American Ethnologist* 14 (1): 126–39. https://doi.org/10.1525/ae.1987.14.1.02a00080.

Sherwood, Harriet. 2021. "'Unique Problem': Catholic Bishops Split Over Biden's Support for Abortion Rights." *The Guardian*. June 12, 2021. https://www.theguardian.com/us-news/2021/jun/12/biden-support-abortion-rights-catholic-bishops-split.

Shestopalets, Denys. 2019. "The Ukrainian Orthodox Church of the Moscow Patriarchate, the State and the Russian-Ukrainian Crisis, 2014–2018." *Politics, Religion & Ideology* 20 (1): 42–63. https://doi.org/10.1080/21567689.2018.1554482.

———. 2020a. "Church and State in Ukraine after the Euromaidan: President Poroshenko's Discourse on Religion, 2014–2018." *Politics and Religion* 13 (1): 150–79. https://doi.org/10.1017/S1755048319000221.

———. 2020b. "Religious Freedom, Conspiracies, and Faith: The Geopolitics of Ukrainian Autocephaly." *The Review of Faith & International Affairs* 18 (3): 25–39. https://doi.org/10.1080/15570274.2020.1795441.

Shore, Paul. 2020. "The Years of Jesuit Suppression, 1773–1814: Survival, Setbacks, and Transformation." In *The Years of Jesuit Suppression, 1773–1814: Survival, Setbacks, and Transformation*, 1–117. Lieden: Brill.

Skinner, Barbara. 2005. "The Irreparable Church Schism: Russian Orthodoxy and Its Historical Encounter with Catholicism." In *Polish Encounters, Russian Identity*, edited by David. L. Ransel and Bozena Shallcross. Bloomington, IN: Indiana University Press.

Smart, Ninian. 2003. "The Global Future of Religion." In *Global Religions: An Introduction*, edited by Mark Juergensmeyer, 124–32. Oxford; New York: Oxford University Press.

Smith-Spark, Laura. 2014. "Pope Francis Ditches Bulletproof Popemobile." June 14, 2014. https://edition.cnn.com/2014/06/14/world/europe/pope-francis-interview-popemobile/index.html.

Soage, Ana Belen. 2007. "The Muslim Reaction to Pope Benedict XVI's Regensburg Address." *Totalitarian Movements and Political Religions* 8 (1): 137–43. https://doi.org/10.1080/14690760601121697.

Spadaro, Antonio. 2013a. 'L'Osservatore Romano.' September 21, 2013. https://www.vatican.va/content/francesco/en/speeches/2013/september/documents/papa-francesco_20130921_intervista-spadaro.html.

———. 2013b. "A Big Heart Open to God: An Interview with Pope Francis." *America: The Jesuit Review* 209 (8): 14. https://www.americamagazine.org/faith/2013/09/30/big-heart-open-god-interview-pope-francis

———. 2018a. "The Prosperity Gospel: Dangerous and Different." *La Civiltá Cattolica*. July 18, 2018. https://www.laciviltacattolica.com/the-prosperity-gospel-dangerous-and-different/.

———. 2018b. "The Agreement between China and the Holy See." *La Civiltá Cattolica.* September 25, 2018. https://www.laciviltacattolica.com/the-agreement-between-china-and-the-holy-see/.

———. 2022. "Pope Francis in Conversation with the Editors of European Jesuit Journals." *La Civiltá Cattolica.* June 14, 2022. https://www.laciviltacattolica.com/pope-francis-in-conversation-european-jesuit-journals/.

Spadaro, Antonio, and Marcelo Figueroa. 2017. "Evangelical Fundamentalism and Catholic Integralism in the USA: A Surprising Ecumenism." *La Civiltá Cattolica.* July 13, 2017. https://www.laciviltacattolica.com/evangelical-fundamentalism-and-catholic-integralism-in-the-usa-a-surprising-ecumenism/.

Spadaro, Antonio, and S. Whiteside (trans.). 2013. *My Door Is Always Open: A Conversation on Faith, Hope, and the Church in a Time of Change.* London: Bloomsbury.

St Ignatius Loyola., and George E. Ganns (trans.). 1970. *The Constitutions of the Society of Jesus.* St Louis: The Institute of Jesuit Sources.

Stafford, Edward. 2016. "The Vatican's Role in the Reconciliation Between the US and Cuba". *Hemisferio - Revista Del Colegio Interamericano De Defensa* 2 (1): 149-60. https://doi.org/10.59848/16.1207.HV2n9.

Stein, Chris, and Sengupta, Somini. "In Africa, Pope Francis Makes His First Visit to a War Zone". *The New York Times.* November 29, 2015. https://www.nytimes.com/2015/11/30/world/africa/in-africa-pope-makes-first-visit-to-a-war-zone.html

The State Council (People's Republic of China). 2017. "China Revises Regulation on Religious Affairs." September 7, 2017. http://english.www.gov.cn/policies/latest_releases/2017/09/07/content_28 1475842719170.htm.

Tido, Anna. 2018. "Where Does Russia End and the West Start?" *E-International Relations*. April 22, 2018. https://www.e-ir.info/2018/04/22/where-does-russia-end-and-the-west-start/.

Tong, John. 2013. "The Church from 1949 to 1990." In *The Catholic Church in Modern China: Perspectives*, edited by Edmond Tang and Jean-Paul Wiest, 7–27. Eugene, OR: Wipf and Stock Publishers.

Toulmin, Stephen. 1992. *Cosmopolis: The Hidden Agenda of Modernity*. Chicago: University of Chicago Press.

Troy, Jodok. 2017. "Global Politics According to Pope Francis." https://papers.ssrn.com/sol3/papers.cfm?abstract_id=2978140

— — —. 2018. "'The Pope's Own Hand Outstretched': Holy See Diplomacy as a Hybrid Mode of Diplomatic Agency." *The British Journal of Politics and International Relations* 20 (3): 521–39. https://doi.org/10.1177/1369148118772247.

— — —. 2021. "International Politics as Global Politics from Below: Pope Francis on Global Politics." *Journal of International Relations and Development* 24 (3): 555–73. https://doi.org/10.1057/s41268-020-00202-y.

Tsygankov, Andrei. P. 2019. *Russia's Foreign Policy: Change and Continuity in National Identity*. Lanham: Rowman & Littlefield del Turco, Arielle. 2020. "China to Christians: We're Rewriting the Bible, and You'll Use It or Else." Family Research Council. October 26, 2020. https://www.frc.org/op-eds/china-to-christians-were-rewriting-the-bible-and-youll-use-it-or-else.

Tutino, Stefania. 2019. "Jesuit Accommodation, Dissimulation, Mental Reservation." In *The Oxford Handbook of the Jesuits*, edited by Ines G. Zupanov, 215–40. New York: Oxford University Press. https://doi.org/10.1093/oxfordhb/9780190639631.013.10.

UCA News. 2021. "Pope Wants to Continue Dialogue with China Despite Challenges." *UCA News*. September 2, 2021. https://www.ucanews.com/news/pope-wants-to-continue-dialogue-with-china-despite-challenges/93983.

Union of Catholic Asian News. 1999. "Vatican's Reported Desire to Move China Nunciature to Beijing Stirs Reactions." *Union of Catholic Asian News*. April 14, 1999.
https://www.ucanews.com/story-archive/?post_name=/1999/02/15/vaticans-reported-desire-to-move-china-nunciature-to-beijing-stirs-reactions&post_id=13032.

Upadhyay, Archana. 2021. "Religion in Russia's Strategic Thinking: Internal and External Dimensions." In *Transitions in Post-Soviet Eurasia*, edited by Archana Upadhyay, 181–99. India: Routledge.

Urio, Paolo. 2018. *China Reclaims World Power Status: Putting an End to the World America Made*. London: Routledge.
https://doi.org/10.4324/9781315174747.

US White House. 2017. "National Security Strategy of the United States of America." December 2017.
https://history.defense.gov/Portals/70/Documents/nss/NSS2017.pdf?ver=CnFwURrw09pJ0q5EogFpwg%3d%3d.

US State Department. 2021. "China (Includes Hong Kong, Macau, and Tibet) – United States Department of State." 2021 Country Reports on Human Rights Practices: China. 2021.
https://www.state.gov/reports/2021-country-reports-on-human-rights-practices/china/.

Uzzell, Lawrence. 2002. "Russians and Catholics." *First Things*, 21.

Valente, Gianni. 2018. "Parolin, 'Why We Are in Dialogue with China'." *La Stampa*. February 1, 2018. https://www.lastampa.it/vatican-insider/en/2018/02/01/news/parolin-why-we-are-in-dialogue-with-china-1.33974144.

Ventresca, Robert A. 2013. *Soldier of Christ: The Life of Pius XXII*. Cambridge: Harvard University Press.

Vourvoulias, S. 2015. "'Not a Sphere but a Polyhedron': The Sacred Geometry of Pope Francis." Al Dia. September 27, 2015. https://aldianews.com/en/thought-leaders/thought-leaders/not-sphere.

Vukicevic, Boris. 2015. "Pope Francis and the Challenges of Inter-Civilization Diplomacy." *Revista Brasileira de Política Internacional* 58 (2): 65–79. https://doi.org/10.1590/0034-7329201500204.

Vatican News. 2022. "Holy See: 'Surprise and Regret' at Installation of Bishop in China." *Vatican News*, November 26, 2022. https://www.vaticannews.va/en/vatican-city/news/2022-11/vatican-surprise-and-regret-installation-chinese-bishop.html.

———. 2023a. "Global Catholic population rising as number of priests, religious falls." *Vatican News.* October 20, 2023. https://www.vaticannews.va/en/church/news/2023-10/fides-catholic-church-statistics-world-mission-sunday.html.

———. 2023b. "Pope at Audience: Matteo Ricci's love for the Chinese people, a source of inspiration." *Vatican News.* May 31, 2023. https://www.vaticannews.va/en/pope/news/2023-05/pope-at-audience-st-francis-xavier211.html.

———. 2025. "Biography of Pope Leo XIV, Born Robert Francis Prevost." *Vatican News*. May 8, 2025. https://www.vaticannews.va/en/pope/news/2025-05/biography-of-robert-francis-prevost-pope-leo-xiv.html.

de Volder, Jan. 2019. "Francis's Ideosyncratic Approach to Vatican Geopolitics: An Introduction." In *The Geopolitics of Pope Francis*, edited by Jan de Volder, 1–24. Leuven: Peeters.

Wan, William. 2014. "Pope Francis Reaches out to China as He Begins Asia Trip." The Washington Post. August 14, 2014. https://www.washingtonpost.com/world/asia_pacific/pope-francis-reaches-out-to-china-as-he-begins-asia-trip/2014/08/14/cb60be66-239b-11e4-86ca-6f03cbd15c1a_story.html?utm_term=.c885e3676fd6.

Wang, Jianlang, and Li Tong (trans.). 2000. *Unequal Treaties and China (Volume 1)*. Honolulu: Silkroad Press.

Wang, Jianwei. 2019. "Xi Jinping's 'Major Country Diplomacy:' A Paradigm Shift?" *Journal of Contemporary China* 28 (115): 15–30. https://doi.org/10.1080/10670564.2018.1497907.

Wang, Maya. 2018. "'Eradicating Ideological Viruses': China's Campaign of Repression Against Xinjiang's Muslims." *Human Rights Watch*. September 9, 2018. https://www.hrw.org/report/2018/09/09/eradicating-ideological-viruses/chinas-campaign-repression-against-xinjiangs.

Washburn, Christian. 2016. "The First Vatican Council, Archbishop Henry Manning, and Papal Infallibility." *The Catholic Historical Review* 102 (4): 712–45.

Watkins, Devin. 2023. "Cardinal Zuppi visits Washington DC as part of peace mission for Ukraine." *Vatican News*. July 2023. https://www.vaticannews.va/en/pope/news/2023-07/pope-francis-sends-cardinal-zuppi-usa-peace-mission-ukraine.html.

Wessel, Susan. 2008. *Leo the Great and the Spiritual Rebuilding of a Universal Rome*. Leiden: Brill. https://doi.org/10.1163/ej.9789004170520.i-422.

Wetzel, Dominic. 2020. "The Rise of the Catholic Alt-Right." *Journal of Labor and Society* 23 (1): 31–55.

Whalen, Brett E. 2014. *The Medieval Papacy*. Basingstoke: Palgrave Macmillan.

White, Christopher. 2021. "What Does Catholic President Biden Need in His Vatican Ambassador?." *National Catholic Reporter* 57 (15): 1–7.

———. 2022a. "Pope Francis Visits Russian Embassy to Holy See to Express Concerns Over War." *National Catholic Reporter*, February 25, 2022. https://www.ncronline.org/news/vatican/pope-francis-visits-russian-embassy-holy-see-express-concerns-over-war.

———. 2022b. "Pope Francis in Video Conference with Russian Patriarch Kirill Rejects Religious Defense of Invasion." *National Catholic Reporter*. March 16, 2022. https://www.ncronline.org/news/vatican/pope-francis-video-conference-russian-patriarch-kirill-rejects-religious-defense.

———. 2022c. "Pope Francis Says He Has Asked to Meet Putin in Moscow." National Catholic Reporter. May 3, 2022. https://www.ncronline.org/news/vatican/pope-francis-says-he-has-asked-meet-putin-moscow.

———. 2023. "10 years later, Pope Francis' Lampedusa 'cry' offers renewed call to welcome migrants." *National Catholic Reporter*. July 6, 2023.

Wiest, Nailene C. 2005. "New Pope, Old Story in Beijing." *Far Eastern Economic Review* 168 (8): 40–43.

Winfield, Nicole. 2025. "Pope prays for Chinese Catholics to be in communion with Rome in first comments on thorny issues." *Associated Press*. May 25, 2025. https://apnews.com/article/vatican-pope-leo-china-390c31434783eb8ff06c14547ab0f08b

Winters, Michael Sean. 2015. "Tim Busch, the Koch Brothers, capitalism and Catholicism." *National Catholic Reporter*. January 28, 2015. https://www.ncronline.org/blogs/distinctly-catholic/tim-busch-koch-brothers-capitalism-and-catholicism.

———. 2022. "Some Conservative Catholics' Apologies for Putin Reveal Fascist Sympathies." *National Catholic Reporter*. March 2, 2022. https://www.ncronline.org/news/opinion/some-conservative-catholics-apologies-putin-reveal-fascist-sympathies.

Wilde, Melissa J. 2020. *Vatican II: A Sociological Analysis of Religious Change*. Princeton: Princeton University Press.

Wooden, Cindy. 2017. "Cardinal Parolin Visits Russia, Focuses on Ecumenism and Peace." *America: The Jesuit Review*, August.

———. 2019a. "Pope Reflects on Changed Attitudes toward Liberation Theology." Crux. February 14, 2019. https://cruxnow.com/vatican/2019/02/pope-reflects-on-changed-attitudes-toward-liberation-theology.

———. 2019b. "Pope Francis Lifts Suspension Imposed on Nicaragua's Ernesto Cardenal." *America: The Jesuit Review*, February.

———. 2021. "Pope Francis: My Spirituality Comes Directly from Vatican II." America: *The Jesuit Review*. September 28, 2021. https://www.americamagazine.org/faith/2021/09/28/pope-francis-vatican-ii-241520.

———. 2022. "A Ukrainian and a Russian Were Invited to Lead the Vatican's Via Crucis. Ukraine Wants Pope Francis to Reconsider." *America: The Jesuit Review*, April.

Wright, Jonathon. 2004. *God's Soldiers: Adventure, Politics, Intrigue, and Power; A History of the Jesuits*. New York: Doubleday.

Wright IV, William M. 2017. "Dei Verbum." In *The Reception of Vatican II*, edited by Matthew Lamb and Matthew Levering. Oxford: Oxford University Press.

Xiang, Lanxin. 2018. "China and the Vatican." *Survival* 60 (3): 87–94. https://doi.org/10.1080/00396338.2018.1470757.

Yang, Fenggang. 2012. *Religion in China: Survival and Revival Under Communist Rule*. New York: Oxford University Press.

Yang, Yi. 2017. "Between God and Caesar: The Catholic Bishops' Election and Consecration in China." *Journal of Contemporary China* 26 (107): 741–55. https://doi.org/10.1080/10670564.2017.1305491.

Young, Neil J. 2022. "Did Donald Trump End the Religious Right?" In *Catholics and US Politics After the 2020 Elections: Biden Chases the "Swing Vote,"* edited by Marie Gayte, Blandine Chelini-Pont, and Mark J. Rozell, 77–99. Cham: Palgrave Macmillan. https://doi.org/10.1007/978-3-030-82212-5.

Zenit. 2016. "Pope Francis' Interview with Asia Times." *Zenit*. February 2, 2016. https://zenit.org/2016/02/02/pope-francis-interview-with-asia-times/.

Zhao, Minghao. 2019. "Is a New Cold War Inevitable? Chinese Perspectives on US-China Strategic Competition." *The Chinese Journal of International Politics* 12 (3): 371–94. https://doi.org/10.1093/cjip/poz010.

Zhao, Suisheng. 2022. "The US–China Rivalry in the Emerging Bipolar World: Hostility, Alignment, and Power Balance." *Journal of Contemporary China* 31 (134): 169–85. https://doi.org/10.1080/10670564.2021.1945733.

Zhu, Rachel Xiaohong. 2017. "The Division of the Roman Catholic Church in Mainland China: History and Challenges." *Religions* 8 (3): 39. https://doi.org/10.3390/rel8030039.

Zhu, Zhiqun. 2021. "China's Grand Strategy toward North America." In *China's Grand Strategy: A Roadmap to Global Power?* edited by David. B. H. Denoon, 212–32. New York: New York University Press.

Zimmermann, Jens. 2012. *Humanism and Religion*. Oxford: Oxford University Press. https://doi.org/10.1093/acprof:oso/9780199697755.001.0001.

de Zoysa, Richard. 2005. "America's Foreign Policy: Manifest Destiny or Great Satan?" *Contemporary Politics* 11 (2–3): 133–56. https://doi.org/10.1080/13569770500275130.

Zonova, Tatiana, Andrea Giannotti, and Roman Reinhardt. 2023. "The Russian Orthodox Church and the World: Mapping the Theme for IR Studies." In *The Routledge Handbook of Russian International relations Studies*, edited by Maria Lagutina, Natalia Tsvetkova, and Alexander Sergunin, 1st ed., 417–27. London: Routledge.

Zupanov, Ines G. 2019. "Introduction: Is One World Enough for the Jesuits?" In *The Oxford Handbook of the Jesuits*, edited by Ines G. Zupanov, 1–32. Oxford University Press.

www.ingramcontent.com/pod-product-compliance
Lightning Source LLC
Chambersburg PA
CBHW031145020426
42333CB00013B/516